Marshall Hall

A Law unto Himself

Marshall Hall

A Law unto Himself

Sally Smith

Wildy, Simmonds & Hill Publishing

© Sally Smith 2016

ISBN: 978 0 85490 187 6

British Library Cataloguing in Publication Data

A catalogue record for this book is available from the British Library

First published in 2016 by

Wildy, Simmonds & Hill Publishing
58 Carey Street
London WC2A 2JF
England
www.wildy.com

Reprinted 2017

Typeset by Heather Jones, North Petherton, Somerset.
Printed in Great Britain by CPI Antony Rowe, Chippenham, Wiltshire.

Contents

PART IV
FAME

List of Illustrations

SECTION ONE
EMH AND HIS LIFE

Dr Alfred Hall, Marshall's much loved father, in his consulting rooms

Julia Hall, Marshall's much loved mother

Ada Labouchere, Marshall's favourite sister

Marshall as a schoolboy

Marshall in his house cricket team at Rugby: seated middle row, far right

Marshall whilst working at a tea merchants in the City of London

Marshall on his call to the Bar in 1883

Marshall as a young man, the matinee idol looks becoming apparent

Count Raoul de Vismes et de Ponthieu, the lover of Marshall's first wife, Ethel

Hetty, Marshall's second wife, with their new-born daughter, Elna, always known as 'Baba'

Marshall at various stages in his life; universally said to be the handsomest man at the Bar – and frequently the handsomest in England

Marshall, Hetty, Elna and the chauffeur in the 1906 Vulcan motor car adorned with electioneering ribbons

Marshall's electioneering photograph for the 1910 election

Marshall on the campaign trail

A 1907 portrait of Marshall painted by Robert Wood, the accused in the Camden Town murder

The photograph of Marguerite Fahmy which she sent to Marshall after the trial. It joined all the other trophies of his triumphs that hung on his chambers wall

Edward Marshall Hall KC

SECTION TWO
PRESS CUTTINGS FROM MARSHALL HALL'S COLLECTION

The 'Brides in the Bath' murder

The 'Green Bicycle' murder

The poisoning of Mabel Greenwood

The Crumbles murder

The murder at the Savoy

Foreword

The Edwardian England of Edward Marshall Hall. For the criminal barrister, if not necessarily the criminals, those were the days. And Marshall Hall was some knight.

In this detailed biography of Sir Edward Marshall Hall, KC, MP, Sally Smith, QC looks back to a time before TV and Twitter, when a barrister practising in criminal law could yet gain showbiz levels of fame. The man at the centre of her study, the legendary Marshall Hall, was leading counsel with the following of a matinee idol. If not quite a KC Kardashian, Hall's success did depend on his impressive physical bearing and striking good looks, almost as much as his skills as an advocate.

How different from our own dear Queen's Counsel. There are no doubt many good-looking, skilful barristers appearing regularly in the Central Criminal Court today, but how many of them are known by name or by reputation, or at all to the general public?

The most famous Old Bailey barrister of recent years is probably Horace Rumpole, and he was the fictional creation of John Mortimer, QC. Mortimer himself gained a wide reputation as an entertaining courtroom performer, especially in his days appearing in the obscenity trials of the 1960s and 1970s; but he is probably best remembered as a man of letters than simply as a man of the law.

Marshall Hall was no real-life Rumpole, but John Mortimer did give to Rumpole Marshall Hall's technique of deliberately annoying the trial judge in order to gain the sympathy of the jury who were to rule on the guilt of his client.

Hall was grand enough (son of an eminent physician; Rugby and St John's, Cambridge) to fit into the class-conscious world of the Bar to which he was called in 1883. But there was enough of the rebel about him to suit the character of the criminal defence counsel taking on the establishment on behalf of the prisoner sitting in the dock of the Bailey.

In Victorian and Edwardian England, the art of the advocate and the skills of an actor were seen to be much of a muchness. And Hall might have had a career on stage but, apart from anything else, was not good enough at learning lines. As it happens, he was not particularly good at learning the law either. Nor did he know much about Greek or Latin, which was usually seen as a *sine qua non* for a legal career.

He had a better understanding of maths and science which helped with cross-examining experts about ballistics, poisons, blood stains, and so on – the bread and butter of a juicy murder.

He also had a ready wit. The original of a much used and adapted courtroom favourite is attributed to him: when asked by a pompous judge, 'Is your client [an Irish labourer] not familiar with the maxim *res ipsa loquitur*?', Hall replied, 'My lord, on the remote hillside in County Donegal where my client comes from, they talk of little else'.

But good-looking and witty might not have been enough to have won over so many juries and gained him such a name with the general public, who fed on the details of his cases which were routinely reported at length in all the newspapers. He had, in addition, what nowadays might be described as emotional intelligence.

Sally Smith explores the ups and downs of Hall's personal life.

He was obliged to leave Rugby school a couple of terms early – he fell out with his house master – and when he eventually made his way to Cambridge he interrupted his studies with two years' travelling abroad as he recovered from romantic upset and mental turmoil. He married young, but his first marriage was desperately unhappy and after a few years he and his wife Ethel agreed to a separation; not long after that she died as the result of a botched abortion.

These distressing life events, the author argues, may well have helped Hall to relate at a human level to the emotions of the oppressed women and desperate men he was briefed to represent. He was certainly able to induce an emotional reaction from the juries he was addressing on their behalf. He put all of himself into cases, performing in a way which Sally Smith suggests anticipated the method acting techniques developed by actors in the theatre and on film years later.

Marshall Hall did not only do criminal work and did not always win his cases, and his success at the Bar did not lead to judicial office. He was elected to Parliament, but his oratory did not carry him anything like as far in politics as it did in the law courts.

Above all, he is remembered for his spectacular successes in court, which, in trials for murder really were a matter of life and death.

The role of the star advocate is somewhat troubling.

If cunning cross-examination, or an emotional closing speech gains an acquittal against the weight of the evidence, it is surely a triumph for defence counsel but have the wider interests of justice been served? And what of the prisoner in the next-door courtroom, condemned to the gallows because he did not have a Marshall Hall to tip the scales of justice in his favour?

Lawyers and non-lawyers may approach these questions in different ways, but to both, Marshall Hall's was a fascinating life and career. And through his trials and tribulations we can also learn much about the high and low life of a previous age, illuminated by this full account of a by-gone style of advocate and advocacy.

Clive Anderson

Preface

Showman, opportunist, crusader, genius, Marshall Hall was all of these things, frequently all at the same time.

He may not have been the handsomest or most eloquent man at the Bar, though many said he was, but he was certainly the most famous. In a profession in which fame is transient, dispersed as soon as the case that generates it is over, Marshall stands out as a colossus. His principal claim to fame, that he defended in more capital trials and saved more people from the hangman's noose than any other known barrister, is almost eclipsed in the general aura of celebrity with which he surrounded himself. His successes in court were greeted with hysterical adulation, his failures simply made him more lovable. He was adored by the public. Those who heard him in action were transported; observers reported unbearable tension, muffled sobs, breathless attention, hysterics and ecstatic applause. Rhapsodic accounts in newspapers and subsequent reminiscences by his contemporaries all suggest that his advocacy was unique. Thousands gathered outside the Old Bailey to hear the verdicts in his great trials. News of those verdicts stopped the traffic from the Old Bailey to Trafalgar Square and curtains were brought down, mid-performance, in West End theatres to announce them.

As soon as he died, in February 1927, a biography was immediately commissioned and was published two years later. It sold in its tens of thousands and is generally held to be the most famous legal biography ever written. Published so soon after Marshall's death, it lacked historical perspective and had all the reticence in relation to his private life typical of its period; but it was a wonderful story, told in the heroic tradition, of a man who struggled against the odds and triumphed, and it crystallised Marshall Hall's image in the public mind. Many famous names in the law, amongst them John Mortimer, the creator of Rumpole, and Lord Scarman, a distinguished law lord, attributed their decision to go to the Bar to reading it at an impressionable age, and it embodies all that is most glamorous about the job in one man's extraordinary life. Edward Marjoribanks' (pronounced 'Marchbanks') representation of Marshall Hall as an almost ludicrously melodramatic if charismatic advocate, a poor lawyer, a naive, volatile personality, and an intellectually superficial man profoundly emotionally involved in his cases, had become the 'real' Marshall Hall.

In all the hype, truth and myth and lies and legend had become inextricably entwined. I wondered if they could be unravelled; the wondering turned into idle googling and the googling into something more serious. The references to Marshall Hall are legion; but the vast majority cite Marjoribanks' biography as their source. Then one morning I had a breakthrough: amongst the lots sold a short time before at an auction house in Gloucestershire was one containing some items belonging to Sir Edward Marshall Hall. Feeling slightly foolish, I wrote to the vendor via the auction house.

Two weeks later the telephone rang. It was the vendor, whose family had inherited from Marshall Hall's daughter the contents of her house. Elna Marshall Hall had died a spinster. Amateur psychology is always dangerous but it is the case that Marshall Hall, much publicised as the most charming and handsome man in England, would have been a hard act to follow, and Elna had devoted a large part of her life to keeping his legacy alive. 'We still have a lot of papers if you are interested,' said my caller.

I drove down to Wales and came back with a crown of rhubarb now flourishing in our vegetable garden and a boot full of papers. Some, but not all, of these papers had been used by Edward Marjoribanks for his book and they included some of his own correspondence with the family after Marshall Hall's death. My search began to feel like a new journey rather than simply a walk in the footsteps of my famous predecessor.

Through some more elaborate detective work I found the papers of Marshall Hall's closest friend, Sir Charles Gill KC. Gill had kept a vast quantity of documents including briefs in some of the great trials in which he prosecuted against Marshall Hall. I untied pink tape which had clearly never been undone since Gill had tied it up at the conclusion of each case nearly a hundred years before. He had also kept a bundle of Marshall Hall's letters to him. Marshall's charm and humour bounces off the pages but the letters also reveal the unimaginable strain under which these men lived.

I knew in theory, of course, the extraordinary background to capital trials in the late nineteenth and early twentieth centuries, when there were no real forensics, the accused could not give evidence in his own defence (prior to

1898) and there was no Court of Criminal Appeal. Pardons were arbitrary and unpredictable, judges reactionary, juries sternly moralistic and hanging followed a short three weeks after conviction. Nothing stood between the accused and the gallows but the advocacy of his barrister. But it was not until one sunny afternoon when I was researching for this book in Inner Temple library, pouring over an 1890s edition of *Archbold's Criminal Pleading Evidence and Practice*, the criminal practitioner's bible since its first publication in 1836 to the present day, that I suddenly experienced what it must have felt like for Marshall Hall and his contemporaries to puzzle over the law relating to the killing of another human being. 'There are very many nice distinctions,' Archbold informs us cheerily after no less than seventeen pages of close analysis. There certainly are. But at the end of the section, after all the subtleties and ambiguities it seeks to explain, there is one resounding certainty: 'Penalty; Death by Hanging'.

Marshall Hall lived with that certainty for decades and countered it with the only things he had: the force of his personality, the cadences of his own voice and his understanding of human psychology. His stamina and courage were unrivalled; his advocacy, whilst histrionic by the standards of today, was not the barnstorming of the previous generation of barristers as it is sometimes now reported; it was unclassifiably his own. I came to the conclusion that he might truly be a hero albeit not quite the kind depicted in Marjoribanks' famous biography. He was a man whose personality and achievements merited looking at in the context of his social and historical background. This book attempts to do that.

As a personality, Marshall Hall was sophisticated and complex, capable of being a cynical self-publicist and a consummate manipulator of others. No one with this last characteristic accompanied by legendary looks and charm could have anything but a complicated personal life. Marshall's was undoubtedly that. The tragedy of his first marriage and his subsequent complicated domestic arrangements accompanied by all the reverses in his professional life in the end made him a consummate psychologist not only of others but also of himself. It was this that was reflected in his advocacy and as a result his powers of persuasion were frequently quite literally irresistible.

Marshall Hall's life was ultimately about timing. He came to the Bar in its golden age, when the romance surrounding barristers and their cases was at its height. He practised during the period when two of the most major reforms of criminal law occurred: the accused was permitted for the first time in history to give evidence in his own defence; and the principle, if not the economics, of the need for public funding for the defence of accused persons was at last recognised. His great trials were conducted at a time when forensic scientific evidence was just being introduced and blood grouping, fingerprinting and the analysis of poisons were all new toys. He was at the vanguard in recognising and embracing the opportunities for publicity provided by the newly powerful popular press. Above all else, as is always the case with great orators, it was the innate timing in his advocacy that provided the key to his charismatic performances.

It does not take very long at the Bar to learn that there is no such thing as truth. There are only versions of events, selective and subjective, manipulated whether consciously or sub-consciously into whatever truth the teller wants to reveal and then evaluated and spun by the listener into whatever truth he wants to hear. I never thought I would discover 'the truth' about Marshall Hall: but I hoped to achieve a sort of just resolution of a life distorted by the legends he and others had woven around it. In the process I have come to realise that biography writing is as much the province of the lawyer as the historian, both disciplines involving the analysis of anecdotal and documentary evidence and its cobbling together into a kind of truth.

The law as referred to in the book is of course the law of the relevant time. There have been many iterations since; I have not embarked on explanations of these since to do so would have been to turn the book into a textbook; those interested will find detailed commentaries in the books listed under 'Legal background' in the select bibliography. In order to retain the period flavour, I have referred to people throughout the book, and in particular in relation to the trials, by the names by which they were commonly referred to in newspaper and other contemporary reports.

I am sure I have made errors of both fact and judgement. I comfort myself with the thought that Marshall Hall would have forgiven me, even if no one else does. He knew better than most just how unreliable 'evidence' can be.

PART I

OBSCURITY

CHAPTER 1

'The last moment'

On 18 December 1907 a young artist called Robert Wood, charged with murder, stood waiting in the dock of court number one at the Old Bailey. After six days of evidence and only seventeen minutes of deliberations, the jury had reached its verdict. It was just before eight o'clock in the evening and the panelled court was shadowy in the inadequate newly installed electric lighting. About ten minutes were to elapse before the verdict was pronounced. Acquittal meant immediate release into the freedom of the cold Christmas crowds of London; conviction was an unimaginable alternative. Executions followed three clear Sundays after sentence with no hangings on a Monday. It needed a lawyer to work out when it was going to happen. The last walk from the condemned cell to the execution shed in Pentonville prison yard was seventy-five feet. You had to walk it in all weathers in those days. Not that the weather mattered much. Before you began the walk your arms were tied behind your back and your collar was undone to bare your neck. That was to minimise the time you stood on the drop. By then it would be exactly 8am. They always came for you at 8am. The chaplain walked with you, chanting the prayers for the dead. After all, he was only a few minutes premature. Then feet on the drop on the designated chalk marks. Legs pinioned. Bag over the head. The rope. You wouldn't see it, but you'd be able to feel it.

Even to Wood, a man of quite remarkable self-possession, it must have seemed a very long ten minutes. He spent it doing the thing he loved most, drawing. Under a technically accomplished little sketch of the judge in full regalia he wrote in a steady hand, 'The last moment; Old Bailey Dec. 18 '07.' For others, the minutes were filled with ritual. The foreman of the jury told the jury bailiff that the jury had reached its decision. The jury bailiff told the gaoler. The judge, waiting in his chambers, reminded himself from a transcript of the solemn words of the pronouncement of death. The chaplain stood by, his job to add the 'amen' that put God's consoling seal of approval on the sentence of the court. The judge's clerk waited, black cap in hand, ready to usher his master back into court. Counsel for the prosecution and for the defence, lounging in the friendly litter of the cramped robing room, stubbed out their half-smoked cigars, abandoned their half-told reminiscences, slapped their wigs back on their heads and took their places in a court vibrating with tension. The public, amongst them many novelists, dramatists and leaders of society, scrambled into the public gallery if they were famous enough or lucky enough to have had seats reserved for them, or pressed closer to the doors of the court, the better to hear as soon as possible. The press, in a hungry, unruly pack, indifferent as to the result, since either way it would be next morning's sensation, took their places in the seats allocated to them.

When all were settled, the jury, a stolid, respectable-looking bunch of men, filed back in. The simultaneous beating of the hearts of those with a role to play in the state-imposed killing of a healthy human being was palpable in the hush. Into that breathless silence, silence was nonetheless called for. The clerk requested the jury foreman to stand and asked for the verdict. There is always a little pause; it seems as deliberate as that of the modern television presenter announcing the winner of a competition.

'Not guilty.'

The court erupted into a great wave of sound, so loud that it was heard by the people waiting outside in the darkness, an incredible 10,000 in number, and taken up by them. It continued during Mr Justice Grantham's release of Wood from the dock and his thanks to a jury who had, as he told them, 'been engaged in one of the most remarkable trials that is to be found in the annals of the criminal courts of England for many years' and whom he now, in recognition of their dedication to their duty, exempted from further jury service for ten years. The crowd outside, however, cared nothing for the formalities ending the trial. Carried along on a massive wave of hysteria they were cheering for Robert Wood, the first man ever to be acquitted after giving evidence in his own defence in a capital case, and for the jury, whose collective courage had resulted in that acquittal. But most of all they were yelling for defence counsel Edward Marshall Hall KC, the handsome, magnetic crowd puller who had achieved the astonishing victory. Vans, cabs and lamp-posts were appropriated as people fought for a good vantage point. An Italian chestnut seller was pushed aside, his roaster with its coals still burning flung to the ground and the barrow on which it had rested used as a grandstand. Hats and handkerchiefs were thrown into the air. Sticks were brandished. Fireworks were let off. Women screamed. A hopelessly inadequate fifty mounted policemen tried to hold back the crowd.[1]

Marshall Hall was nothing if not a showman; he appeared like a king at a window above the roaring crowd, his dazed client by his side. Minutes later, Wood was spirited away invisible in the phalanx of policemen surrounding him, whilst Marshall Hall, who always ensured he was very visible, descended the steps of the court to meet his public. He was forty-nine years old, six feet three inches tall at a time when the average height for a man was five feet eight inches, immaculately turned out, with strikingly dark eyes and patrician features, his dark hair streaked with silver. 'No-one', said the rather less physically impressive F E Smith wistfully, 'could have been as wonderful as Marshall Hall then looked.'[2] But the public thought he was just as wonderful. They saw what he intended them to see, the glamorous embodiment of a glamorous profession and not the turmoil that lay beneath. The sickening pre-trial stage fright, the naked ambition, the breathless gamble with his client's life, the ruthless triumph of winning combined with manic elation and extreme exhaustion were all carefully hidden beneath that immaculate façade.

Nor did the crowds know what Marshall Hall knew: that this was his last chance. It was not his first taste of fame, but previously it had been dashed away time and again. Domestic scandal and tragedy, flaming rows with judges, vendettas by the press and the envy of colleagues had all led in the end to what he regarded as the bitterest disgrace there could be, that of professional obscurity. This time, though, the pedestal upon which press and public had put him really did feel stable. And this time he was determined to cherish his fame with all the tenderness he lavished on his renowned collection of eighteenth-century snuff boxes: to gloat over it, burnish it, augment it at every opportunity. All those years of quixotic optimism in the face of disaster and sheer bloody-minded egotism were going to pay off.

The Wood trial was over. The victim lay, her throat cut from ear to ear so savagely that her head was only just attached to her body, in a quiet grave in Finchley. Robert Wood was to live the rest of his life in the forgotten shadows inhabited by the controversially acquitted. But for Marshall Hall the trial had to be not an end, but a beginning.

Back in his chambers in the Temple the congratulations were piling up from colleagues at the Bar and his many friends, actors and journalists, politicians and peers, and there were the invitations from the newly attentive society hostesses. They all had to be answered. He prided himself on his little personal notes, charming, self-deprecatory; he had always believed in the importance of making people feel special. Then there were the Wood trial press cuttings to add to his neatly catalogued albums. That, if he was honest, was what made him feel special.

His love affair with publicity had begun at the outset of his career, back in 1884. Every time his name was so much as mentioned in a newspaper, however obscure, he had lovingly stuck the cutting into the ever-increasing volumes. By now, in 1907, there were eight of them, a relentless whirl of thefts and assaults, perjury and blackmail, carnal knowledge and horse stealing, bigamy and breaches of promise, attempted suicide and selling beer without a licence, the occasional terrible murder: all the trivial and tragic transgressions that comprise a barrister's experience.

Now they invoked all those dawn trains from London stations, lugging wig and gown, books and briefs all over England. They conjured up for him those first trials in dim stuffy local courts and then the solemn rituals of the bigger trials in the great assize courts, the horrible accuracy of prosecuting counsel, his own frequent naked insolence to obscure judges, some long dead, and the competition and camaraderie of his contemporaries. Feuds and friendships made for a lifetime. All that early promise and then all those failures. The pages smelled to him of thwarted ambition and of nostalgia.

To his regret there were very few reports amongst them of the massively lucrative briefs that had eventually come the way of many of those contemporaries. Little or no commercial work, or disputes involving wills or land, or even murders committed by those with money to pay and society reputations to defend. Not until now. Robert Wood had been employed by a highly fashionable company producing etched glass in the new Art Nouveau style. The company, anxious to avoid the publicity of one of its top designers on the gallows, had written a handsome cheque for Wood's defence, one of the largest Marshall Hall had ever received.[3]

His life so far, like that of all barristers, had been characterised by the waiting: waiting for trains, waiting for cases to be called into court, waiting for verdicts, waiting for cheques. Now there was the wait for the next big opportunity. Somewhere soon some other fractured lives would lead to another sensational trial and now this one remarkable success would mean that his name would be foremost in the mind of every solicitor in England looking to brief defence counsel. No one could ever say of him that he had not fought passionately, all his working life, for the underdog, quite irrespective of personal gain. He had represented the bad, the mad, the innocent, the guilty in accordance with the ethics of his profession but also with a passionate conviction and an utter disregard for personal cost. Few of those colleagues carefully forging their careers with an eye on pocket and advancement could say as much. That did not mean he was indifferent to money, though. On the contrary, he wanted a lot of it.

Ever since his call to the Bar, twenty-five years earlier, money had been a constant worry. Until recently, there had been no public defence funding and even now it was pitifully inadequate. The lifestyle so important to his carefully nurtured image was increasingly expensive and the Inland Revenue was constantly on his back.[4] He was not sure how long he could maintain his little family in the stuccoed staffed grandeur of Cambridge Terrace, Bayswater,[5] what with the ever-growing art and antique collections, Hetty's entertaining and dresses, the governess for Elna, now ten, and the carriage horses eating their heads off in the mews behind the house, not to mention Elna's beloved donkey. Despite the income from his sideline dealing in jewellery and antiques, he had begun to think something would have to go.

It was probably time for the horses to go anyway. The new motor car had certainly attracted a few headlines and now he knew he could afford not only to run it, but to employ his own chauffeur as well. It really did seem as though, at last, a career of crime might be going to pay. Crime in the professional sense, that is, of course. He had only ever actually committed one himself and that had been forty years earlier. He must have been eight or nine at the time; a good-looking little boy, chunkily built with the co-ordinated agility of the brilliant sportsman he was to become, the thick dark hair partly concealing a picturesque scar on his forehead inflicted when he was a toddler by the challenge of a table far too high to climb onto. He was bright eyed with intelligence; self-confident with the security born of the devoted love, prosperity and social standing of his parents; outgoing; and bursting with a contempt for authority that because of his charm, grown-ups indulgently labelled as mischief.

Only on this occasion, he had been guilty of rather more than mischief, although it was never of course the attempted murder his victim had alleged. It had truly been an accident, the first of many occasions on which he was to run that particular defence to a gun crime.

The scene of the crime had been the Old Chain Pier[6] in Brighton, a stone's throw from his home in Old Steine, and the weapon had been his newly acquired pistol.[7] He had loved that pistol with a passion and never really got over its loss.

The Chain Pier was an irresistible lure to the young Edward. Racing along the promenade he spurned the entertainments laid on there for children; not even the rides in little wooden carts pulled by goats had the appeal of the pier with its grown-up attractions and potential for danger. Sneaking unnoticed past the toll booth at the entrance was easy enough when you knew how.

And then you were on the pier itself, which spanned the beach below with its beguiling mix of ragged fishing boats and bathing cabins (ladies to the east of the pier, gentlemen to the west) and stretched out into the sea, allowing glimpses of heaving waves to sparkle in the gaps of the decking floor.

Along its length, in the bases of the iron towers from which the suspension rods and chains were hung, were irresistible delights: a camera obscura and a silhouette artist, souvenir shops and a sweet kiosk manned by Mrs Terry, who doted on him, bestower of sticky ecstasy in the form of treacle fudge, marzipan and brandy balls. Not all those working on the pier were as benevolent as Mrs Terry; the pier master had reason to love him rather less. There had been some unfortunate incidents involving Edward's perilous fishing activities and, worse, his deliberate losing of a pail full of crabs onto the decking, causing the promenading ladies to scream and lift up their skirts, exhibiting forbidden glimpses of ankles to the hidden Edward. But on this occasion, the pier master was elsewhere. Pistol in hand and already on the way to becoming a consummate shot, Edward had looked around for something to aim at. Glistening with gold paint the 'o' of the word 'Royal' emblazoned on a wooden advertising sign on the beach below was irresistible. How satisfying a neat black hole would look in the centre of that 'o' and how sure he was he could get it right in the middle. He aimed and fired. It was a good shot.

How on earth could he have known that the sign was painted on the back of a bathing machine? Or that the bathing machine at that moment concealed a fat man with few clothes on?

Fright had a strong effect on them both. Even the intrepid Edward was alarmed out of his usual defiance as the fat man, beside himself with rage, dragged him off down the pier, destined for the police station. It was fortunate that Mrs Terry witnessed the scene from her sweet kiosk. No trained advocate had ever mastered a brief more quickly and effectively than did Mrs Terry. She hurled herself between the two and into passionate oratory on Edward's behalf. A lightning assessment of the evidence (small boy holding a literally smoking gun) and of the characteristics of the victim (outrage oozing from every naked pore but in fact unhurt) made Mrs Terry realise that salvation for Edward lay in mitigation. This little boy was a dear little boy; this was not a little boy to be dragged to the police station like any ragamuffin off the streets of Brighton. This was a little boy whose distinguished father could be relied upon to deal with him. And so on, until at last the fat man was defeated by consummate advocacy and, the beloved pistol confiscated, Edward was allowed to go home.

That night as he went to bed after the loving discipline of father and mother, so infinitely preferable to the terrors of the Brighton Constabulary, he had learned a great truth. When in trouble, there is no comfort in the world greater than the passionate support of a really good advocate. He never forgot it.

Father was Dr Alfred Hall MD FRCP, descended from a family of landowners in Derbyshire. The Cressy Halls of Alfreton were an old and proud dynasty. Business and law ran in the family. The family money derived from business interests in one of the nearby collieries and Alfred's father, John Cressy Hall, had his own trading wharf, Hall's Wharf, on the Cromford Canal at Langley Mill. John had trained as a lawyer, been called to the Bar in Gray's Inn and subsequently practised as a local attorney, the equivalent of a modern-day solicitor. Active in local Conservative politics, he brought up his family in a house described at the time as a neat modern mansion in its own park, Swanwick Grange.[8] Of his three sons Gervase and Frederick both trained as lawyers but Alfred, stepping outside the family tradition, had studied medicine at Edinburgh University. Now Alfred was one of the most eminent physicians in Brighton: vice-president of the Obstetrical Society of London, with a large private practice as well as a charitable post at the local hospital; spearhead of the campaign to improve the town drainage system; president of the Natural History Society; much-loved pillar of the community; handsome, clever, sensible and kind. Whilst working as a general practitioner in Glasgow he had met and married Edward's mother Julia, beautiful, loving and deeply devout. She was the daughter of the head postmaster in Glasgow and their first six children were born there. After a brief move to London, where two more babies were born, Alfred had taken the family to live in Brighton. And there Edward was born. He was just Edward Hall, born on 16 September 1858, the tail end of a family of nine. To Julia and Alfred he was infinitely precious. The previous three babies had all died and the remaining children were growing up fast. James was fifteen, Alfred fourteen, Ada thirteen, Julia twelve and Annie ten when Edward arrived.

In contrast to all the other children, home for Edward had always been number 30, one of the largest houses on Old Steine. The Steine was a middle-class enclave[9] of large professional families and number 30 a beautiful house with Regency bones and Victorian additions, dominant in its position close to the sea with a bow-fronted façade, a gracious staircase crying out to all small boys to be slid down and, on the ground floor, his father's private consulting rooms, full of the fascinating potions and poisons of his profession.

Snug in his third-floor nursery in the care of Eliza his nursemaid Edward lived out the rhythms of his infant life to the music of Brighton, lulled to sleep by the strains of the dance band from the nearby bandstand, woken by the incessant crying of seagulls and the constant drag of sea on pebbles. Through his windows would have wafted the smell of salt and crowds and food and, as soon as he was tall enough to see out of them, there waiting to be discovered was restless, rowdy, stylish Brighton, his early playground. By 1858 it had acquired most of the characteristics it has today, the vivid layers of its history on show like the strata in a geological specimen: hard-working fishing port, aristocratic Regency mecca for fashion and vice, genteel Victorian spa town and now, with the arrival of the railway, favourite destination for London day trippers out for a good time.

Its raffish past and cosmopolitan itinerant population, the non-stop theatres and music halls, the meretricious charms of its pier and bands and seaside souvenirs, its froth and showmanship and its underbelly of illicit sex and crime provided the backdrop of his childhood, its diversions his lifelong fascinations. Drawn to the intricate lanes with their jewellery and junk shops he began his obsessive collecting, and penetrating the backstreets he must have caught glimpses of the seediness, sensed rather than understood, of the beer shops, brothels and betting rings which operated behind the alluring glitter.

Then, when he was thirteen, Edward discovered for the first time the thrill, which lasted his whole life, of sensational crime. A world of insanity, poison and sexual passion opened up on his doorstep, in all its drama and pathos, reality brought home by the involvement of people and places he knew intimately.

In June of 1871 a little boy had come to Brighton with his parents for a holiday by the sea. He lived in Clapham and he was four years old. His very name, Sidney Albert Barker, conjures up a little figure in cap and knickerbockers and brings a lump to the throat. During his holiday his Uncle Charles, his mother's brother, came for a visit and passing Maynard's sweet shop in West Street, bought Sidney a bag of Mr Maynard's best chocolate creams. Uncle Charles ate one of them and Sidney quite a few. Uncle Charles felt very unwell. Sidney was dead within twenty minutes. The post mortem revealed that Sidney's small stomach was full of chocolate creams and strychnine.

An inquest was held and interestingly a lady, a Miss Christiana Edmunds, came forward. Miss Edmunds was the daughter of a well-known local architect, privately educated, of independent means, living with her mother in Gloucester Place, Brighton, and her evidence carried weight. Miss Edmunds told the coroner that she too had bought and eaten Mr Maynard's chocolates and been very unwell. The chocolates were not made by Mr

Maynard; he bought them from a chocolate maker in London. The coroner heard that the London chocolatiers had been troubled by rats and laid down rat poison. A conclusion was reached that somehow some of the poison had got into the chocolates. A verdict of death by misadventure was recorded and Mr Maynard undertook to destroy the remaining chocolates.

That would have been the end of it had there not then begun an extraordinary chain of events that rocked Brighton. The town was hit by a wave of poisonings: small boys stopped in the street and given sweets by a heavily veiled lady became violently sick; poisoned chocolates were left around town in places where they were found and eaten. Dogs died in mysterious circumstances. As time passed the campaign stepped up. No one felt safe. Mr Maynard feared for the future of his shop. Sidney's father received a spate of anonymous letters and Brighton's chief constable put an advert in the local paper pleading for information.

In August 1871, the perpetrator indulged in a positive orgy of poisonings. A number of prominent Brighton residents were sent parcels of luxury foods; the poisoner had now added arsenic as well as strychnine to his recipe and had moved his centre of operations to London, sending the parcels by train from Victoria station. They were accompanied by notes, retrospectively full of menace: 'flavoured on purpose for you to enjoy' and 'the last of my debt and the first of the fruit from my garden'. Many people were ill and the servant of a Dr and Mrs Beard nearly died of convulsions after eating some of the cake sent to her mistress.

At this point Dr Beard contacted the police to tell them that more than two years previously one of his patients had conceived an obsessive passion for him. The patient was none other than Miss Christiana Edmunds, the witness at Sidney Barker's inquest. The degree to which Dr Beard reciprocated the obsession is uncertain but at any rate Christiana had become intimate with his family and in September 1870, nine months before Sidney's death, had given a present of chocolates to Dr Beard's wife Emily, which had made her ill. Dr Beard's medical knowledge, and possibly a guilty conscience, caused him to be suspicious and he accused Christiana of trying to murder his wife. Despite her hot denials he brought the relationship to an end and banned her from his house. Christiana had bombarded him with letters, some referring to the mysterious poisonings and to her role in the inquest, and these he now handed to the police.

The investigations which ensued were of the most laborious kind as the police tried to fit together the pieces of the complex jigsaw into a coherent pattern of evidence which would ultimately lead to Christiana's door and to her arrest. Quite why she had embarked on her poisoning campaign was anyone's guess. One theory was that she sought to direct suspicion from her original attempt on Mrs Beard's life by creating the myth of a motiveless poisoner at large in the town: another that she was 'trying out' doses for her next attempt on Mrs Beard. It may well be simply that thwarted passion had turned into a universal hatred of mankind.

The medical fraternity of Victorian Brighton was a close knit one. Mr Blaker, a surgeon living at number 29 Old Steine, next door to the Halls, was the doctor called to treat Mrs Beard's convulsing maid and another doctor also living in Old Steine was a recipient of one of the deadly parcels. Fevered speculation as to the nature of Dr Beard's involvement with Christiana Edmunds, his patient, was rife, as was prurient fascination with the sufferings of the victims.

Hundreds gathered outside Brighton Town Hall for the preliminary committal proceedings in the police court.[10] Amongst those who gained the prized seats was Alfred Hall, who took Edward with him. It was strong entertainment for a young boy; but it was after all, a brutal age. Public hangings had only been abolished three years previously in 1868 and lunatics were still regarded as good entertainment. There, in the stuffy police court, Edward sat through the detailed analysis of train tickets and journeys and boarding house registers that placed Christiana in London on the days the parcels were sent from Victoria. He listened to the identification evidence given haltingly by small boys and confidently by chemists and to the handwriting experts who linked the writing on the parcels with the chemists' receipts and the love letters to Dr Beard. Despite the dry technical detail Edward was captivated by the forensic skill that built the terrible conclusive picture and fascinated by the ordinariness of the perpetrator. There sat a woman who might have been his mother or sister, discreetly dressed in a black silk dress, demure beneath the veil of her bonnet. Had she really put strychnine in the sweets destined for little children and sent arsenic-laden parcels to the neighbours with whom she socialised? And if so must she be mad? Or bad? Or both? Or neither? The questions were to become the preoccupation of his career.

The Old Bailey jury who eventually determined the question in Christiana's case decided she was bad. She was found guilty of murder and sentenced to death. The subsequent reports of two doctors as to her demeanour as she awaited her punishment at last persuaded the Home Secretary of her insanity and the death sentence was substituted with life in Broadmoor. Her greatest claim to fame was the public debate she had triggered on the nature of free will and evil, a debate foreshadowing Edward Marshall Hall's great trials thirty years later.

These tales of a prosperous Brighton childhood were those that Sir Edward Marshall Hall KC MP immortalised by repetition over the decades of his fame.[11] An accomplished raconteur, renowned for his charm, cigar in hand and foot on fender of the society drawing rooms and gentlemen's clubs of London, he recreated this picture: the enchantingly naughty little boy, shaped by his love of Brighton, his knowledge of medicine and of poisons learned at his distinguished father's knee, and of ballistics through his precocious passion for target practice, who had vowed to become a barrister as he sat entranced in the Brighton Police Court listening to the unfolding of one of the great crimes of the Victorian age and who had never looked back. Describing a seamless transition to school at Rugby, university at Cambridge, a trip abroad and then the professional delights of the Inner Temple, and the domestic harmony of Cambridge Terrace, he told of the privileged and predictable life of an eminent KC with just enough individuality thrown in to captivate his audience.

The stories were true; but they were highly selective, chronologically massaged and very far indeed from the whole truth.

CHAPTER 2

'Splendid types of English public school life'

Edward was seven when things changed. His beloved sister Ada, then aged twenty-one, whom he regarded as a second mother, abandoned him. Always there, always on his side, Ada, beautiful and feted, only did what everyone else had expected, and found herself a rich and eligible suitor. In 1865 she married Arthur Labouchere[1] in St Nicholas, Brighton's foremost church, the venue befitting the grandeur of the match. Arthur was the son of a rich Huguenot banker brought up in a 54-bedroomed pile in Coldharbour, Surrey[2] and now, nominally at least, employed by his father's bank, though in practice so little inclined to work that his father paid him to stay away.[3] On their marriage, he and Ada set up home in style in nearby Horsham. Alfred and Julia were delighted. To Edward it was betrayal. Eternally optimistic, he never expected anything other than happiness. Blows when they came not only upset him, they astonished him. This was the first one. His passion and despair were accompanied, as they would be throughout his life, by a breakdown in his physical health. Jaundice, scarlet fever, typhoid and mumps followed one after the other. His behaviour became increasingly difficult to handle and even his mother, devoted as she was, described his temper as ungovernable.[4] Boarding school was the answer.

It was not his first experience of school. As a very small boy he had gone to a local nursery school in Brighton along with the other children living in Old Steine. His natural restlessness confined by authority and his small wooden desk, he had simmered with resentment and only two memories remained: his sweet vulnerable classmate Ethel Moon, aged four, who lived down the road at 9 Old Steine, and the picture on the schoolhouse wall of David and Goliath with Goliath getting very much the worst of it.[5] Both pretty Ethel and the bloodied Goliath had roused for the first time the protective instincts, inexplicable and inconvenient though he found them, that were to dog his life.

This time, though, school was a lot more challenging. Before he knew it he was on his way to St Andrew's College, Chardstock, buried in the Dorset countryside 150 miles from the urban delights of Brighton, accompanied by two pairs of sheets, two pillow cases, six towels, knife, fork and spoon and brushes for hair, teeth and nails.[6] Away from beloved family and home he nonetheless maintained his unquenchable optimism. Under his new five-shilling college cap[7] was a head full of dreams of triumph culled from his favourite book, *Tom Brown's Schooldays*, the rollicking novel by Thomas Hughes published in 1857 and telling the story of young Tom's experiences at Rugby in the 1830s. The fictional Tom, attractive, brave, energetic, kind hearted and intellectually incurious, bore a strong resemblance to Edward and Tom's father's attitude in the novel to his son's education might, judging by the choice of St Andrew's College, have been Alfred's attitude to Edward's: 'I don't care a straw for Greek particles … no more does his mother … if he'll only turn out a brave helpful truth telling Englishman and a gentleman and a Christian, that's all I want.'

On any other basis, St Andrew's was a very odd choice indeed. Built in 1834 by an eccentric vicar it was one of the new 'middle schools', a term derived from the original 'middle class school'. A number of these opened in the nineteenth century aiming to provide a practical education to boys of all ages, the sons of the growing commercial class who would follow their fathers into business. But St Andrew's was also a unique social experiment. Alongside the middle school was an industrial school, run as a charitable institution funded by the proceeds of the middle school, which provided a rudimentary education for working-class children of both sexes, mainly orphans destined to go into farming or domestic service. Opinion seems ultimately divided as to whether the worthy aims of the industrial school were in fact honoured or whether the orphans quickly degenerated into unpaid servants for the vicarage and the college: but the school thrived, and by Edward's time it had, in addition to the gothic-looking Spartan accommodation of all boys' schools of the period, a playground, an equipped gymnasium, a cricket ground and a bathing pool in the nearby river Kit.[8]

The pragmatic education offered is apparent from the syllabus with its emphasis on reading, writing and arithmetic, book keeping, grammar and geography. Attendance in the so-called Classical Department was a guinea (twenty-one shillings or £1.05 in today's terms) a term extra and very much an afterthought.[9]

The consequences for Edward were far reaching. The despised 'Greek particles' in *Tom Brown's Schooldays* were a shorthand reference to the minute scholarly investigations which formed the essence of a classical education. A sound grounding in the language, literature, philosophy and culture of ancient Greece and Rome was the cornerstone of all upper-class boys' education, begun at preparatory school and continued at all the big public schools with an assumption of proficiency by the time of advanced studies at Oxford or Cambridge. The disciplined mind trained in the classical stages of logic and rhetoric and possessing a good knowledge of Latin was taken for granted at the Bar, the exclusivity of the profession perpetuated by the fact that its members literally spoke the same language. It was a language Edward never properly learned.[10] At St Andrew's, a big fish in a small pond, he learned instead the language of populism. Mixing with boys from backgrounds very different from his own, handsome, extrovert and charismatic, he was soundly whipped for disobedience, became hero worshipped for his sporting prowess, and was appointed head boy at fourteen despite the presence of many older boys. He ultimately left believing that charm combined with brilliance at cricket would see him through pretty well anything and with an addiction to the heady drug of popularity that never left him.

It was not until September 1874, aged sixteen, that he went on to the public school which in his stories of his youth figures as an essential requirement to success at the Bar. In truth he was at Rugby for only two years and left in disgrace.

The Rugby he arrived at was not of course Tom Brown's Rugby. But thirty years on the ethos of the school, as promulgated in Hughes's novel, was still very much intact; so-called 'muscular Christianity', with an emphasis on wholesomeness of body and mind, embracing both athletic prowess and an adherence to Christian values. To Edward, who had already begun to identify fitness with happiness, it was an appealing philosophy and one he seems to have taken rather too literally. God and sport, though not always in that order, became his abiding passions. It all started well. Joining Philpott's House[11] under its popular housemaster, Mr Philpott, he must have been entranced to have his school career begin exactly as Tom Brown's had begun, with a hare-and-hounds run. But scholastically, his lack of a sound classical grounding at St Andrew's became immediately apparent. Too late to catch up, he was allowed to substitute further mathematics for Latin and Greek. He excelled at it, winning both the Upper School Mathematical Prize and the form prize at the end of his first year, but his ignorance of the classics did little to endear him to his new housemaster, Henry Lee Warner, a distinguished classicist who took over on Philpott's retirement.

Lee Warner was generally thought by the boys to be a good sort: 'He is gaining the affection of the house by the most hearty joining in both work and games … his anxious care and unceasing labour for the good of the house as a whole and all the members of it individually,' gushes the head of house in the house year book shortly after his appointment;[12] and this accolade seems borne out by Lee Warner's support for sporting events, spelling bees and the new debating society, at which 'a good debate was carried on about "Trial by Jury"', we are told in the year book. Edward's contribution to a subject on which he was to become one of the greatest experts of all time is not recorded.

Edward despised Lee Warner and a mutual loathing grew. Lee Warner may have detected and distrusted the lack of conformity lurking beneath the surface of Edward's apparently conventional schoolboy exterior. His now well-developed passion for trading in jewellery and guns was extraordinarily precocious; he had graduated from the silver fourpenny pieces collected in Brighton junk shops to small antiques, holding auctions in his study and buying and selling from dealers in Brighton in the school holidays. His fellow schoolboys were no match for him; a stamp collection bought from one of them for five pounds Edward immediately sold for fifty. Physically and emotionally he was mature for his age; he fiercely resented authority and was quite incapable of disguising the contempt he felt or the terms in which he expressed it. Curiously reckless and self-destructive, as senior judges were later to discover, he either did not recognise or did not care that those in authority usually held the upper hand. Most dangerously of all he was a natural leader.

All in all he was a type particularly distrusted by schoolmasters, and Lee Warner may well have categorised his influence, compounded as it was by his reputation as a wonderful cricketer, as a subversive one. The boy's successes on the cricket field only seem to have irritated his housemaster further. He went from strength to strength, culminating in the magnificent achievement in a house match of taking eight wickets in the first innings and five in the second. A house picture of Edward, by then seventeen, shows the mature face of a sensitive young man surprisingly guarded, somehow apart from his fellow boyish contemporaries. Perhaps he sensed the end was in sight. Only a few months later Lee Warner told the Halls that further education at Rugby was wasted on their son. Edward was interested only in achieving a summer term of glory on the cricket field and not in work, he said, and at the conclusion of the Christmas term 1876 the house book tersely records: 'E M Hall left the school.' He was leaving two terms early and he never forgave the man who had deprived him of the long-awaited triumphs of his school career: captain of his house, playing cricket for the school, the centre of attention.[13] The resounding fictional achievements of Tom Brown had been within his grasp and had been snatched from him.

In his later pursuit of a seat in Parliament and shameless courting of popularity, Edward claimed early ambitions for quite a number of careers, as a businessman and a craftsman as well as a lawyer. But in the cultivation of his racy image, he was less inclined to admit to the truth. Whether it stemmed from his devotion to his mother and hers to God, or from a subliminal recognition that his talent lay in persuasive oratory, is uncertain, but he left Rugby determined on the Church as a career. His doting mother was ecstatic; his equally doting sister Ada, derisive nonetheless as sisters are, greeted with scepticism the news that the rebellious Edward had decided to become a clergyman. Alfred, sharing her doubts, was anyway angry at the ignominious end to Edward's school days. Determined to teach his son a lesson in the need for hard work he sent him to gain commercial experience in the City. Edward came, after all, from a family of successful businessmen and his eldest brother, James, was by now setting an example as a prosperous forage merchant with a house in Park Lane to show for it.

In January 1877 Alfred sent Edward to work at Shepherd and Co, tea merchants in the commercial heart of London. Shepherd's was situated in Mincing Lane, a thoroughfare known then as 'the street of tea'. Tea merchants had settled there around the London Commercial Salerooms in order to be on the spot for the weekly tea auctions, chaotic affairs at which the world's tea was traded at furious speed and the tops of voices. The environment was not without romance but it was not one to which Edward, forcibly removed from Rugby, was receptive. The experiment was short lived and the commercial experience he gained was more likely to have arisen as a result of the opportunity to acquaint himself with London jewellers and antique dealers than from the world of tea. By the early summer of 1877 he was seeking comfort on the cricket field, playing for the Gentlemen of Sussex and regretting the end of his studies.

Old Rugby friends now planning their futures at university made him realise what he was missing. Aware of his academic inadequacies he embarked on a series of anxious letters to St John's College, Cambridge, the college his uncle Frederick, now a well-known lawyer, had attended. With the guidance of the college and the assistance of a home tutor he applied himself earnestly to the studies of the classics which then formed the bedrock of the university entrance requirements.

It is striking that all the arrangements required for entry to St John's were made by the eighteen-year-old Edward himself rather than, as was customary, by parent or school tutor.[14] It was certainly not a measure of any lack of interest on his family's part; Alfred was by now convinced that his son was destined to follow his Uncle Frederick to the Bar. Nor had Rugby washed its hands of him; Henry Lee Warner, his loathed housemaster, had relented sufficiently to provide a lukewarm but adequate reference.[15] It seems more likely to have been another indicator of the fierce independence and early maturity which had been his downfall at Rugby and ultimately led to all the adventure and tragedy of his young life.

In October 1877 Edward went up to St John's, to a spacious set of rooms with stone-mullioned windows framing the Second Court quadrangle and the tower of St John's Chapel.[16] Three years in that privileged environment, surrounded by old school friends, stretched ahead of him.

Later as a famous man, he eulogised the benefits of undergraduate life.[17] In truth, he left after just over a year, at the end of Michaelmas term 1878, and did not return for two years. No college or university records provide the reason for his sudden departure. According to his first biographer, Edward Marjoribanks, Edward had declared his love for Ethel Moon, his nursery school playmate, now seventeen. Devastated by her rejection, we are told he had a breakdown. There is no doubt that at some point Edward fell passionately in love with her, and ultimately she became his wife. It seems probable that she did indeed play a part in his decision to leave Cambridge. By now it was apparent that he took rejection very hard and his reaction to it was frequently physical illness. But there must have been other factors as well.

He was already showing a taste for rebellion. He resented structured environments and authority; now he had tasted freedom and the adult world of employment. He had more confidence in his commercial abilities. His love of sophisticated London was growing. His broken heart, like the ill-advised beard he briefly wore, may have seemed a symbol of manhood. The world was calling too urgently to resist and after whiling away the summer of 1878 playing cricket for the Gentlemen of Sussex, he responded to the call, leaving with no plans for Paris. He was still only nineteen, universally held to be exceptionally handsome, radiating energy and personality, greedy for experience. Unsurprisingly, no records exist relating to the year he spent there, though there are arch hints at a bohemian lifestyle in Marjoribanks' biography.

He became a *flâneur*, a kind of deliberate drifter for which there is no exactly equivalent English word but a role for which there was a well-established nineteenth century tradition. For Edward this time as an idler with a purpose was hugely significant. Merging into the crowds as an anonymous observer, cut loose from the labels attaching to him as an upper-class English schoolboy, he became the personification of Baudelaire's classic description:[18] the passionate spectator who sets up home in the crowd, away from home and yet feeling at home, a connoisseur of empathy, entering into the crowd, reflecting it like a mirror, endlessly reassembling the individual characteristics of its constituents like a kaleidoscope.

Whilst his contemporaries settled into their Cambridge rooms, reassuringly like those of Rugby, and continued their schoolboy friendships and habits of study, Edward drifted around the Latin Quarter. He was restless and rootless, probably genuinely heartbroken but perhaps a little self-consciously revelling in his heartbroken state, an outsider and observer and all the while, unknowingly, mirror and kaleidoscope, developing the extraordinary understanding of human psychology which he was to turn into his greatest asset.

With his particular brand of dash and pragmatism, he threw himself into the lives of the bohemian artists living in attics in romantic penury, but at the same time did rather well for himself trading in jewellery in the smart arcades. Paris was home to some of the greatest jewellers in the world – Boucheron, Cartier, Chaumet, Mauboussin, all glittering in Rue de la Paix and Place Vendôme – as well as to smaller backstreet dealers. Edward developed a lifelong hunger for their wares and a way of assuaging it. Jewels fed his eyes and soul and pocket. By a mixture of instinct and knowledge he dealt successfully, buying from the smaller dealers and selling to the larger ones, and he made money. Reluctant to come home and conform, hungry for adventure, he set his sights on Australia.

The journey he embarked upon was neither the privileged foreign tour of the young aristocrat nor the cushioned gap year of the modern student, but a final journey into adulthood. He went with the style that was typical of him. The privations of second class were not for Edward, nor was the pragmatism of the steam ship. There were plenty of these taking passengers from England to Australia but the *Hydaspes*, on which Edward travelled, was something very special. Iron hulled, she had been built in 1852 as just another steam-propelled ship destined for the mail run between Plymouth and Calcutta. In 1868, however, she was sold to new owners who removed her engines and converted her into a sailing ship. Now reinvented as a three-masted, massively canvassed 'tall ship', the *Hydaspes* was captained by the fabled Edwin Babot, who had built her reputation into one of legendary grace and speed. The sight of her, moored at Chatham docks, ready to set sail, would have stirred to adventure far more prosaic spirits than that of the romantic young Edward. It is not known whether, prior to sailing, he had availed himself of the owners' invitation to all prospective saloon passengers to inspect the 'unequalled passenger accommodation' with every 'convenience and ventilation thoroughly provided',[19] or whether he had his first sight of his ship only when he went aboard at Chatham, a day or so before departure.

No considerations of customs and excise or health and safety legislation dispelled the romance of that departure. Accompanied by the shouted commands of the sailors and the cries of the seagulls, it was all crammed on board: livestock for eating, pet dogs for company, fighting cocks, musical instruments and cricket bats for entertainment, Bibles for spiritual ills, potions for bodily ones, the trunks of the saloon passengers and the bundles of the poor. Along with them went Edward, with his portmanteau, gun and fishing tackle.

The actual date of a ship's departure was frequently different to that advertised as the captain waited for the most favourable combination of wind and tide, and Edward's voyage began on 30 July 1879 when the *Hydaspes* set sail, bearing her sixty-six passengers (sixteen saloon passengers and fifty second and steerage class) and a heavy cargo.

Hugging the Kent coast until she reached Deal she seemed almost as reluctant to say goodbye to England as many of the emigrant passengers cooped up in steerage but at last she turned out into the Channel, Australia bound.[20] She passed the Eddystone lighthouse on 3 August and now, after the pilots who had accompanied her had been dropped, she became a tilting independent little world of straining canvas and creaking spars, with her own surgeon and clergyman, sail makers and cooks and her own laws and traditions.

It was not unusual for ships encountering each other by chance to sail in company for a day or two; but not the *Hydaspes*. Captain Babot regarded the sighting of another ship sailing in the same direction as a personal challenge. Extra sails were hoisted and the crew doubled their exertions, relaxing only when the rival had been left far behind and nothing but the interminable swell stretched ahead.

During the long days at sea Edward kept a journal,[21] as was commonplace amongst both saloon and steerage passengers, in which the tedium magnified humdrum occurrences into excitements.

Monotony was punctuated by ritual; prayers and Bible classes were held daily. There were weekly entertainments, cock fights, minstrel shows put on by the sailors and concerts by the saloon passengers. The crossing of the equator was particularly celebrated by a dinner with champagne and equatorial pudding[22] but amongst the saloon passengers all events were seized upon as subjects for celebrations. On 16 September 1879, Edward's twenty-first birthday was one of them.

A weekly ship's newspaper, the *Hydaspes Gazette*, was a tradition on every voyage, compiled by the saloon passengers and edited by one of their number elected during the first week out. Predictably, though one of the youngest of the saloon passengers, Edward was chosen for the honour during his voyage. The paper always followed a well-established format and one example from a previous voyage survives in the National Archives of Australia.[23] It is written in a heavily facetious style and laden with puns, italicised to ensure they were not missed. ('The publishers hope none on *board* will be *bored* by it'.) It makes enchanting reading; a Births and Deaths column records the two sons born on board to Mrs Feline, the sad demise of Miss Budgere Gar and the suicide of two ducks destined for the dinner table who chose instead to commit their bodies to the deep. For entertainment there are short stories, puzzles and concert programmes for the 'Hydaspes Theatre Royal'. There is the report of a mock trial which was held in front of a jury of four ladies and there was even a cricket match on a deck transformed into the 'Hydaspes Oval'. Beautifying seaweed cream, stout and claret were advertised for sale in the ship's stores along with items signifying the ship's progress towards the equator, sales of rugs, sea boots and fur caps giving way to those of calicos, lace and lemonade. Cambric handkerchiefs and onyx studs were Lost and Found; correspondents consulted an agony columnist and a young man with 'light brown hair, whiskers and slightly inclined to embonpoint'[24] sought an amiable loving wife; perhaps unsurprisingly with that description, without success. More seriously the designated shipping reporter provided a weekly record of the weather and the ship's progress towards her destination.

As the shipping records show, the voyages were not all fun. Even for the saloon passengers the discomforts were considerable. The weather ruled all activities: it was uncomfortably cold or far too hot; fog led to the ringing of bells and blowing of trumpets night and day; the rolling seas made exercise difficult and resulted in the constant precipitation of belongings across cabins and the upturning of dinner tables. Passengers wedged themselves into their berths with carpet bags and their sleep was constantly disturbed by the ship's rats. ('The public are cautioned against a disreputable individual,' said the *Hydaspes Gazette*; 'he has a long peaked face and large whiskers, wears a rough brown long tailed coat and goes without shoes.'[25]) Shooting the rats was a popular sport for the young men on board. Never one to be outdone, Edward later insisted that the rat he potted was of enormous size.

The indignities and hardships suffered by the emigrants in steerage were far worse. Treated almost like convicts, subject to rations and roll calls, their days were supervised by a government matron and they were confined to their berths as soon as darkness fell. Religious instruction was almost constant. Disturbances broke out and malefactors were confined in makeshift cells. Sickness was rife and resulted in strict segregation from those in the saloon.

Sometimes there was very real danger, and fear united passengers of all classes, as they prayed for safety. Occasional sightings of masts sticking out of the water, grave markers of previous voyages, were reminders of the ship's vulnerability. Flat calms were ominous in a different way, when there were finite provisions on board and the constant threat of infection if the cramped intimacy became too prolonged. Hundreds had lost their lives on the Australia run through shipwrecks or fever.

Edward only just had a safe passage himself; on her very next trip out to Melbourne the *Hydaspes* collided with another ship and sank.[26] Edward's voyage, however, seems to have passed uneventfully and energetically. In addition to his newspaper-editing duties, he recited at concerts, shot seabirds and caught passing fish. His fellow saloon passengers were a mixed bunch: there were several single young men and some families including two Baptist ministers and their wives and children. The ministers may have offered sympathetic ears to Edward's religious ambitions but are unlikely to have been much fun. They were travelling out to bring sobriety to Melbourne: 'This young country is too given up to pleasure,' the Melbourne church leaders are reported as saying in welcoming them.[27] Despite the narrowness of the community with whom he lived so closely, Edward appears to have enjoyed the saloon society and there would have been no reason for him to observe the lives of those in steerage, separated by the planks of the saloon floor and by an uncrossable social gulf. But it seems, nonetheless, that he did watch and learn. More than thirty years later when the *Titanic* went down, it was Sir Edward Marshall Hall KC, the by then famous defender of the underdog, who took the sensational step of demanding publicly that her steerage passengers, reportedly kept behind locked doors whilst the gentry crowded onto the lifeboats, should be represented at the Board of Trade inquiry. No one else had even considered that they should have a voice.

The *Hydaspes* reached her destination eighty days after leaving England, on 18 October 1879.[28] Melbourne, founded only forty-five years previously, was vibrating with the frenzy of the Victorian Gold Rush and fast becoming the richest city in the world. It was right up Edward's street, Brighton on a bigger, brasher scale. Speculative developments were sprouting everywhere with prestigious hotels, coffee palaces and opulent mansions appearing almost overnight. The raw new city was buzzing with excitement and the explosion of wealth brought what it always brings: a sector of the community keen to establish themselves as the elite. English society was their model, with balls, cricket matches and a Henley regatta on the Yarra River. Smart visitors from England were especially welcome. When ships arrived a list of the saloon passengers was published in Melbourne newspapers and a whirl of activity in Melbourne society resulted.

Four years before Edward's arrival, two young Englishmen arriving in Australia to live and work, 'splendid types of English public school life' as one memoir describes them,[29] had set up the Bohemians Club for the purposes of cricket in the summer and theatricals in aid of charitable causes in the winter. The club prided itself on its free spirit. Its motto was 'Peradventure' and it had no clubhouse, no subscription or entrance fee and a highly exclusive membership, the criterion for which, other than the necessary social standing, was that a member was a good cricketer, or 'if a pretty bad bat then a pretty good singer or actor'.

It was a club tailor made for Edward and as its guest, he joined in the summer activities. The Bohemians toured the Western District for matches in various far-flung areas with lyrical names, Geelong, Colac, Campertown and Warrnambool, and then travelled on to Tasmania, where their critics, who initially mocked them for their immaculate appearance – hair parted in the middle, wearing clean linen – quickly became impressed with the quality of their cricket. The hospitality was overwhelming and when Edward was not playing cricket he was shooting birds, rabbits, wild duck and kangaroo and falling in love with the Australian bush. On his journeys he befriended a travelling jewellery salesman and got involved in a fist fight from which he emerged the victor; and all these experiences joined his growing collection of good stories embellished with a lot of imagination and lashings of charm.

In the spring Edward returned to Melbourne to start his journey home, speedier and less romantic than the voyage out. He travelled by steamship, the SS *Deccan*, via the Suez Canal, leaving Melbourne on a calm showery Friday in March 1880,[30] along with the London-bound Australian mail, a cargo of household goods, one dog and a diverse group of passengers, bound variously for Adelaide, Ceylon, Bombay and Venice as well as London.

Edward had changed. Nearly two years older, polished by Paris, toughened by the Australian bush, fluent in French with an already slightly shadowy past, he was no longer just another personable public schoolboy but a travelled, charming man who had, as he later said, 'learned that England, great though she is, is not the only country in the world'.[31] But two things had not changed. He still wanted to marry Ethel. And he still wanted to be a clergyman. The first desire proved stronger than the second.

Shortly after his return he proposed and was accepted. Ethel was nineteen years old and Edward had yearned for her since their kindergarten meeting.

Superficially her family was very like his. Her father, Henry Moon, was also a doctor and she was almost the girl next door, living at 9 Old Steine. In reality, her background was very different and it was on that basis that Edward's family were disappointed in the match.

The Moon family is an enormous one, deeply rooted in the yeoman class of Sussex. In training to become a doctor, Henry had stepped outside family tradition. His career was extremely worthy; he worked for many years as a general physician at the local hospital and was engaged in such social causes as the inoculation of the poor, but he had neither the professional nor the social standing of Alfred Hall. Furthermore there were Moon family connections with a tannery business in Horsham. Edward's sister Ada, now settled in her palatial country house just outside the town, was particularly unenthusiastic about the prospect of too close an association with the Moons, afraid it would reflect on her standing in local society.

In spite of, or perhaps more accurately because of, the later appalling scandal that attached to her name, Ethel is a shadowy figure. Her father married three times and was widowed twice. Her mother was Henry's second wife, Caroline. Ethel was born into a household already including four grown-up children from Henry's first marriage; Mary was twenty-four, Myra sixteen, Alfred fifteen and Sarah fourteen. She also had a full brother and sister, Nathaniel, eight, and Caroline, four. Packed into the narrow home in addition were a nurse and under-nurse, a cook and a housemaid. For Ethel as the youngest it must have seemed a bewildering environment. When she was five, at around the time she must have been attending kindergarten with Edward, disaster struck when Nathaniel died aged fourteen, followed less than a year later by her mother. She remained motherless, in the care of a governess and housekeeper, until her father married for a third time when she was eleven years old.

A few months prior to Edward's proposal her father also had died. Alone, vulnerable and by all accounts strikingly beautiful in a fragile willowy sort of way,[32] it is not hard to see why Ethel the orphan appealed to the protective chivalrous Edward. In his interactions in his public life his chivalry was of the elaborately punctilious kind which verged, even by the standards of his own day, on the patronising. Privately it went far deeper; he yearned to protect and Ethel's attraction probably arose from her need for protection. Perhaps that need also fuelled her own feelings towards him. Whatever the motives, they had each chosen their partner for the dance. It was to prove disastrous.

A prospective wife to support made Edward abandon thoughts of the Church. He decided at last to follow what his father believed to be his destiny and train for the Bar. Returning to Cambridge in October 1880, he was formally admitted to the Inner Temple as a prospective law student a month later. This time at Cambridge he seems to have had the detachment of the mature student, living in digs outside college and rushing through a law degree in two years. Save for winning his college cricket colours he left little impact. He graduated in 1882; his prolonged absence from the university and resultant failure to take the mathematical tripos resulted inevitably in a 'poll' degree, a pass without honours.[33]

Within days of leaving Cambridge he was married. The tenth of June 1882 was, symbolically enough, a warm day with the threat of thunder in the air.[34] But for Edward no clouds hovered on the horizon. The short walk from the porch of St Andrew Old Church, Hove, to the lychgate where the carriage was waiting is only about thirty yards but it was thirty yards to a sparkling future. Edward had married Ethel as he had yearned to for years; they were both young and beautiful; a honeymoon in Paris, the city he had claimed as his own, was to follow; a new flat in Seymour Street, just off Marble Arch, had been rented for the couple to live in on their return; the Bar already promised to be a career suited to his independent spirit and persuasive charm. If the sun was not actually shining it must have seemed to be doing so to Edward.

As they drove away from the church, Ethel told him she could never love him as he loved her. At least that is what she said. What she probably meant was that she had no intention of consummating her marriage.

CHAPTER 3

'Words can never tell my grief'

H e took her to Paris as planned, of course; what else could he do? And as planned they stayed in a central hotel and explored together the romance that characterised the City of Light of the 1880s. It was the very height of the Belle Epoque when the arts were flourishing, haute couture had just been invented, French cuisine was the best in the world and the production of champagne had been recently perfected. There was Maxim's and the Ritz Hotel and operettas and cabarets. Everywhere was adorned with orchids cultivated in the new glasshouses. The boulevards were beautiful, the colonnaded shopping arcades irresistible and the cobbled alleys of the Latin Quarter enticing. By Ethel's side was her new husband, handsome enough to turn heads in the street. He spoke French like a native, knew Paris intimately, and was greeted by name in the alluring little jewellery shops. He loved beautiful things and flowers and giving presents. His knowledge of fine wines and cigars and good food was ever-increasing. He adored her. No girl could have asked for a better lover to introduce her to Paris. And Ethel was miserable and quarrelsome and querulous.

In a painfully intimate diary[1] Edward recorded the meltdown of his honeymoon. Within two days of their marriage he was writing of her cruelty to him and his determination despite it 'to try and make her love me by kindness'. 'She is a dear little thing,' he recorded with his resolute optimism. But Ethel was not a dear little thing. She was capricious, spoilt and demanding and complained of illness most of the time.

He persevered with all the planned treats. During the days of that early summer they went for long walks down Rue de Rivoli through the heart of Paris and for long drives in a horse-drawn carriage through the Bois de Boulogne to the suburbs of Longchamps and Neuilly. They went down the Seine in a steamer and visited Fontainebleau and Versailles. There were cherries growing on trees. There was moonlight and the smell of fresh hay. And Ethel was low spirited and unkind and made scenes and told her new husband she did not love him; or, almost worse, that she would 'try' to do so. On one occasion she went out alone and he lost her. Having searched Paris all day, distracted by despair, he eventually found her in the late afternoon sauntering down the colonnaded Rue Castiglione absorbed in her misery, oblivious or indifferent to the anguish she had caused. 'I induced her to have some dinner and then pacified her a little, but I fear her love for me is almost gone for ever. I wish I were dead. Words can never tell my grief,' he wrote after that episode.

What was the problem? Given the immediacy of the onset, Edward's desperation and the timing of the quarrels in the early mornings and the evenings when they 'stay in' after dinner, the overwhelming probability is that they were sexual in origin and the marriage was not properly consummated. 'Poor little child how I wish I could make her happy. She does not seem to care for me much and I cannot make a difference. Spent a wretched evening,' he wrote. But why on earth should Ethel have taken such a stance with this kind, handsome young man whom she had known all her life and been engaged to for two years? It has been the subject of considerable speculation and some wild theories, but the probable reality is now clarified by newly researched evidence. Ethel was morbidly terrified of pregnancy and childbirth to the point of phobia. Her one confidant seems to have been her brother in law James Robinson, the sober solicitor married to her half-sister Mary. She had told him on many occasions that she dreaded having a child. Ultimately five years into her (childless) marriage she told Robinson that her doctor had confirmed to her that an anatomical deformity meant a child would cost her her life. This was not true though it may well be that she believed it.[2]

Today phobic fear of pregnancy is a recognised psychological disorder with a name (tokophobia) and a support group. Then, it would just have been blind lonely terror. Poor Ethel, with no mother in whom to confide, almost certainly ignorant of even the most rudimentary forms of birth control, may well have thought abstention was the only answer and it seems probable that faced at last with the reality of her imminent wedding night, she panicked with the violence of the phobic.

It was no better on their return to the new rooms in Seymour Street. The misery continued, their lives dominated by Ethel's moods and demands. By now of course it was not one sided. Frustration and anger at his crumbling dream made the always hot-tempered Edward retaliate; he was beginning to discover the savagery of words that could fall like blows, a talent that did not improve his personal relationships.

Professionally of course it was a talent that was to prove useful and now he had a living to earn. 'If I were asked to say what are the requirements of success at the Bar, I should be inclined to mention three ... the young barrister should have a good deal of ambition, secondly he should have very little money, thirdly he should be very much in love,' said Sir Edward Clarke KC in his Victorian memoirs.[3] Edward met all the criteria. It was just a pity that he was also so desperately miserable.

At the beginning of the Michaelmas term in October 1882 he paid his 100-guinea pupillage fee to his new pupil master, Henry Tindal Atkinson, and started his apprenticeship in Atkinson's chambers in the Inner Temple. Leaving his domestic problems behind for a while, immaculate in a dark suit, starched linen, a silk top hat and a velvet-collared overcoat, he travelled on a horse-drawn bus from Marble Arch to Fleet Street. Once he had alighted onto the wooden pavement and crossed the muddy and manure-strewn road he turned in through the vast gates that led to Middle Temple Lane and fell, like Alice down the rabbit hole, into his own particular wonderland, the sudden beauty and quiet of the Temple, that tight cloistered little world of ancient buildings, gardens and squares and cobbled alleys that lies hidden between Fleet Street and the Embankment. There he was to find like so many before and after him a refuge and solace, a second home away from the demands and miseries of the real one.

The Temple comprises two of the four Inns of Court, the Inner Temple and the Middle Temple,[4] fiercely individual though geographically conjoined. All the Inns operate independently on a collegiate system, offering barristers working and sometimes residential chambers, along with facilities for education and dining. At the time when Edward became a barrister they retained what they have only recently, at last, completely lost, a slightly amateurish dilettante charm arising from their fourteenth-century origins as what were, in effect, finishing schools for the sons of gentlemen, providing dancing lessons along with a rudimentary legal education. The tranquil surroundings so reminiscent of the ancient public schools and universities from which their members then came nonetheless had a sophistication to them which gave them their particular appeal. It was as though the stone fabric was somehow steeped not only in learning but in the crime, commerce and human conflicts which have been the business of the Bar for centuries. They provided as a result a unique brand of worldly escapism, cloistered as a monastery but with a romantic hint of the French Foreign Legion.

Life within the Inns was a curious comforting one, defined by rituals and ceremonies, time parcelled into the manageable bites of the legal terms – Hilary, Easter, Trinity and Michaelmas – punctuated by (very) long vacations.

In 1882 when Edward came to the Bar, the summer vacation lasted from 8 August to 2 November and the total vacations took up four and a half months of the year. Proposals to shorten them had met with judicial outrage.[5]

All possible loneliness was cushioned by the total lack of formal retirement requirements or even expectations. Octogenarian judges and QCs tottered into dinner at hall high table every day, never having to relinquish their hold on the life they had always known, the students eating below them at the refectory tables in a consoling continuum. It was a tiny world, exclusively masculine, cliquey, gossipy, protective towards its own.

The number of practising barristers has always been difficult to estimate since historical records made no distinction between those who practised and those who did not. The profession for centuries included a great many of the latter, young men who qualified only for social reasons. Nowadays there are more than 15,000 practising barristers. When Edward began his career the practising Bar was numbered in the hundreds and the criminal Bar was a very small proportion of those hundreds. As a result, the same men appeared very frequently on opposite sides of cases and it is unsurprising that intense friendships and animosities flourished, as they exploited each other's weaknesses and recognised each other's strengths, locked in the intimate rivalry of a lifetime of forensic battles.

There were few formal rules of conduct though many rigid and unspoken conventions rooted in the universally understood expectations of the behaviour of gentlemen. Edward himself, with all the casual arrogance of his class and time, emphasised in an article the necessity of a public school education: 'An uncouth man would not be at home in the Temple; he has to practise with gentlemen. The Bar must of necessity be a profession of gentlemen because the only control of the barrister's conduct is moral control. The sole restrictions upon the members are those imposed by gentlemen who are innately gentlemen.'[6] In the mid-1880s, judging by their father's professions, compulsorily recorded, 75 per cent of those called to the Bar came from the upper classes and in the Inner Temple 90 per cent were Oxford or Cambridge graduates. No considerations of diversity disturbed the little world in which these men operated, comfortable in the comradeship of innate superiority, applying to their working lives the schoolboy standards of honour, fair play and covert intolerance inculcated into them from their earliest years.

Members of the Bar have always had specialist subjects, but the particular specialisation that united them was that of advocacy, the persuasive presentation of a case in court. Barristers were generally employed because of their expertise in the art of advocacy; the subject matter was secondary.

Edward joined during a golden age; the social and intellectual superiority of senior barristers was unquestioned by the world as well as by themselves. The successful were accorded huge honours and respect and massive fees; knighthoods were conferred on most of those who reached the status of Queen's (or King's) Counsel; passports into high society and membership of the House of Commons were almost guaranteed to those who wanted them and ultimate progress to the Bench was the culmination of successful careers.

Getting there was, however, another matter; the journey involved a notoriously slow start and there are literally dozens of nineteenth-century memoirs recounting the pitiless drudgery of early years at the Bar, of young men wedged into shared desks in sunless back rooms slaving over the legal problems of their elders whilst struggling to make ends meet, sometimes for years on end. Those without private means supplemented their incomes by writing legal textbooks whilst a few of the more adventurous, lured by the proximity of Fleet Street, resorted to journalism. The fabled breaks at the Bar were elusive; it was hard to stand out of that crowd 'united by the common tie of paucity of means and alertness of intellect'.[7]

Edward tackled the problem with the skills of a brand manager of today. Rejecting the worthy activities of his colleagues he funded his enterprise by exploiting yet another of his singular interests. Having learned a bit about cigars from a Mr Dash, a tobacconist in Brighton, he bought 10,000 of a certain brand whose potential he recognised, kept 2,000 for the personal consumption that was to become one of his trademarks and sold the rest for a hefty profit. When that ran out he traded in jewellery of ever-increasing value. His appearance was always immaculate; his manner always assured. Recognising the importance of a memorable name he changed his. He had been christened Edward Marshall, his second name after the distinguished Dr Marshall Hall,[8] famous as the so-called father of neurology, and so professionally he now used his full name, Edward Marshall Hall. He quickly became known universally amongst his colleagues as 'Marshall', as he is for the rest of this book.

And as Marshall he became popular and admired by his contemporaries. He was dashing and amusing, always up for a game of tennis in the Temple gardens, ready with his invitations to home-made lemonade afterwards, apparently contemptuous of study and industry whenever there was a theatre or music hall to tempt him away, quick to inveigle others to go with him.

His new pupil master, Atkinson, was then forty-one, the cultivated son of one of the last serjeants at law.[9] He had a busy general practice and a deep understanding of the law. But if Marshall was hoping to see exciting cases he was to be disappointed. Most of his master's work during that year involved civil disputes heard in the superior courts of common law in Westminster Hall, the home of civil justice since medieval times. The superiority did not extend to the facilities. Westminster Hall was dark and fuggy, lit by smoking oil lamps and inadequately heated by open fires, though change was imminent. Young Marshall was amongst the very last intake of barristers to travel there by boat, in the centuries-old tradition. He would have made the trip up the Thames from the Temple Steps to Westminster Bridge on the penny steamer. It must have been a windblown journey and he would have had to clutch his hat on his head with one hand whilst holding the traditional blue bag containing his new wig and gown in the other.

It was at Westminster Hall that he listened to the great *cause célèbre* of the day: Richard Claude Belt, the fashionable sculptor of the 1880s whose sculptures of Baron Rothschild, Charles Kingsley and Lord Byron were much admired, was publicly accused by *Vanity Fair* magazine of being a fraud whose works were in fact sculpted by his backroom partner, a Mr Verhyden. The many society figures who had sat for Belt were loud in his support whilst the artistic elite of the Royal Academy turned on him. The ensuing complex legal proceedings were presided over by Baron Huddleston,[10] one of the most famous of the old order of Victorian judges who attracted much criticism in this case for his partisanship towards Belt. Egged on by his wife, Lady Diana Huddleston, who sat beside him, the judge invited the society witnesses who supported Belt to come and join the couple on the Bench after they had given evidence. It was an unedifying display of establishment manipulation of the proceedings and young Marshall watching it cannot have been very impressed. The case was planned to be the last in Westminster Hall. Half way through it was adjourned. The other half, to demonstrate the seamless administration of justice, was to be heard in the new law courts in the Strand.

On 4 December 1882, in a moment of increasingly rare domestic harmony, Marshall and Ethel stood at a window of Cogswell and Harrison, a department store in the Strand, looking down at the gaily decorated street, loud with church bells and cheering, as a procession headed by Queen Victoria and William Gladstone, the then Prime Minister, filed slowly into the new court. The massive new palace of justice stretched along 500 feet of the Strand in an orgy of turrets and buttresses, its thousand rooms including nineteen imposing courtrooms built to provide a suitable setting for a new era of more dignified dispensation of justice. With the move came the introduction of a system recognisable by the standards of today. There was a consolidation of the untidy overlapping of courts and jurisdictions. New procedural rules were introduced. There was a daily cause list, naming the cases to be heard that day; the public began to know at last where they were. The judges knew where they were too: on chairs for the first time in history. The old benches on which they had traditionally sat were thrown out along with the pewter stands containing wafers and sand; only blotting paper was good enough for the new law courts.

It was all very grand and there were rich pickings for young barristers in the disputes as to land rights, wills and property increasing with the growing middle class, and in the burgeoning commercial work following on the heels of the industrial revolution; but Marshall, almost despite himself, was drawn instead to the Central Criminal Court, housed in the squalid Old Bailey buildings at the far end of Fleet Street.

The Old Bailey courthouse was hopelessly cramped outside and in. The narrow alley on which it was situated was constantly clogged up with horse-drawn vans lumbering to nearby Smithfield market and the street outside the courtroom windows was liberally strewn with straw in an attempt to deaden the sound of hooves that disrupted the proceedings inside. On all sides were taverns where accused, witnesses and legal clerks congregated. You could get more than ale and pies here if you knew who to ask and the price was right; there were plenty of volunteers to be alibis or witnesses or to swear documents. Inside the courthouse it was just as bad. The best that could be said of the Old Bailey was that the practice of criminal work was not quite as corrupt as it had been fifty years before. The vicious reputation of the barristers who practised there had diminished. On its way out was the bullying of witnesses and verbal and sometimes even physical abuse of opponents which had given the Old Bailey Bar a lower reputation than the criminals it represented. The buildings, however, were worse than ever. Separated only by a courtyard and an underground stone passage from the grim walls of Newgate prison, the Old Bailey had, with an increasing workload during the Victorian era, become oppressively overcrowded. The lighting was poor; huge reflectors were hung in front of the windows to try and capture every ray. The pea-souper fogs made it still darker, on bad days infiltrating the courtroom with an atmospheric haze which the inadequate ventilation, itself a health hazard, could not dispel. The accommodation for the Bar was squalid. The Bench dined lavishly alongside the most eminent and favoured counsel but mess facilities for the rest of the Bar consisted of cauldrons of gravy and potatoes, the smell, along with that of misery and poverty, pervading the dark corridors.

Protests about the cruel and oppressive conditions were constant and now, at last, the inadequacies had been recognised,[11] though there was little incentive for change in a system in which criminals were treated with contempt. It is easy to forget that although crime may be as old as mankind, its regulation through a humane system of trial and punishment is relatively recent in England. All the most significant reforms, which transformed it from a biblical system to one in which there was a clear concept of fairness to the accused and humanity in his punishment, only really began during the second half of the nineteenth century and the reform of the legal system lagged far behind progress in other areas. It is an astonishing fact that people would have been able to travel by Underground (first in use in 1863) to witness a public hanging (the last of which was in 1867). The last hanging, drawing and quartering (in practice by then, hanging and beheading) was carried out in 1820, less than forty years before Marshall was born; young children were being hanged until 1833; the last public whippings took place when Marshall was three years old and the last public hangings when he was ten. The more enlightened system in which Marshall worked was therefore relatively new and a culture of brutality was still very close to the surface. Floggings, hard labour, solitary confinement, savage sentences for minor offences, cruel oppression of the poor and weak were still part of the daily business of the criminal courts and over it all hung the shadow of the noose.

For Marshall, already addicted to the theatre, the trials were revelations, the pity of the human condition laid bare with all the drama of the stage but with the savagery of reality thrown in. Here was the costumed ritual he loved; here was the mannered oratory of the Victorian drama; here the adulation of the star performers and the frantic scrabble for tickets to listen to them.[12] Here was the admiring audience; here occasionally was even the applause although that was now frowned upon by the judges and quickly suppressed. Here too were often the stock characters of melodrama: hero, hero's friend, girl, villain. But the plots were real and there was nothing artificial about the passion; real stories of lust, greed, hatred, love and sacrifice were being played out in all their compelling truth. Many years later, addressing a Playgoers Club dinner, Marshall reminisced about how he had learned how undramatic theatre was compared with real life and told the little story that exemplified that: a young man had assumed his brother's identity, stood trial for his brother's crime and served a prison sentence on his brother's behalf. The judge asked why he had done it. 'He married my girl and I ain't got no kids,' he said simply.

All his working life Marshall revelled in the drama of crime as he revelled in his evenings at the theatre, his responses to the two almost indistinguishable. Ultimately, in 1920, in a merging of life and art which made it impossible to know which was imitating which, he made an application on behalf of two film producers from Gaumont-British Pictures for seats close to the dock at the announcement of a death sentence in order that they could observe and realistically reproduce on film the facial expressions of judge and defendant at this most theatrical of moments. Mr Justice Darling, to whom the application was made, dealt with it in the best traditions of assumed judicial ignorance of popular culture. He was appalled at the suggestion, he said, and dismissed the application. 'What is a film producer anyway?' he asked.[13]

It was in the Old Bailey that Marshall himself witnessed for the first time that moment of pure drama that was the passing of the death sentence.

At the beginning of the Michaelmas term of 1884 Marshall had nothing to do. He was at the end of his pupillage, with no work; no permanent place in chambers; no real interest, he had discovered, in the academic side of the law. Nothing really but this restless yearning for passion and drama. He had spent a morning wistfully watching some of the great names conducting a case at the Old Bailey and now, when he was sitting in the robing room, a prosperous young barrister, enviably preoccupied, accosted him.

Forrest Fulton was a persuasive orator with a reputation for competence rather than brilliance and a way with juries: 'good looks, good figure, good manners, good voice – and a good working knowledge of the criminal law', as a contemporary described him.[14] Fulton was in court that afternoon and he needed help in getting up a brief for a trial the next morning. The trial was a sensational and very serious one: the fatal shooting of a young police officer in the course of investigating a burglary on his beat. It speaks volumes for the rough and ready approach of the law at that time that the barrister who was to conduct the defence should receive his brief the day before the trial and should then delegate to an unknown novice the task of preparing it.

In fact, Forrest Fulton had fallen on his feet. Marshall, hungry for work, with an already extensive understanding of ballistics, discovered a new skill for intricate analysis. He embarked on a note of the facts, a task which sounds simple but is in fact one of the most important in a criminal trial; Marshall later attributed his skill in it to his study of mathematics and he exhibited the same love of order that manifested itself in his meticulous collecting and display of small exquisite antiques. Something about the dry task of arranging from the chaos of overlapping and contradictory evidence a neat clear chronological parcel, impeccably accurate, covertly partisan, appealed to him and it was to become one of his greatest skills, as vital to his success as the brilliant oratory that hid the pedestrian toiling over detail.

The case in which he was to extract and analyse the salient points was one which must have reminded him of his schoolboy fascination with the Brighton chocolate poisoner Christiana Edmunds. In this case also, the prosecution had to rely upon the stitching together of fragments of circumstantial evidence into a plausible case against the defendant. On a dark and foggy night in east Dalston, a young police officer, Police Constable Cole, twenty-six years old and newly married, was shot apparently whilst attempting to arrest a man who was in the process of breaking into a chapel. Other officers arriving on the scene after hearing gunshots found PC Cole dying on the ground and lying by the low window of the chapel a chisel with the word 'ROCK' scratched on the handle.

Many months later, acting on information received, the police caught up with two men who confessed to acting as accomplices that night to a friend who was attempting to burgle a chapel. The friend was a Thomas Orrock, who, they said, possessed a gun and who had subsequently admitted to them the shooting, which they had not seen. Their evidence as accomplices required corroboration. Microscopic examination of the chisel handle revealed that two letters preceded those already seen, 'OR'. Further investigations ascertained that Orrock had bought a gun (thrown away by him and never found) and the bullet extracted from PC Cole's head was of the same type as the ammunition Orrock's gun would have discharged. Orrock confessed to the burglary but denied the shooting. Marshall's subsequent account that Orrock was 'hanged on the evidence of a scratch on the chisel'[15] was, like many of his observations, poetic but inaccurate. The circumstantial evidence, far more extensive than set out here, was, if not the well-worn 'overwhelming', at least sufficiently striking for a conviction.

Marshall's assistance was rewarded with a very minor role in the trial, taking notes of the evidence. It was not what he dreamed of, but it was a beginning.

The trial was a classic example of its time, appalling to the modern eye in the inequality of arms. Heard by Mr Justice Hawkins (later Lord Brampton), the archetypal 'hanging judge', it took only two days in total. Nowadays it would take at least two weeks. The prosecution case consisted of rousing speeches and a succession of witnesses giving rapid evidence superficially dealt with. The defendant in those days had no right to give evidence in his own defence and his theoretical right to call witnesses was in reality frequently frustrated by poverty, both his own and that of the witnesses. His life rested on the speech by his advocate, supposing, as in this case, he was fortunate enough to have one. Forrest Fulton did his eloquent best but the proximity in time and geography of burglary and murder made it a hopeless task.

Thomas Orrock, aged twenty-one, was found guilty and Marshall, three days after his twenty-sixth birthday, heard for the first time the passing of the death sentence heralded by the resonant proclamation of the judge's clerk: 'My lords, the Queen's Justice do strictly charge and command all persons to keep silence whilst the sentence of death is passed upon the prisoner at the bar.' Mr Justice Hawkins was never one to exercise restraint. He was a good lawyer but he combined it with a callousness that made him more feared than respected. Autocratic in the extreme, he sat in broiling courtrooms all windows closed to avoid draughts and dispensed savage sentences with an uncomfortable mixture of brutality, self-righteousness and Victorian sentimentality.

Now he put on the black cap. It was part of his performance to speak so softly that the defendant, already nearly senseless with terror, had to strain to hear his fate:

> You now stand justly righteously convicted of the crime of wilful murder. You slew … a brave young officer. You cut short his days by your murderous hand. There is … no escape for you from the doom that awaits you … the law says you must die … henceforth this world is no more for you and when you descend the steps from the dock where you now stand turn your thoughts to almighty God and pray for forgiveness for your great sin.

Only then did he actually get round to the sentence of death:

> It remains only for me to pass upon you the heaviest sentence of the law, which is that you be taken from hence to the place from whence you came and from thence to a lawful place of execution and there you be hanged by your neck until you are dead; and when you are dead that your body be buried within the precincts of that prison within the walls of which you shall have been confined last … and may the Lord have mercy upon your soul.

Delivered in dim courts, these sentences even when uttered by kinder men seemed utterly God-like; it was hard to believe that any other Day of Judgment was necessary. It is no wonder that the judges who pronounced them came to believe so implicitly in their own power and to wield it so confidently. There are many stories of early nineteenth-century judges sobbing as they delivered a death penalty. But this was not the case at the beginning of Marshall's era; decades of rigid Victorian morality and settled ideas of just retribution for sin had made them less merciful.

These displays of hubris inspired in the young Marshall the lifelong irreverence for which he became famous. From his very earliest years, whilst his contemporaries assiduously sought the judicial approval that ensured comfortable trials and professional advancement, Marshall baited judges, teasing, harassing, badgering, cutting down to size, to the fury of the Bench and the delight of juries. Delivering death sentences might not have caused the Bench to break into sobs but poor old Judge Field at the Sussex quarter sessions was reportedly frequently near tears of rage at Marshall's impudence.

Unimpressed as he was by displays of judicial power, Marshall was nonetheless hooked. Hooked by the drama. Hooked by the horrid mix of prurience and pity which affects the spectator of a major criminal trial. Hooked by the car crashes that were the protagonists' lives, defendant and victim somehow joined in one defining aftermath. 'I mean to specialise in the two biggest gambles there are,' he told a friend, 'life and death – freedom and imprisonment. Facts not principles for me. I don't know much law but I can learn what there is to be known about men and women.'[16]

Fulton was to give him his opportunity. Shortly after the trial he wrote offering Marshall a place in his chambers in Fountain Court. He had never heard Marshall utter a word in court but he recognised a winner when he saw one. Marshall settled happily there in the autumn of 1884 and began the slow business of building a career. The work was spasmodic; he still spent a lot of time playing tennis with his new room-mate, Edward Pleydell-Bouverie. It was a pastime that proved profitable for one of them; Pleydell-Bouverie, the son of the Liberal politician of the same name, made quite a name for himself in 1890 with his book on lawn tennis. Marshall meanwhile undertook 'devilling' (preparing briefs, writing opinions and drafting documents) for others. He began to hold very junior briefs in bigger criminal cases. His talents as an advocate were not the only ones recognised around this time. The American jewellers Tiffany's, about to open their first London branch, offered him a job as manager. He refused it; much as he loved jewels there was something that fascinated him more.

Terrible crime had become part of his life and he was increasingly preoccupied by motive and troubled by those cases where it seemed absent. Apparently sane defendants who, like the Brighton chocolate cream poisoner of his childhood, committed crimes of madness held a sort of compulsive attraction for him: Harry Patrick, who cut the throat of his beloved girlfriend with a Japanese dagger; Mrs Taylor, a grocer's widow and apparently steady mother, who did the same to her three daughters with a razor. Holding junior briefs in each, the first prosecuting, the second defending, he listened to the unsophisticated evidence and began to doubt the law relating to criminal insanity. Surely in these cases of infinite tragedy and pity medicine should play a greater part in the understanding of irresistible impulse? Surely things should be done differently?

Even more than the cases he became fascinated by the psychology of the jury. In Marshall's day most litigants whether in civil disputes or criminal trials had the right to trial by jury. Ancient though this right was, deeply and romantically embedded in the law of England, barristers had not traditionally applied much thought to the best way to the hearts and minds of these twelve random men entrusted for a few days with absolute power over the fortune and life of a fellow human being. They regarded themselves as infinitely the social and intellectual superior of the jurors and subjected them to theatrical performances more concerned with impressing them than persuading them. Thanks to the qualifications for jury service there was in Marshall's day a remarkable uniformity amongst jurors; selected from a narrow band of society, male householders, none was under twenty-one or over sixty and the upper middle classes were excepted almost in their entirety. No peers or MPs or doctors or lawyers. No clergymen or vets or soldiers or sailors. Jurors were 'middle aged, middle class and middle minded'.[17] If England was a nation of shopkeepers, most of them ended up on juries.

Marshall soon recognised that with the obvious disadvantages a great advantage lay in the consequent uniformity of psychology. It was a relatively easy task to identify and analyse the forces that drove them but no one had ever done it as effectively as he was to do. Nowadays identification with the psyche of the jury, hard though it is with the diversity they have, is commonplace. Then it was revolutionary. Marshall did not perform in front of them, he aligned himself with them.

He slowly began to be briefed in his own right and he loved it. The camaraderie, the rivalry, the constant stress and travel, the adrenalin rushes, even the penury, carrying as it did the potential for the earnings and lavish lifestyle of the leaders of the Bar – the Queen's Counsel – who seemed to him to have it all. Meanwhile he tried his hand at everything: crime, divorce, personal injury, breach of contract.

At the Old Bailey the good looks regarded as little short of staggering were constantly remarked upon. One of the old Newgate prison warders described his personality as so strong it was almost audible. The young Marshall was like a lion, the old man reminisced: arrogant, powerful, menacing in court, yet with the warmest of hearts, always ready with a joke. Into the Bailey he would storm in the mornings, depositing in the warder's office for safekeeping a piece of silver purchased on the way to court, full of information about gems and weapons and astronomy and astonishing facts that had just caught his interest. Once, the old man said, young

Marshall had penetrated the office to teach him the jiu-jitsu moves he had just learned.[18]

In Sussex this blazing personality combined with his father's well-known name won him solicitors anxious to send him the cases that would give him his chance in court. He quickly began to be noticed by the court reporters. This was partly attributable to his trick, infuriating to his colleagues, of starting even the most humdrum case with a ringing reference, calculated to rouse the reporters' attention, to the sensational nature of the evidence he proposed to call; but nonetheless the admiration was genuine. 'This popular member of the Sussex Bar has been in great demand in the courts lately. Nature has been bountiful in her gifts to him. He has a fine presence, an admirable voice and a great flow of words,' cooed an Eastbourne newspaper. Amongst his contemporaries Marshall was beginning to be regarded as a dangerously effective opponent; amongst more senior members of the Bar he had been noticed; and most of the Sussex and Bailey judges were rendered apoplectic at the mention of his name.

The future, professionally at least, looked promising. Personally, too, things were improving; not at home in Seymour Street, where they seemed to be going from bad to worse, but as a result of a new world that was opening up. The Orrock trial had resulted in an unexpected connection.

CHAPTER 4

'Violent passionate extraordinary advocacy'

Above the raffish Folly Theatre, charmingly painted and panelled, in William IV Street by Charing Cross station was the (literally) green room, which reverberated with the sounds from the music halls, burlesque and new light French operas known as *opéras bouffes* being played out on the stage below. It was in that room in 1876 that the Beefsteak Club[1] had held its inaugural meeting. Amongst the founder members who paid the eight-guinea entrance fee were W S Gilbert, Arthur Sullivan, Henry Irving, Corney Grain the comedian, John Hare, a distinguished actor-manager, and F C Burnand, soon to be editor of *Punch*. 'The better class of Bohemianism all well-known and clubbable,' said Gilbert.[2] Open from 3pm to 3am, the club became the meeting place of actors and favoured members of audiences after the curtains had come down. (All men of course; the wives were sent home in the brougham once the performance was over.)

By Marshall's day the list of Beefsteak members reads like an encapsulation of the late Victorian London social scene, representing clubland at its most intoxicating fringes where bohemia (as long as it was embodied in someone beautiful or talented enough) met landed aristocracy and those of the distinguished professional classes interested in the arts. The club prided itself on its iconoclastic inclusive reputation although in the eyes of today its membership and the casual arrogance of its rules (all waiters to be called 'Charles' for ease of reference of its members) hardly exemplify that image.

One of the stalwarts of the club was slim, moustached, debonair Montague Williams QC, who had been leading counsel for the prosecution in the Orrock trial. Williams straddled two worlds: he had been an actor in his youth and married an actress, the daughter of Robert Keeley, a great actor-manager of the day. Early widowed, Montague Williams had made the Beefsteak a home from home. In 1885 he proposed Marshall for membership, the proposal seconded by Charles Gill, a barrister whom Marshall had met at the Sussex quarter sessions and who was to become one of his closest friends.

The unknown Marshall was at twenty-seven very young for membership of such a club and his sudden trajectory into high Victorian society is striking. Few achieve such an exalted social circle, from a relatively obscure beginning, so young; and if they do, they usually work very hard for it. Marshall's looks and charm must have been his passport, since he had no other. He is unlikely to have been unaware of his impact on the famous old actors and actor-managers, many of whom had never married, who dominated the Beefsteak membership.

Whatever the reason for his election, Marshall was born to be a London clubman, drawn to domestic comfort without domestic restraint, to the relaxation of the company of other men and to the traditional platform of the consummate raconteur. The Beefsteak connections led on to a proposal for membership to the larger and more famous Garrick Club, the two clubs having a significant crossover of membership. Through members of both and the invitations leading on from those members he developed a vast theatrical network, so becoming intimate with a world far removed from that of his hard-working and generally sober contemporaries at the Bar, most of whom would have regarded with horror the idea of sitting up half the night and appearing in court the next morning. It never bothered Marshall. The great names of the theatre of his day,[3] playwrights and writers,[4] satirists and cartoonists,[5] all became part of his social circle along with the more unconventional of the politicians, aristocrats and senior members of his own profession. It was a heady environment and one which gave Marshall polish and confidence and confirmed in him his predilection for high living.

His advocacy also began to be influenced by these theatrical friendships. There was nothing new about his recognition of a close association between advocacy and stagecraft. The Bar had traditionally looked to the stage for ideas; up to the mid-nineteenth century young barristers were being taught the rudiments of declamatory rhetoric, many taking their lessons from John Cooper, an actor who taught aspirants to both stage and Bar;[6] and as late as 1882 *The Times* reported that it was envisaged that the new School of Dramatic Art would be open not only to would-be actors but to barristers and curates, all those proposing to earn their livings by the techniques of persuasion being taught under one roof.[7]

A misconception commonly held latterly is that Marshall's technique was a throwback to that of the advocates of a generation before, a style which emulated the Victorian stage, ludicrously melodramatic, embarrassingly mannered.[8] The mid-Victorian advocates had thrown themselves around courts, wringing their hands, rolling their eyes and making lachrymose pleas to the heavens, bellowing for justice, or in cases where that might be inconvenient, for mercy. Had that been Marshall's style he would have been one of many; his oratory would never have resonated down the decades in the way that it has. Admittedly histrionic by today's understated standards, nonetheless he was learning the new styles adopted on the stage by Irving and others in which artifice was abandoned in favour of the application of technique to real emotion born of personal experience and memory. Years before Stanislavsky invented the technique and decades before Strasberg developed it, Marshall was becoming a method actor.

As his domestic unhappiness grew so his contemporaries began to remark on his 'violent passionate extraordinary advocacy'.[9] Through his own emotional experience he was beginning to build a unique style. He was not to be given the case in which he perfected it for some years, but the building blocks were all in place now. All the experiences and memories of his unconventional past and miserable present, both so different from those of most of his contemporaries, were now called into play. The school friends at St Andrew's, his social inferiors by the standards of the day; the bitter clash with authority at Rugby; life as a City clerk; the relaxed morality of bohemian Paris; the rugged privations of the *Hydaspes*; the novelty of distant foreign cultures; above all the humiliations of his marriage; he drew on it all. And without even knowing why, juries responded to it. This was not another young toff in a wig and gown displaying from the great heights of intellectual and social superiority the charged rhetoric of the Victorian melodrama; this was a man who had suffered. His views were worth listening to.

Meanwhile he and Ethel soldiered on, outward appearances maintained: they attended Temple Church every Sunday for divine service, Marshall in his top hat and Ethel her Sunday best and when they emerged into the courtyard afterwards they walked past the admiring working people who lived in the alleys around Fleet Street and who congregated there on Sundays to watch their red carpet equivalent, the judges and QCs who were the great names of the legal world.[10] In the afternoon the two of them walked in the park. They toured Europe for their first summer holiday and went into society together. Together they entertained the friends Marshall met through his Beefsteak connections, many of whom were to become his closest confidants. Ellen Terry visited them and other famous names of the late

Victorian theatre. But none of these entertaining friends, nor the theatres and concerts she was taken to, nor the diamond star brooch bought for her, nor Marshall's DIY to embellish her home made any difference to Ethel's feelings.

The Beefsteak was enormous fun and home was utterly miserable. Marshall relied more and more on club life and on friends, on the stimulating conversations which were honing his advocacy skills, on intimate little dinners at the Beefsteak with Charles Gill, his club seconder, and on the soothing qualities of cricket and shooting on aristocratic estates. Ethel, in her turn, relied more and more on the outlet of demanding scenes, long periods of illness and the soothing qualities of chloral hydrate,[11] a sedative and sleeping draught. Marshall was away a lot both for work on circuit and for amusement. Despite her coldness to him Ethel liked to be pampered and fiercely resented his absence and the increasing demands of his work. In sharp contrast to his home life he had forged a professional and social life where he felt appreciated, recognition and admiration fuelling his ever-increasing lust for self-promotion.

It was probably this lust, along with a recognition that crime was not where the money was to be made, that motivated his move, in 1886, to a new address in King's Bench Walk in the Inner Temple. He went at the invitation of Henry Bargrave Deane, a junior barrister who was shortly afterwards instructed with Sir Walter Phillimore QC in one of the most sensational cases of the century, and Marshall joined the team of advocates as the most junior member.

The terrible downfall of Sir Charles Dilke serves as an archetype of the cataclysmic but transient political scandal, regarded at the time as of huge constitutional importance, now long forgotten. In 1886 Dilke was a forty-two-year-old Cabinet minister, widely tipped to succeed Gladstone as Prime Minister, when he was cited as co-respondent in the divorce between a fellow MP, Donald Crawford, and his wife. Crawford had been a political protégé of Dilke and had married a nineteen-year-old girl in 1882. In 1885 she told her husband she had been seduced by Dilke in the first year of her marriage and had since carried on an intermittent affair with him. Crawford sued for divorce and a judge, in reliance on Crawford's (hearsay) account of what his wife had told him, granted a decree nisi on the basis of her adultery whilst inconsistently in the public's eyes, if not the lawyers', acknowledging that there was no hard evidence to suggest any impropriety by Dilke. Had Dilke had a grain of sense, or been properly advised, that would have been that. Instead he sought, disastrously, to clear his name, by invoking the aid of an official known as the Queen's Proctor. This official is entitled, on behalf of the Crown, to prevent a divorce decree becoming absolute in circumstances where a court may have been misled into granting the first stage, the decree nisi. The Queen's Proctor was represented by the team in which Marshall was the most junior. The result was a lengthy hearing in which Crawford's wife gave evidence but Dilke, who was not a party, nor strictly speaking represented, could not cross-examine her.

A breathless public was treated by the newspapers to a salacious story which read like one of the pornographic novels concealed in the libraries of respectable Victorian gentlemen, the illusion enhanced by the (real) names of the female protagonists. The reluctant quivering new bride, Virginia, said she had been persuaded by Dilke, her own mother's ex-lover, to meet him for trysts in an anonymous house in Warren Street, where, his carriage waiting outside, he introduced her to 'every kind of French vice', culminating in naked romps between the two of them and a maidservant called Fanny.

Many thought the story was either Virginia's fevered fantasy or part of a smear campaign by Dilke's political enemies. Nonetheless, the judge and jury believed it and granted the decree absolute. Dilke was ruined, the recipient, it was widely said at the time, of the worst legal advice ever given.

The role Marshall played in the case was too junior for his reputation to be tainted by the errors of judgement made by his team. On the contrary the kudos of involvement in a case of such importance, and including such names, enhanced his growing reputation both as a successful barrister and as one who was moving in high social circles.[12]

They were about to get even higher. A few years before Marshall came to the Bar, there had been a modern addition to the sixteenth- and seventeenth-century buildings in the Temple, erected on land reclaimed when the Thames Embankment was built. The new Temple Gardens buildings were designed by Sir Charles Barry and his son Edward in the highly romantic neo-classical style described as French Renaissance. Into number 3 Temple Gardens, bent on establishing a select hand-picked chambers, went Charles Hall QC. No relation to Marshall, Charles (later Sir Charles) was the son of a distinguished judge of the same name. He was educated at Harrow and Trinity College, Cambridge and was a close friend and confidant of the Prince of Wales, the future Edward VII. Ultimately, in 1877 he had been appointed his Attorney General.[13] The cachet of 3 Temple Gardens was from the outset considerably enhanced by the frequent sight of the Prince of Wales in his carriage bowling down the new Embankment and up Middle Temple Lane to the impressive doorway. There, he ascended the green tiled staircase to visit his attorney, sometimes for legal advice but more often for social reasons. 'Charley' Hall was a member of the Marlborough House set, the racy coterie surrounding the prince, a fashionable man about town, a distinguished collector of art and antiques and a member of the Carlton Club, White's, the Garrick, and the Royal Yacht Squadron. He lived in Mount Street, off Berkeley Square, when not on the continent for what were said to be health reasons. He was a very confirmed bachelor.

The young Marshall, we are told, 'attracted his fancy'.[14] Since Charles Hall's practice was principally in the Admiralty courts, a particularly arcane and academic branch of the law, it is unlikely to have been Marshall's intellectual abilities that made Hall think he would be a valuable addition to his chambers. Whatever the reasons for the invitation, for Marshall it was a career-defining moment. He joined 3 Temple Gardens in November 1888 and when Hall ultimately went to the Bench in 1892, Marshall took over as head of chambers with Edward Sands as his clerk. He remained there until his death in 1927, his beloved room becoming over the years more home to him than anywhere else, his growing reputation given social gloss by his smart address.

It was amidst all this glitter, in which he revelled, that Marshall, always drawn back despite himself towards criminal work, began to develop really rather an inconvenient social conscience. The tragedies of passion and of poverty which are the bread and butter of young barristers moved him to a degree he could not ignore. His compulsion to protect others, so constantly thwarted by his wife, and his increasing personal experience of deep unhappiness drew him to the underdog.

The cartoon of a severe lawyer leaning across his desk to the anxious client sitting opposite and saying 'Just how much justice can you afford, Mr Smith?' was never more apt than at the end of the nineteenth century. Defendants in criminal trials had had the legal right to be represented since 1836. What most of them did not have was the money to pay for it. In Marshall's day the majority of those who appeared in court accused of crimes were undefended and campaigns for state-provided criminal defence funds had been fruitless. It was to be another fifteen years before any provision was made for central defence funds. Even then they were hopelessly inadequate and available only to those prepared to prove their entitlement by disclosing their defence in advance, thereby losing the precious advantage of surprise on the day of trial.

As a result of the lack of formal funding, pragmatic schemes had evolved to help poor prisoners. Judges in a practice known as assignment sometimes took it upon themselves to ask one of the unemployed counsel sitting in court hopeful for a remunerative brief to undertake a defence without a fee. Counsel, whether motivated by altruism, a desire for experience or an unwillingness to fall out with a judge upon whom his professional advancement might depend, would usually agree. Alternatively there was the dock brief tradition whereby, despite the professional rules of etiquette that prohibited counsel from accepting a brief direct from a client rather than through a solicitor, the accused in the dock could choose in open court a barrister not already engaged in a case and pay him directly a guinea, the minimum fee a barrister was permitted to accept.

Marshall had his first dock brief early in his career; he was picked out by the accused from the row of pristine wigs waiting in counsel's row only to discover that the man had just fifteen shillings to pay him. With a characteristic disregard for the then inviolable rule of professional etiquette and with the noisy expansive compassion for which he was loved by many and despised by a few, Marshall accepted the brief. And in a forerunner of what was to come, against all the odds he got him acquitted as well, the only one of the four co-defendants to walk free. It was a practice he was to continue for the rest of his life; in 1926, the year before he died, two astonished small boys charged with a minor offence at the Manchester quarter sessions got the benefit of free representation by the most famous barrister in the land when Marshall, waiting for his own case to come on, spotted that they were in need of assistance.[15] But this sort of haphazard representation was hardly the answer to a problem of these dimensions.

Terrible injustices frequently arose from these makeshift schemes for representation and Marshall was not alone in revolting against the system. With the case about to begin, the barrister would receive hissed and minimal instructions from the dock with no opportunity to seek clarification, documentation or witnesses. An impassioned plea for a Poor Prisoners Defence Fund appeared in the Press in 1887.[16] It drew the contrast between two men, one a labourer and one a doctor, charged with the same unspecified ('revolting') sexual offence. The unrepresented labourer was sent to prison. The doctor, represented by three counsel (including, coincidentally, Marshall), was let off scot free. But despite articles such as these no official steps were taken to remedy the situation. Like all bad systems, it took a case that fired public imagination to bring about some change.

In 1888 a young girl of nineteen called Sabina Tilley, a waitress in a London coffee shop, discovered she was pregnant. She hid it for as long as she could but in the end, confronted by her employer, she confessed. He was not unkind; he paid her a week's wages, arranged for her luggage to be transported to the railway station and wrote down for her the details of the journey home to her mother. But Sabina did not go home. In her shame she travelled to Brighton and there in the workhouse gave birth to twin girls,

Edith Martha and Daisy Eliza. It was a bitterly cold winter's day when in a scene no less terrible for being a Dickensian cliché, she left the workhouse and made her way, carrying the two blanketed bundles in her arms, down the bleak exposed road to the town.

A few days later she returned to her former employer. Her child had died, she told him. Could she have her job back? The corpses of the two babies were subsequently found in a wicker hamper in the compartment of the train in which she had travelled back to London. They had died of cold, Sabina said; she had squeezed them to her breast to suckle them and keep them warm but they were then nearly dead. She was charged with their murder.

Any defence would be complex and would require specialist medical knowledge and expensive medical expert witnesses. Had it not been for the enterprise of the *Sussex Daily News*, Sabina would have joined that legion of unrepresented victims who hanged because they were too poor to pay for representation and too inarticulate, whether through terror or lack of education, to get across their own defence. The *Sussex Daily News* was certainly one of the first and probably the very first newspaper to recognise the power of the press to raise defence funds from the public,[17] its aim to raise enough money to instruct counsel of the newspaper's choice. Research by journalists into pretty Sabina's background suggested that despite her transgression she was a likely candidate to attract public support. And attract it she certainly did. Overnight the headlines changed from 'Terrible double murder' to 'A pathetic story' and the campaign for her defence hotted up. It exposed an evil and touched a public nerve:

> Agitated, ignorant, bewildered, the prisoner's chances of acquittal are reduced by one half [if he is unrepresented] and it only needs that every reader of the sad story of Sabina Tilley should contribute to a defence fund to secure that this young country girl, deeply wronged as she has been, sinful it is true, but sinned against also, should be carefully and properly defended at her trial.

The subscriptions poured in; local aristocracy and councillors, celebrities from the Brighton theatres, groups of tradesmen, families, shop assistants, butchers, vicars, army officers and anonymous donors all responded to the appeal, their names faithfully listed in column after column, filling pages of the broadsheet newspaper. As a result, the newspaper pledged, Sabina's case could be submitted with all the eloquence, persuasiveness and power that professional representation could bring to it.

What the *Sussex Daily News* wanted of course was a performance that gave them something to report. The chosen counsel, technically instructed not by the accused herself but by 'the subscribers of the Sabina Tilley Defence Fund', were Charles Gill, an established member of the Sussex Bar, and the up-and-coming junior Marshall Hall, already gaining a name for his expertise in medical matters. Marshall and Gill were by now the firmest of friends. It was an unlikely partnership; seven years older, Gill was as different from Marshall as a man could be. A quiet conscientious worrier, plain featured and plain speaking, he was nonetheless an extremely effective advocate in a dogged sort of way and had an established reputation and a large Sussex practice. A few years later when Marshall's fame was so much greater than Gill's, the gossip in the Temple was that he had got his break by pinching Gill's Sussex practice. Both Gill and Marshall rejected the notion; they remained close and loyal friends for the rest of their lives.[18]

Now Gill, with Marshall as his junior, mounted a compelling case for Sabina: the congestion of the babies' lungs attributed to deliberate suffocation could equally have been due to pneumonia; and in any event babies with lungs already congested through cold would be more vulnerable to smothering by a mother desperately clutching them to her breast. The jury, already disposed to mercy, acquitted. And didn't the *Sussex Daily News* make the most of it:

> Her mother and her sisters stood waiting for her at the door leading from the cells … as the door was flung back and the girl came forth into the open air a scene of strange pathos was witnessed. The liberated girl with a cry of happiness that was yet more than half a sob and uttering one word: one word only – 'Mother' – almost leapt forward into her mother's arms … and mother and child clung to each other and sobbed out their gratitude … to the kind readers of the *Sussex Daily News*.

The defence of Sabina Tilley ticked all the boxes. It was ingenious and persuasive, it provided sensational sound bites for the local press and it saved her life. It also heralded a whole new world of funding for serious crime. Marshall became one of the greatest exponents of the power of the press in fund raising and ironically, since his motives had been entirely altruistic, later in his career he became one of the greatest beneficiaries. By the early twentieth century, bypassing public appeals, national newspapers were themselves funding fashionable barristers to conduct defences. Marshall, who could be relied upon to deliver the goods, was their first choice. The reply written to him by the editor of the *Sussex Daily News*, to whom Marshall had sent his thanks after the trial, just about sums it up: 'There is nothing to thank me for. I am as much indebted to you as you are to me so we will call it quits.'[19] It was the beginning of a pact with the devil.

Marshall's domestic miseries meanwhile were continuing relentlessly downhill. Between 1886 and 1888, he and Ethel rowed and reconciled and rowed again; Ethel underwent an operation in an attempt to deal with the heavy painful menstruation that was now the main focus of her constant ill health;[20] they moved to Kensington; the differences between them became so bitter that on one occasion Ethel flounced out, but with nowhere to go but Marshall's parents she was persuaded back. She began to make friends of her own and developed a taste for the vicious company that was to prove her downfall. On 31 December 1887 Marshall celebrated the new year with a heavy heart and a domestic horizon he described in his diary as 'more cloudy than ever'. His forebodings were accurate.

It was the beginning of miseries piling one on top of another. His beloved mother, always his confidante, became terminally ill. His parents moved to Tunbridge Wells in the hopes that the benefit of the spa would help her but she died less than a year later.[21] His older brother James, the once highly successful businessman, was ruined and fled to South Africa. And Marshall's doomed marriage came to an end when Ethel flounced out for the last time.

Marshall, with his eternal optimism, would not consider the annulment which was probably open to him, but ultimately he entered into a deed of separation,[22] its terms plainly drafted in the hope of her ultimate return to him. The document refers only to 'unhappy differences' between them and allows for possible reconciliation. By now, Marshall knew Ethel to be flighty, unreliable and vulnerable. He pledged to pay her a quarter of his annual income, already becoming substantial; he appointed trustees and advisers through whom the money was to be paid to her; he wrote to Dr Phillips, the doctor who had operated on her two years previously, asking him to attend her professionally whenever she required.[23] He did all he could to protect her. It was not enough.

PART II
NOTORIETY

CHAPTER 5

'Mysterious death of a barrister's wife'

Marshall played no part in the dreadful ending to Ethel's story. Nonetheless the manner of her death dominated his life; many blamed him for it and until his own death nearly forty years later he suffered from the backlash of tragedy and scandal. Paradoxically, the events seem also to have been the making of the electrifying emotional power of his advocacy. In the case in which he subsequently made his name he poured into his oratory all the pent-up miseries of his disastrous marriage. His impassioned description of the inexorable descent into disaster of women who chose to step outside the expectations of respectable society has never been forgotten. Although in that case he was talking about his prostitute client, it was about Ethel too, their childhood romance, his idealistic marriage to her and her sordid fate.

By 1889 Marshall was living alone in lodgings just off the Strand and close to his chambers, longing for Ethel's return and keeping intermittently in touch with her. He last saw her in April 1890 when she was living in Carlos Place, near Grosvenor Square; but she left that address shortly after and did not tell him where she was going. Unbelievably, less than six weeks later, beguiling, headstrong, twenty-nine years old, she was dead.[1]

The circumstances of her death brought together in one sensational story the preoccupations of a prurient Victorian society. A beautiful victim, a handsome wronged husband, a dissolute aristocrat, a brazen prostitute and a drug-addicted doctor all played their parts against the backdrop of that den of vice, the Alhambra Theatre. It was an irresistible combination.

By 1889, Ethel was living a discontented life moving from lodging to lodging, spurning the protection of husband or family. Beautiful, emotionally fragile, susceptible to flattery, like many a Jemima Puddle-Duck before her she was ripe to meet her fox. Count Raoul Guy Richard de Vismes et de Ponthieu was a twenty-six-year-old army officer on leave in England and living with his widowed mother and two sisters in St Leonards-on-Sea, near Hastings. He was five feet eight inches tall,[2] with a moustache and a dashing uniform No intellectual, he had gone straight from school to the Royal Military College, Sandhurst, leaving to join the Northamptonshire Regiment with an unenthusiastic 'inclined to be thoughtless' on his conduct record.[3] In 1885 de Ponthieu had been seconded for service to the Bombay Staff Corps. Now, ostensibly learning Russian in anticipation for his next posting, he was out for a good time.

Ethel met him on 13 December 1889 in Bournemouth. The circumstances of the meeting are unknown and only one thing is clear: somehow he ignited in her a reckless passion that her tall, handsome, clever, husband had failed to rouse. By mid-April she was disastrously pregnant. Within the respectable framework of marriage Ethel's terror of childbirth had dominated. Outside that framework the combination of terror and shame were unendurable and for de Ponthieu the financial implications were alarming. Her allowance from Marshall continued, according to the terms of the agreement, only whilst she remained chaste and led a virtuous life.

De Ponthieu's income was modest and he had other reasons for being appalled at the prospect of a scandal. His family, Huguenot on his father's side and English landed gentry on his mother's, were not of the type to weather it. Had they been as aristocratic as they wished to appear perhaps they might have been. As it was, they had been bombarding the Prime Minister and College of Arms for decades in the obsessive pursuit of English recognition of their foreign titles. Despite threats, cajoling and an offer of payment into the privy purse they had been unsuccessful. They had clung doggedly over the generations to an ever-increasing number of exotic European names and titles, continuing to style themselves princes and counts, but the reality was that their lifestyle never quite matched their aspirations. Social irregularities were the last thing they wanted.

On an afternoon in early May 1890 de Ponthieu took Ethel to a consultation with Dr Achille Vintras in Hanover Square, introducing her as his wife. Dr Vintras was a distinguished physician. He had a large practice amongst French residents in London, was physician to the French embassy, and had written an elegant little book, *A Medical Guide to the Mineral Waters of France and Its Wintering Stations*. In what must have been a well-rehearsed story, Ethel told the doctor that her husband had a government appointment in Persia. Her period was two weeks overdue. It would be awkward for her to travel with him if she was pregnant. Furthermore, she was constipated: she needed something to unblock her bowels. Dr Vintras grasped the high level of anxiety but appears to have missed the sub-plot. He gave her a prescription for her constipation; it contained aloe, no doubt what she was after since it was a well-recognised abortifacient, but he prescribed it in the tiny dose also well recognised as a laxative. If she hoped it would do the trick, she was inevitably to be disappointed. He then conducted an interview alone with de Ponthieu. Ethel needed taking out of herself; escort her out and about and to the theatre, the urbane Dr Vintras suggested. Amuse her and divert her. As to the pregnancy, time would tell.

Diversion and amusement were not what Ethel wanted and time was what she did not have. She wanted a solution and above all she wanted to be reassured that she would not be dumped by her lover. She would not, as he later told the police, let him out of her sight. Cornered by her demands, he agreed to find lodgings with her.

Only a few days after the visit to Dr Vintras, de Ponthieu paid a visit to the Alhambra Theatre. In a city full of theatres and music halls, the Alhambra had for nearly fifty years been the most popular and latterly the most disreputable. Its unlikely Moorish façade, all turrets and twiddles, dominated the east side of Leicester Square. It personified the rowdy itinerant cosmopolitan character of the square, packed with cafés, gin houses, Turkish baths and doubtful lodgings, grubby by day and tawdry by night, heady with the smell of sweat and garlic and tobacco, crowded at all hours.

Once inside the entrance, the interior of the Alhambra lived up to its exotic façade, rich with elaborate fretwork, oriental window treatments and gigantic chandeliers glittering in the smoky perfume-laden atmosphere. Excess was its byword. The sheer size of the building lent itself to performances on the most spectacular scale for audiences of more than 3,000. Chorus lines 200 dancers long, vast ballets, music hall and variety shows, operas, acrobats and jugglers, minstrels, melodramas and slapstick comedy, all had a place at the Alhambra. But whatever the spectacle on the stage, there was always an even more popular one off it. In the long intervals, hundreds of women congregated in the open promenade, dressed in tawdry finery, brazen in purpose. Over the years sporadic attempts were made to clean it up but to no avail; on the Alhambra lumbered, shameless and notorious, catering on a mass scale for the sale of sex.

It was here that de Ponthieu picked up Mrs Hermione Grandt. Estranged from her respectable husband, Hermione had come to London to fend for herself. Her card described her as a teacher of music, but she supplemented her income, as she coyly admitted in court later, by frequenting the music halls and on occasion misconducting herself. Yes, she took men home and they gave her money. No, she acknowledged in answer to the sort of facetious overkill in cross-examination beloved of barristers throughout the centuries, she did not take men home for the night in order to give them music lessons. In fact her principal means of earning her living was apparent from her very presence, dressed to kill (an apt phrase, as it turned out) at the Alhambra. De Ponthieu took Hermione out to supper and then went home with her to her house at 78 Berners Street, just off Oxford Street. Since he spent all night there, it seems safe to assume that this was an occasion when Hermione was persuaded to misconduct herself. She did so to such good effect that he was only able to tear himself away in time to keep an appointment with the (presumably unknowing) Ethel at noon the next day. Before he left he asked Hermione if she could let a room in her house to him and a lady friend. The startling inappropriateness of this suggestion does not seem to have occurred to him. Hermione offered a single room and the very night that he saw it, 6 May, he and Ethel, whom Hermione knew as 'Mrs Marshall', moved into it. Ethel's speedy descent into the misery and vice of Victorian London's underbelly began almost at once.

On 14 May, Ethel went to her bank and drew a cheque for twenty pounds on the allowance Marshall paid to her. On the same day, a telegram was sent to a Dr Laermann at the White Lion Dispensary, 116 Pimlico Road. Laermann, though Ethel did not know it, was another of Hermione's clients. The telegram was written by de Ponthieu in Hermione's name, noticeably anonymous in its content: 'My lady friend coming today at 5 o'clock according to promise.'

In the late nineteenth century contraception was frowned upon by the Church and the medical profession, and abortion was a thriving business. Ethel could have found thinly disguised advertisements in all the ladies' magazines: pills to remove 'obstructions' were easily obtainable, at best ineffective and at worst, and cheapest, poisonous. There is some evidence that she tried one of these methods first, but now with the help of her new acquaintances she resorted to more drastic measures.

Since the 1861 Offences Against the Person Act, performing an abortion carried a sentence of life imprisonment. Secretly a few doctors would follow the dictates of their consciences and abort when they believed the mother's life to be in danger, but it was to be well into the twentieth century before even this practice was publicly acknowledged. Those prepared to carry out a termination in circumstances such as Ethel's employed methods which were always surreptitious and frequently insanitary and unskilled. All the same, there was money to be made and most successful backstreet abortionists were not backstreet at all. Middle-class women prepared to pay were reassured by the outward appearance of a premises which even if not located there, had a whiff of Harley Street about it.

Thirty-four-year-old Dr Albert Laermann was a Belgian. The White Lion Dispensary, which was also his home, was a slick-looking outfit. It had a plaque outside the door with his name on it, Dr Laermann MD, and his brougham was parked outside. He employed his own private coachman, a housekeeper/receptionist and an assistant/secretary. The business had been previously owned by an eminently respectable doctor, Richard Jack. Jack had employed Laermann as his assistant, on the strength of a diploma evidencing his qualification as a doctor in Brussels. The work had been principally as an accoucheur, the equivalent of a male midwife.

Ultimately Laermann had bought the practice. It may be that acting as a society accoucheur he had discovered that some babies were less welcome than others and thus started to respond to a growing demand. Ethel is unlikely to have been the first woman for whom he offered to 'remove polypus' for fifteen pounds (a sum roughly equivalent to £1,750 today), as he later recorded in his account books.

On 14 May, whilst de Ponthieu waited outside, Ethel and Hermione were ushered in by the housekeeper to a room on the first floor furnished with a sofa and a piano. The latter was to have a later horrid significance. In a rather striking departure from normal medical practice, the three of them then drank a great deal of wine.

There were no witnesses to what happened next. Laermann invited Hermione to go and admire the view from the window and whilst she gazed dutifully out over the grounds of Chelsea Hospital, he hitched up Ethel's skirts and performed a procedure using a pair of tongs; it was sufficiently quick and rough to make her cry out. They all had some more wine, and were then ushered out to the waiting de Ponthieu and returned in a hansom cab to Berners Street.

The procedure did not lead to the required result and the next day Ethel moved yet again, to lodgings at 21 Duke Street, a short distance from Berners Street. The Countess de Vismes et de Ponthieu and her two spinster daughters Elise and Berthe were arriving from St Leonards-on-Sea to stay with the count. They would certainly have taken a dim view of the Berners Street set-up. The new Duke Street lodgings were more spacious, consisting of a bedroom and sitting room on the second floor of a terraced house. For two guineas a week Ethel was to have the landlady cook for her and the maid of the house wait on her. But she did not want to live there without her lover. Terrified of abandonment, panic made her demanding. She made de

Ponthieu swear he would come to see her twice a day and introduced him to her new landlady as her brother to explain the frequency of his attendance.

A pattern had been set. Over the next two weeks a series of visits were paid by Ethel and Hermione to the Pimlico Road consulting rooms, preceded on each occasion by a telegram in Hermione's name and Ethel's hand, its terms almost identical to the first. There was still no result. Ethel became increasingly desperate, increasingly sore and inflamed by the repeated attempts and an embarrassment to her accomplices.

On 24 May the two women visited 116 Pimlico Road for what was to be the last time and Laermann decided on drastic measures. Ethel's anaesthetic this time was champagne chased with tumblers full of green chartreuse. There was no looking out of windows to admire the view and no observing of niceties this time. Ethel lay on the sofa and Hermione held her down. Her skirts were hitched up and fastened with her scarf pin. Laermann then proceeded to inject acid nitrate of mercury into her vagina. Mercury is not a recognised abortifacient; it is a powerful corrosive locally (a drop on a fingernail would eat through it rapidly) and a powerful poison when absorbed into the system. The agony must have been unimaginable. Whilst she lay screaming, in a bizarre performance, apparently to drown the sound, Laermann played the piano and Hermione sang. 'It may be that the notes of the piano drowned the remonstrances of his own conscience as well as the cries of Mrs Hall,' one newspaper later observed sententiously. With a sort of ghastly solicitousness Laermann administered a large dose of morphine and replaced Ethel's scarf pin in its rightful place. She could not by then have done it for herself.

Twenty minutes later she was carted down the stairs by Hermione who got her home to Duke Street with difficulty. It took her six days to die.

When de Ponthieu arrived that evening he found Hermione drunk and Ethel clearly desperately ill, vomiting, passing copious blood-stained diarrhoea and haemorrhaging vaginally. It was not quite what he had imagined for his stays at Duke Street. He wrote a letter for Dr Laermann: 'I am afraid there is danger. For God's sake hurry up.' All the same, he kept his head sufficiently to sign it in Hermione's name.

The next morning he turned to the nearby Wigmore Institution for Resident Nurses; he needed a nurse for his sister, he told them, as she seemed to have taken a chill. Nurse Charlotte Ironmonger attended 21 Duke Street and found not a sister with a chill but a woman in agony and, it seemed to her, under the influence of opiates. Ethel had dysentery, Laermann told her; there was a lot of it about. But then, though he had promised to call again that evening, he disappeared having been arrested for forgery.

'Dr' Albert Laermann was not what he seemed. The cheque with which he had purchased the practice in Pimlico Road was forged. He was not a doctor: the diploma of qualification in Brussels was a forgery too. Furthermore, his life was dominated by his massive drug habit: he existed on a cocktail of Indian hemp, cocaine and, as he himself described it, enough morphine to kill a horse. In his pockets on his arrest was a packet of it, and deprived of it by the police, he quickly slipped into a state of acute withdrawal. Brought immediately before the magistrate, even hardened police court reporters were shocked as he was carried into the dock, unable to walk and screaming for morphine. He was remanded in custody.

Meanwhile, Ethel was dying. There was only one doctor left to call upon, Dr John Phillips, an old friend of Marshall's who had looked after Ethel for the preceding three years and whose services to her Marshall had retained in their deed of separation. He went at once to 21 Duke Street. Ethel was wandering in her speech but at his gentle questioning out it all came, in all its pathos, sufficient for the doctor to form a coherent picture. She had gone wrong, she told him. She could not bear being alone or the shame. She knew she was dying. She would not tell him who the father of her child was nor who gave her the recommendation to Laermann. 'I won't incriminate anybody,' she said.

Dr Phillips did not mince his words in his subsequent interview with de Ponthieu: in the event of Ethel's death, he told him, he would refuse a death certificate. An inquest should be held. Did de Ponthieu accept responsibility for Ethel's ghastly state? Yes, said de Ponthieu, he did; but now he had to go home to St Leonards. By the next day he had made a plan of action, polished his account and returned to 21 Duke Street. It was 29 May.

During that day Ethel lay haemorrhaging, exhausted but still lucid. De Ponthieu's main concern seems to have been alarm that she might have been fit enough to make a statement. Ethel's brother in law James Robinson, now her closest surviving male relative, had come in answer to a telegram. They had always been close and it was not the deathbed scene for any respectable woman to attend. Ethel deeply regretted her past, she told James. She begged him to bring Marshall to her. She knew how desperately he wanted her back. But Marshall was in Paris for the legal spring vacation. Whatever it was she wanted to say, there was no time left to say it.

Ethel died at seven o'clock the next morning. She was still pregnant. De Ponthieu called at eight. The maid opened the door and told him Ethel was dead. He left, saying he would go for a doctor, and never returned. On 30 May in the early summer beauty of Paris Marshall opened the telegram informing him of Ethel's death and returned at once to London.[4]

The laborious wheels of the legal system began to turn. Over the next five weeks, proceedings in the coroner's court and committal proceedings in the police court dominated the headlines: 'Mysterious death of a barrister's wife'; 'Doctor in police court'; 'Officer arrested'. Marshall's namesake, Dr Marshall Hall, of whose friendship his father had been so proud, had a grandson who wrote sniffily to *The Times*: 'Sir – with regard to the publicity afforded in your columns to the mysterious death of a lady, I should be obliged if you would make known that the Mr Edward Marshall Hall has no connection with the family of the late Dr Marshall Hall ...'[5] It was the ultimate humiliation. The Bar was agog. If young Marshall's name had not been universally known in the Temple before, it certainly was now.

On 3 June the coroner opened an inquest on the body of Grace Ethel Hall, late wife of Mr Edward Marshall Hall, barrister at law. The first hearing was brief; de Ponthieu, the central witness, had not responded, having left for Russia, ordered to do so, he later said, by the War Office to perfect his Russian. He found time to consult solicitors before he left and police inquiries ascertained that no such order had been issued. His leave, which expired at the end of the month, could have been extended had he requested it. He must have left for Russia as soon as Ethel's death was confirmed. It did not look good. He seems to have thought so himself, for having got as far as Berlin he saw in an English newspaper that his presence was required and made his way back to England. He presented himself voluntarily to the Westminster coroner on 10 June.

The coroner's proceedings were only part of the legal process now in train. Laermann, already under arrest for forgery, was now charged with the use of an instrument and drugs with intent to procure an abortion, and on 11 June Inspector Bonner and Detective Sergeant MacGuire of the Metropolitan Police travelled to St Leonards to arrest de Ponthieu. Arriving at his mother's home at 8.30 in the evening, they were ushered in by a maid and de Ponthieu received them and immediately telegraphed his solicitor.

The coroner's inquest into the cause of Ethel's death proceeded. Laermann, in custody awaiting the police court proceedings, was not present. De Ponthieu on bail attended willingly as a witness. Despite the coroner's caution that his evidence might be used against him in subsequent criminal proceedings, under the canny guidance of his solicitor he expressed a positive eagerness to tell his story. Now this was clever; remember that in criminal proceedings at that time a defendant had no right to give evidence in his own defence. The inquest enabled him to tell his story in response to the friendly questioning of his own lawyer without any testing of its vulnerabilities in cross-examination. Polished, highly selective, de Ponthieu gave his unchallenged account. No explanation at all was given of his initial motive in introducing Ethel to Hermione whom he blamed for all the ensuing arrangements. He had assumed Laermann to be a respectable practitioner; he had attended only on the first occasion and thought she was merely being examined. She was subsequently treated without his knowledge; he thought she was suffering from dysentery; he had been sincerely attached to Mrs Hall.

The coroner, concerned only to establish the cause of death, was more interested in the evidence of Dr Augustus Pepper, the Home Office pathologist. A quiet man, Dr Pepper was not given to drama. In this case, it was not anyway needed to get his message across. A horrified jury listened to his dry description of the state of Ethel's corroded body and of the tools of the abortionist's trade found at Laermann's consulting rooms and returned a verdict against Laermann of wilful murder. The stakes could not now be higher. Both Laermann, charged now with Ethel's murder, and de Ponthieu, charged with being an accessory before the fact and therefore according to the law at the time a principal in the crime, faced the death penalty if convicted.

It was in the criminal proceedings at Westminster Police Court that the real drama unfolded, in front of a packed courtroom presided over by the Westminster magistrate, Louis Tennyson d'Eyncourt. D'Eyncourt had been a magistrate for nearly forty years and was complete master of his court. *Punch* described him as patriarchal. There is no other evidence of his character, but in view of the way he conducted the trial, it is irresistible to record that he came from a family whose social pretensions were legendary. His father, born plain Charles Tennyson, uncle of the poet, had on inheriting a fortune changed his name to reflect his obscure connections with an aristocratic Norman family and turned his modest Lincolnshire family home into a sixty-one-bedroomed neo-Gothic castle, complete with moat and drawbridge.[6] It was to this grandiose lifestyle at Bayons Manor that Louis d'Eyncourt retired aged seventy-six, four months after the Laermann/de Ponthieu trial.

Like most trials in those days, it was dominated by personality. Counsel for the prosecution was Mr Charles 'Willie' Matthews, the child of a theatrical family and a flamboyant advocate, ultimately knighted, and later to become the first independent Director of Public Prosecutions. Laermann was represented by Edward Abinger,[7] then a junior of only three years' experience who never became a QC and whose ultimate distinction lay in the longevity of his practice rather than its quality.[8] In a police court, either a solicitor or a barrister could appear for the accused and de Ponthieu was represented by George Lewis, by that time the most famous solicitor in London. Three years off his knighthood, he was already at the top of his game. He was everything a solicitor should be: fixer, networker, negotiator, with an unparalleled web of informants across London; quiet, competent and above all discreet. Socially, his profile was as high as that of the great names dominating the Bar, but professionally he was content to be the man behind the scenes, his advice practical, tactful and, inevitably, very expensive. Whoever retained him on de Ponthieu's behalf showed great judgement. In addition to his other qualities, Lewis was a superb police court advocate. The skills required were very different from those needed in the higher courts in which the Bar had the monopoly.

The job of the magistrate in the more serious cases in the police courts was simply to determine whether there was sufficient evidence for the matter to be sent for trial by a jury sitting in the next assize court.[9] Given that prior to 1898, the defendant could not give evidence himself in his own defence, the case in committal proceedings consisted largely of a recitation of the prosecution evidence. Defence counsel had the opportunity to test the robustness of this evidence in cross-examination and at its conclusion could either accept that it at least warranted consideration by a jury and keep his powder dry for those proceedings, or submit that there was simply not enough evidence to justify sending the defendant for a jury trial. One of the greatest attributes for defence counsel in committal proceedings was (and is) knowing when to shut up, a quality which requires the self-effacement of which many barristers are incapable. George Lewis had it down to a fine art.

The cards were stacked in de Ponthieu's favour from the outset. On bail, his surety paid for by a friend of the family, the ninth Earl of Northesk, Lewis made an application for him to sit not in the dock but in the well of the court. Laermann stood in the dock. On the actual bench, alongside the magistrate, sat a number of young officer friends of de Ponthieu as well as his surety, the Earl of Northesk. This was not as unthinkable as it would be today; but even in those days of latitude towards the upper classes it was sufficiently unusual to occasion comment in some of the newspapers.

Hermione, resplendent in mauve silk, was the chief prosecution witness, her evidence supported in its basic outline by Laermann's housekeeper, Ethel's landlady, James Robinson and the doctors. Questions relating to her meetings at the Alhambra were disallowed. D'Eyncourt said he could not see their relevance. At the conclusion of the prosecution case, Lewis called General Charles Blowers, who was de Ponthieu's commanding officer on the Afghan frontier ('he was a promising officer'); William de Vismes et de Ponthieu, his brother ('I am interpreter to Her Majesty's legation and British vice-consul in Tangiers'); and General Sir James Fraser Tytler ('I knew de Ponthieu's father'). After this resounding roll call, he made a speech. There was no evidence, he submitted, which would justify the committal of his client for trial; Mrs Grandt, however wicked she was, had said nothing inconsistent with the innocence of de Ponthieu. De Ponthieu had stood by this lady like a man of honour. There had been evidence she was afraid of having a child. It was much in de Ponthieu's favour that he took her to Dr Vintras and introduced her as his wife. The only evidence which could be put against him related to the telegram in his writing before the first visit to Dr Laermann. Even Lewis could not suppress that bit of evidence but he had dealt with it as best he could; de Ponthieu had written it because Mrs Grandt had asked him to. Anyway, he pointed out, getting into his stride, Mrs Grandt was nothing but a drunken Alhambra frequenter and although de Ponthieu could not in this court give evidence in his own defence, he had given his own gentlemanly account of his role in the story in the coroner's court. The magistrate knew that, since he had read the coroner's depositions.

D'Eyncourt proceeded to give his decision; he felt Lieutenant de Ponthieu had acted in a very manly way, he said. There were, he acknowledged, some suspicious things against him, particularly his journey in the cab with the deceased to Laermann's preceded by Mrs Grandt. However, after hearing Mr Lewis, he felt the evidence did not quite justify sending the lieutenant for trial and the charge against him would be dismissed. There were loud cheers from de Ponthieu's young officer friends and Lieutenant de Ponthieu, reported *The Times*, left 'with the Earl of Northesk and numerous other friends'. Laermann, who had conceded there was a case to answer, was committed to the Old Bailey for trial.

Thus it came about that on 1 August 1890, Albert Laermann stood trial alone for Ethel's murder. Charles Matthews prosecuted again, this time with the assistance of Marshall's close friend Charles Gill, whose absolute discretion could be relied upon. The young Abinger was defending alone. No doubt he was all that Laermann could afford. The evidence concluded on the Saturday. In summing up, the trial judge, Mr Justice Grantham, expressed surprise that de Ponthieu was not also standing trial. The evidence, he said, would have fully justified this. The jury in accordance with the barbaric hours then kept at the Old Bailey, retired at 7.35 in the evening to consider their verdict and returned at 11.10. Laermann, like many others before and after him, faced the possibility of a death sentence in a dark court, lit by feeble gas light and candles. The evidence against him was overwhelming but the law clearly caused the jury some difficulty. Although, the judge had told them, it was plain Laermann intended no malice towards Ethel, if the jury concluded that he had attempted an abortion, itself an illegal act, and death had resulted, it was nonetheless murder. The jury returned a verdict of manslaughter. It probably in part reflected an unwillingness to hang a man for a death which did not involve malicious intent but was probably also motivated by the rider they, unusually, added to their verdict: de Ponthieu and Hermione, they said, should have been beside Laermann in the dock.

The newspapers could not get enough of it; day after day throughout the inquest, the police court proceedings and the Old Bailey trial they reported with relish every detail they could and made up for those parts which were unprintable with dark hints of the unspeakable horrors that had befallen Mrs Marshall Hall. To this day, even the Old Bailey records are marked 'unfit for publication'. At the time the whole shameful story was known only to a few and since then the police file has lain deep in the National Archives, misnamed in the Archives catalogue.[10] The trial depositions contain a poignant postscript. During the course of the criminal investigation Hermione told the police that she had always known Ethel's real name because she had seen it embroidered on her chemise. The police duly seized it. Sure enough, inside it was the name 'E Marshall Hall'. But there was also a date: 1882. It must have been part of her trousseau.

Laermann was sentenced to fifteen years' penal servitude. Hermione Grandt had left her address at Berners Street by the time of the next census a year later in 1891 and was probably absorbed back into the life from which she came. De Ponthieu returned to his regiment and to a life in India. Promoted to the rank of major, he became Her Britannic Majesty's Consul in Pondicherry and Karikal and married in Bombay in 1896. He did not escape tragedy; his little daughter Evelyn fell victim to the heat and infections and died when she was a few months old. De Ponthieu himself died in 1901 of sickness, reported as a lung congestion. He was only thirty-seven. He left a young widow and a four-year-old son.

Marshall was left shamed by the public airing of his marital failure, desperate with grief for his loss and corroded with bitterness against de Ponthieu. His profession provided a lifetime of reminders. Countless visits to the dark corridors of the Old Bailey and the grim cells beneath, and countless appearances in the court in which Laermann had been tried;[11] countless appearances in front of Mr Justice Grantham, who had conducted the trial; countless cross-examinations of Dr Pepper, the pathologist who had dissected Ethel's body; countless legal arguments about the niceties of manslaughter and murder; countless social encounters with Charles 'Willie' Matthews at the Garrick and the Beefsteak and with Edward Abinger, a fellow Inner Templar. Despite a tacit understanding at the Bar that the subject should never again be referred to in his presence he never felt he could get away from it.

CHAPTER 6

'God never gave her a chance'

Plenty was being said behind Marshall's back, of course, and he knew it. Young members of the Bar were not generally mixed up with sex and scandal; their marriages were not usually the subject of column after column of salacious speculation in newspapers; their wives, come to that, did not have public affairs (especially not with disreputable foreigners) and get themselves murdered. It was all unseemly and sordid and however blameless Marshall may have been, the generally held view by those unaware of the sterile shell of his marriage was that he should have looked after his wife better. Many of his colleagues began to steer clear of him and judicial eyebrows were raised.

Struggling with the emotional impact of bereavement, Marshall was hardly aware of the depth of the damage done to his career. The optimism that had been one of his defining characteristics had suffered a terrible blow. Faced for the first time with a situation in which hope could play no part, he scarcely knew how to conduct himself. Over the next few years all his energies were taken up in trying to recover his equilibrium. Always deeply superstitious, rather shamefacedly interested in lucky numbers,[1] omens and fortune telling, he now felt vindicated; hadn't Ethel always said that having a child would kill her? Unable to live without some sort of expectation of reconciliation, his conviction grew that he could somehow reconnect with her. He began to explore the beliefs and practices of the spiritualist movement, though he had the sense to keep the fact a secret for many years, until the carnage of the First World War made spiritualism more mainstream.

Always short tempered, he was now more fiery than ever; the newspapers that had originally noted with admiration his temerity with judges still reported it, but were no longer so complimentary. Amongst the references to his good looks and charm were observations less helpful to his reputation:

his impudent manner, bullying of witnesses and displays of temperament all attracted the attention of court reporters. His fellow barristers found him high handed and didactic and his desperate physical restlessness made him an uncomfortable companion. Distracted by his grief, he lost his always tenuous inclination to study. He became uncomfortable about acting for the prosecution in criminal trials, however vile the crime, his faith in a judicial system that had let his wife's lover go unpunished profoundly shaken and his sensibilities heightened by his own suffering.

Those closest to him at the Bar feared for him and supported him. Edward Pleydell-Bouverie bore some of the brunt of his impossibly volatile emotions; Charles Gill, knowing and loving him so well, became his chief confidant. It was Gill who restrained him from carrying into action a romantic plan to bury his grief in jungle isolation and apply for a colonial judicial appointment. 'I don't think it is a good thing for him to do, as he is so much accustomed to civilisation,' he wrote earnestly in a letter to his brother Arthur, also a barrister and friend of Marshall.[2] No doubt he had in mind the wine, the cigars, the evenings at the theatre and the sophisticated little dinners at the Beefsteak.

Gill was right. In the end it was civilisation and a case that saved him. The warm tolerance of club friends and welcoming leather armchairs of the Beefsteak and the Garrick became a deep solace and, just when the damage to his professional reputation threatened to overwhelm him, one solicitor dared to brief him. Many were now very cautious about instructing this young man with a dubious past and a reputation for falling out with judges, but caution was not a word in Arthur Newton's vocabulary. Arthur Newton was extremely able with a large criminal practice, an unparalleled network of contacts in the criminal underworld and a reputation for sailing very close to the wind. He like Marshall was good looking, entertaining and a risk taker. He too had a shady past, having served a six-week prison sentence for his part in helping an aristocratic client to escape to France and so evade prosecution in the so-called Cleveland Street 'rent boys' scandal.[3] Astonishingly Newton had been permitted to return to practise on his release, presumably because he had in truth done the establishment a good turn.

In 1894 Newton was looking for a barrister whose principal qualification was that he was cheap. Desperate for funding, he had on the accused's behalf already sold to Madame Tussauds the blood-stained trunk that was the main exhibit in the case, with a view to display when the trial was over. Nonetheless despite this, the money was tight and Newton could not afford to be picky or to be too concerned that his chosen counsel's name was really only known for disreputable reasons.

The case was too hopeless for it to matter much. Newton briefed Marshall to defend Marie Hermann, an unprepossessing forty-three-year-old prostitute who took home with her to her lodgings in Grafton Street, off the Tottenham Court Road, an apparently blameless old man of seventy-two. Once there, she hit her visitor over the head with a poker at least seven times, crammed his burly body into a trunk and moved to new lodgings, the unwitting removal men transporting the body with her other belongings. A fellow inmate in her original lodging house had heard suspicious noises and later, finding blood on the floor, reported the matter to the police, who on investigation discovered the ghastly contents of the trunk in the new apartment.

Hermann was charged with murder; it was the first time Marshall, still a relatively inexperienced young barrister, defended alone on a capital charge. It was the loneliest place in the world to be. The public's fascination with hanging was not shared by the Bar. Few barristers were prepared to undertake more trials in which the prisoner's life was at stake than the barest minimum that public duty demanded of them, and many barristers of great eminence found that once was enough. Sir Rufus Isaacs, Marshall's contemporary, compelled to do so in his role as Attorney General, prosecuted only one murder and was so unnerved by the experience he swore never to do another.[4] The distinguished Sir Edward Clarke, famous for his disciplined delivery, having secured the acquittal of a young woman charged with poisoning her husband, put his head in his hands in open court and wept with strain and relief.[5] Alongside minimal defence funds were forensic evidence of the most rudimentary kind, unsophisticated juries, reactionary judges and a rigid code of social morality. Nor, until 1908, was there recourse to the Court of Criminal Appeal,[6] and pardons were unpredictable. Hanging usually followed within three short weeks of the verdict. Defence counsel had nothing with which to counter this but the force of their own personalities, the cadences of their own voices and their understanding of human psychology. The advocacy was all, the responsibility unimaginable.

The Hermann case was not one in which a barrister would see many opportunities to shine. The evidence seemed overwhelming; the newspapers had taken universally against the accused; to the respectable all-male jury she was going to be seen as a fallen woman whose depravity put her beyond all compassion; and she was not young or pretty enough to rouse even a salacious interest in her fate.

On that Monday morning in May 1894, as he travelled the short distance down Fleet Street from the Temple to the Old Bailey, Marshall was not the only young barrister facing the day with the beating heart and sweating hands of acute stage fright, and a hopeless case to run. Nonetheless his position was unique. He was starting a trial in a court for which he had developed since the trial of Ethel's killer an almost visceral hatred, those dark claustrophobic chambers filled with the only too familiar avid public and press. Literally girding himself in the robing room for a battle in which death might be the outcome would be Charles 'Willie' Matthews, prosecuting counsel. There was something terrifying about Matthews, so small yet so compelling in his raggedy gown always half off his shoulders, with his high-pitched effeminate voice and his deadly cross-examinations. One of the leading prosecutors of the day, he was an alarming adversary to any young barrister; but he had also been prosecuting counsel in the de Ponthieu and Laermann trials. The junior barrister prosecuting with him was Archibald Bodkin, a future Director of Public Prosecutions and a close friend and contemporary of Marshall. They, like the judge and like most of the lawyers and press in court, knew the degrading pathos of Ethel's death though not the circumstances of his marriage which would have exonerated Marshall from blame. In the brief that Marshall carried to court that morning was a statement in immaculate copperplate from Dr Augustus Pepper the Home Office pathologist, reporting on the post mortem carried out on Marie Hermann's victim. Marshall was going to have to cross-examine the very pathologist who had dissected Ethel's corroded uterus and removed the still intact foetus. Pepper knew better than Marshall himself the secrets of Ethel's body and the agony of her death.

There must be a recognised limit to professional detachment even for the most highly trained. But Marshall either never had or ignored the instincts for self-preservation which would tell him when he had reached that limit. For him there was only Marie Hermann, a victim in her own way, exploited by men, trapped by circumstance, whose life he might be able to save – had to save. It seems to have been for Marshall the moment in which by the most complete sublimation of self he could somehow free himself from the shackles of his own spectacular personal and public failure.

During the trial, armed with all the dirt that Newton, an expert in the art, had managed to dig up, and with the tragic details of Hermann's life, Marshall transformed the victim from an innocent old man with a forgivable, if pathetic, liking for prostitutes into a vicious and violent predator and his attacker into a desperate and unhappy woman, once a respectable governess, the mother of a blind child whom she had to support. The attack itself was turned by Marshall into a frantic struggle for Hermann's own survival. His cross-examination of the medical experts was subtle and ingenious and put the two of them, both acting for the prosecution, at odds about the direction of the fatal blows and the positions of the two protagonists. He identified and exploited the few points in Hermann's favour: the evidence of a fight in the empty blood-soaked lodgings; the bruises on her neck; the belated attempt that had been made at resuscitation with brandy and bandages. He made as light as he could of the evidence of the other occupants of the house who had heard the anguished cries of 'murder'; of the very dead man who had gone out with money in his pocket, no longer to be found on his corpse; of the sudden wealth of the formerly impoverished Hermann; and above all of the determined and horrible concealment of the body. He did a good job, but that after all is what barristers are paid to do; there was nothing exceptional about it.

It was in the end the speech that won the verdict, and it was so astonishing that the legend began. Judge, jury, press and public hardly knew how to define what they were listening to. The three-hour outpouring was unclassifiable, part poetic oratory, part open wound. White faced and motionless Marshall hurled himself into his defence speech, the words pouring out in a torrent, yet always just kept under control. He made a bold and bitter start. Aware of the irritability he had found impossible to contain during the trial, he apologised, attributing it to the cramped grim environs of the court, which he described as 'utterly unfitted for the administration of justice and a positive disgrace to the richest municipality of the world'.[7] It was a brave beginning for a young member of the Bar but it had a dual effect. It won the sympathy of a jury sitting in a jury box too small, in a court too hot, for hours far too long, straining to see in the inadequate light; and it made the somnolent press sit up with a jolt at such an unexpected beginning.

Marshall began with a clear and concise analysis of all the points in his client's favour, easy to understand and completely lacking in the pomposity and patronage of many of his contemporaries. By the time he embarked on an enactment of the crime as he invited the jury to see it they were listening with rapt interest. And then, suddenly, the tall still figure flung himself into frantic activity. No one had ever seen anything like this re-creation of the death struggle. He demonstrated first the savage old man pinioning Hermann to the ground, his hands around her throat, and then Hermann herself, with only her left hand free, seizing an imaginary poker which seemed almost to materialise before the jury's eyes and delivering the ghastly fatal blows. The balletic agility and elegance of Marshall's sportsman's body made the whole thing transfixing theatre rather than the risible charade it could so easily have been. ('A good deal of attention should be given to bodily

71

training,' Irving preached to young actors; 'anything that develops suppleness and elasticity.'⁸)

It was only then that Marshall took on what he knew to be the stickiest point in his defence: the nature of his client's profession. The language reserved for prostitutes in the courts of the late nineteenth century was extreme: they were sinners and degenerates, rotten, brazen, wanton, steeped in vice, daughters of shame, at very best magdalenes and unfortunates. Only the very youngest and prettiest qualified as soiled doves.

'These women', said Marshall baldly, 'are what men made them.' It was a startling concept, arresting in its modernity, its message risky in the extreme to the sensibilities of this all-male jury, righteous in its respectability and property-owning entitlement to judge. Before they had time to bridle he appealed to what he knew they also were: sons, husbands, fathers, brothers. 'There was a time when this woman was as pure and good as any child,' he said in a voice just breaking with emotion. His jury did not know that he was thinking of Ethel, the little girl in the kindergarten, the beautiful bride, the broken body; but as he was thinking of Ethel they began to think of the purity of mothers, wives, daughters and sisters secure and cared for at home.

The speech rose to a crescendo of emotion. Marshall always ended up convincing himself of the righteousness of his cause; surely they were not going to let this woman hang? He did not beg; he never did that. He ended with a challenge that was to become familiar in his speeches: 'Gentlemen, on the evidence before you I almost dare you to find a verdict of murder.' Then he sat down.

The press must have tumbled out at that stage, eager to be the first to give an account of the new phenomenon, for they all missed the last famous words, quoted over the decades sometimes with admiration, sometimes in recent years in parody, but part of such a strong oral tradition that though never reported they must have been said. Catching sight of the sobbing woman huddled in the dock, the ringing peroration seemed to Marshall suddenly to be inadequate. He got to his feet again and uttered the words with which his name has ever after been associated:

> Look at her, members of the jury, look at her; God never gave her a chance. Won't you? Won't you?

The theology may have been a bit dodgy but the psychology was masterly. Put up there with God, twelve stolid householders found mercy in their hearts after all and delivered a remarkable verdict of manslaughter with a strong recommendation to mercy. Marie Hermann faced six years' imprisonment instead of the noose, Marshall's name was made and the blood-stained trunk, minus the corpse, was the chief attraction at Madame Tussauds that summer, attracting thousands of visitors.[9]

What the jury had heard that day was advocacy in its purest form, identification with the interests of another human being which seems to the listener to transcend self. Those hearing it, unable to categorise it with reference to anything else they had ever heard, described it in terms almost of the supernatural, reporting that they were transported in spite of themselves. Words such as 'hypnotic' and 'magnetic' were bandied about. Marshall himself must have recognised that this performance, in which personal grief seeped into his advocacy, was contrary to all the basic principles of the professional advocate. He had been speaking from the heart but all the same, even whilst he had struggled not to break down, the watcher who lurks inside every criminal barrister, one eye on the jury, the other on the public gallery, must have recognised that he had found the key. From then on his unique brand of real emotion and seamless technique was irresistible.

The work flooded in and with the work, stress. Indiscriminate instructions on every legal topic under the sun arrived from solicitors who hoped that this reportedly electrifying advocate would win the day regardless of subject matter and merits. With each case singled out for attention by the press the pressure grew. It was not that he did not know his own limitations; 'I am an advocate not a lawyer,' he always insisted, cheerfully admitting to what he described as a pitiful grasp of the technical aspects of the law. To remedy this weak point he invited Robert Ernest ('R E') Moore to join 3 Temple Gardens, ever after his loyal researcher and interpreter when the technicalities of the law became too challenging. Nonetheless the expectations became intolerable. Marshall relied like a sprinter on the massive short burst of energy dredged up from God knew where which hurled him past the finishing post. The short drama of the sensational criminal trial, in those days seldom lasting more than a few days, suited him down to the ground. He was never a long-distance runner.

In 1895 Marshall was instructed in a case that required weeks of painstaking work leading up to a trial which lasted twenty-two days, during which time it dominated the headlines in column after column of extraordinarily detailed evidence. There is nothing so dull as a dull fraud trial. The evidence is usually far too complex to hold the interest of those not intimately involved and the opportunity for forensic fireworks is non-existent. The so-called Liberator trial was no exception, though the crime had been sensational enough and the main perpetrator a famous personality.

Jabez Balfour was very short, very fat and very rich. The product of non-conformist temperance campaigning parents and brought up in Croydon, Balfour had become a property developer and financier, the mayor of the town and a Liberal MP. His reputation as a philanthropist and man of the people reached its zenith when he set up the Liberator Building Society, its aims to 'liberate' the working man from the insecurity of rented property and tyrannical landlords and enable him to buy his own small piece of England. The shares were sold by intermediaries who were dissenting ministers of religion, thus imbuing the whole enterprise with moral authority, and the scheme captivated the imagination of thousands who rushed to invest.

Over a period of some twenty years Balfour constructed an elaborate business empire operating through a complex series of companies underpinned by a maze of impenetrable accounts. Flamboyant, bluff, superficially amiable, fraudster on a Robert Maxwell scale, the eventual collapse of his empire was met with incredulity and then as the scale of the losses incurred by the investors began to sink in, with despair and suicides. Balfour sneaked out of the back door of his Oxfordshire mansion and did a bunk to Argentina only to be ignominiously brought back by a Scotland Yard detective who became impatient with the delay in extradition proceedings and bundled him into train and ship and so home to face his trial. Alongside him in the dock were four company directors, amongst them George Brock, generally credited as the backroom financial wizard elevated by Balfour from his original position as a lowly clerk and completely in Balfour's thrall.

The case was of immense legal importance, the first criminal prosecution of its kind under the Companies Act, and counsel for the prosecution were the cream of the senior Bar: the Attorney General, who later became Lord Chief Justice; a future Lord Chancellor; a future Director of Public Prosecutions; and a future High Court judge of great eminence.[10] The now penniless Balfour was represented by a senior barrister who was an old friend and Brock, equally impoverished, by Marshall.

Marshall quickly attracted attention. 'The dreariness of the Balfour case was yesterday perceptibly relieved ... while cross-examination was being conducted by Mr Marshall Hall ... He is a young man but he conducts his difficult and complicated case with marked ability.'[11] Then came the speech. Senior counsel must have awaited it with an interest not untinged with malice; dramatic re-enactment and tearing emotion might be all very well in their place but in a dry fraud trial they would be laughable. But Marshall was 'gentle in delivery, eloquent in words, judicious in tone sincere in manner, altogether admirable,'[12] said the reporters.

Oratory is the most ephemeral of the arts; only since recordings have been available have we been able to have an inkling of the true impact of great speeches. Once heard, the words of the speech and the voice that uttered them become indistinguishable: Churchill's determination never to surrender, Martin Luther King's dream, Nehru's tryst with destiny at the midnight hour are impossible to read without hearing them at the same time; but nonetheless the words of great speeches even in their written form have a poetry.

Marshall was recorded only once[13] and exhaustive attempts to find his voice have failed. We know only that it was very deep with a curious break in it and that he spoke (contrary to all the rules of advocacy) very fast. The rhythms of the Liberator trial speech even in print are unmistakably compelling. How much more lyrical must they have been delivered in that singular voice:

> The Defendant stands ready to receive Your Lordship's sentence, bowing his head to it, after a fair and impartial trial, penniless and a bankrupt, ruined alike in credit and in reputation. For years he followed blindly the orders and directions of the men he trusted – bound by the ties of gratitude. I beg Your Lordship to deal justly with this man but in dealing out justice let it be tempered with that quality of mercy which is and always has been so prominent a feature of the judgments of the English Bench.

'The Speech of the Day,' trumpeted the press.[14] The stellar array of counsel in court that day would not have been human had they not found that quite extraordinarily irritating.

Balfour was sentenced to fourteen years' imprisonment. Brock's exceptionally light sentence of nine months was universally attributed to the performance of his counsel.

Marshall finished the case spent with exhaustion, the darling yet again of the press and basking in the admiration, albeit in some cases through gritted teeth, of his colleagues. There was a massive weight of expectation on his shoulders and work filled his horizon. He reacted as he always did, with ill health. Shooting in the rain with Lord Burnham, the proprietor of the *Daily Telegraph*, he contracted pneumonia. It was the beginning of a mysteriously lengthy illness. Pneumonia, in the days before penicillin, was an extremely serious and sometimes fatal disease. Its course could be protracted, frequently lasting several weeks, but Marshall, a young fit man, was away from the Bar for nearly a year. Much of it was spent on the Sussex coast being nursed back to health by his father, who had returned there to a smaller house in Lansdowne Place, Hove, after his wife's death.[15] The length of time Marshall remained there and his past and subsequent history of periods of illness followed by change in direction suggest that his undoubtedly physical illness had a psychological component. Pneumonia provided Marshall not only with a refuge but with opportunities for reinvention.

CHAPTER 7

'Vote for my daddy, Marshall Hall'

On his return to London and the Bar, still fragile from his long illness and in need of pampering, Marshall moved into the Savoy Hotel,[1] a short walk from the Temple. The concept of hotel living for single men was well established in the late nineteenth century. Trollope writes in his novel *The Eustace Diamonds* about Frank Graystock, the archetypal young bachelor barrister, who had 'chambers in the Temple ... lived in rooms which he hired from month to month in one of the big hotels in the West End and dined at his club'. In Graystock's case the hotel was the Grosvenor.

For Marshall it had to be the Savoy. The hotel had opened a few years previously and had quickly become a byword for exactly the kind of glitzy glamour he found irresistible. Built by the impresario Richard D'Oyly Carte with profits from the Gilbert and Sullivan operas staged next door in the Savoy Theatre, it was originally intended to provide overnight accommodation for his audiences but the word had quickly spread. Here was to be found a degree of luxury, including unprecedented hot and cold running water, previously only to be found in American hotels. With the added glamour of Paris provided by the manager, César Ritz, and the sophistication of French cuisine by Auguste Escoffier, it quickly became the haunt of the Prince of Wales, and with him came the racier elements of London society.

Marshall was already familiar with the charms of the Savoy. Shortly after it had opened in August 1889, D'Oyly Carte had introduced the favoured younger members of the Beefsteak, Marshall amongst them, to a secret dining room approached by a side door into the hotel,[2] where those in his inner circle could be wined and dined at a third of the cost of dining in the main restaurant. It had been the beginning of Marshall's association with D'Oyly Carte, Arthur Sullivan and George Grossmith, all investors, shareholders or directors of the hotel. When the directors fell foul of London County Council with a five-foot-high sign on the roof advertising the new restaurant it was Marshall who represented them. Living there in 1896 would certainly have been beyond his means; the strong probability is that he was offered 'mates' rates' in one of the rooms more modestly priced because of its view of the internal courtyard rather than the river and with a bathroom across the corridor.[3]

The arrangement anyway was only to be for a few short months. Marshall had to make other plans for his future rather hastily. He had got a highly respectable girl, the friend of one of his father's patients, pregnant. There was only one course for an honourable man to take.

Henriette Kroeger, always known to Marshall as Hetty, was Austrian by descent, brought up in Germany in Altona, close to Hamburg. Her father, a ship owner, had drowned in an accident at sea, leaving Hetty and her sisters, then small children, to be brought up by their mother. There were English family connections and when she grew up Hetty was a frequent visitor to England. She had met Marshall intermittently over the years when staying in Ramsgate with a family friend, Miss Eliza Freeth, who happened to be one of Alfred Hall's patients. Hetty was small and fair and gentle, pretty in an unthreatening way that was a far cry from Ethel's dangerous beauty, with charmingly accented, fluent English. If at thirty-one she was a little past her sell-by date by the standards of the day, at least her maturity enabled her to cope with the scars of Marshall's past. His first marriage was never to be mentioned by her, and never was.[4]

They married very quietly in Ramsgate Parish church on 2 November 1896 with Eliza as a witness. Hetty was by then four months pregnant. Within a short time, bolstered by a loan from his father, Marshall had established a domestic empire from which to rebuild his practice, a home suitable for just what he wasn't but what he aspired to be, a prosperous, settled family man. Cricket was prohibited since his long illness and now he took up golf, at which he was also to excel. He became a keen bridge player. He rode occasionally on the fashionable Rotten Row in Hyde Park and circulated in the evenings within the narrow social boundaries of his London world: the Savoy, the Garrick, the Beefsteak, the West End theatres and the Café Royal in Piccadilly. He began to entertain on a lavish scale. He obtained the first of many beloved dogs, an Aberdeen terrier who fulfilled the basic requirement in all Marshall's dogs, utter devotion to his master, for whom he would sit waiting for long hours on the doorstep of the new matrimonial home.

Number 75 Cambridge Terrace,[5] Bayswater, was stucco fronted and elegant, five storeys high, staffed with five indoor servants, and with stables in the mews behind which soon housed the family's carriages – the victoria, the station brougham and the governess cart – as well as Skylark and Grayburg, the horses.

More than twenty years of obsessive collecting provided the contents of the house.[6] Marshall's flair for the theatrical enabled him to arrange them for maximum impact. Visitors to the Marshall Halls were led up a staircase lined with museum-quality mezzotints and engravings to the two grand interconnecting first-floor drawing rooms with overmantels designed by Marshall, one made up of the carved wood of old pews and the other with a seventeenth-century French picture frame. Here the walls were literally covered with his massive collection of pictures, engravings, enamels and ivory reliefs. There were cases and tables everywhere, one displaying a huge collection of miniatures, another repeating watches, yet another patch and snuff boxes, needle cases and rings. Locked away in the massive safe was the prized collection of Queen Anne silver. This was the accumulation of an aesthetically inclined jackdaw whose taste teetered on the fine line between eclectic and indiscriminate. Gorgeous, glittering, each object had been obtained for the sheer love of ownership – to stroke, to gaze at, to arrange, and yet frequently to press into the hand of anyone who admired it with an expansive generosity.

Here after the offer of a Havana from an old box that had once belonged to General Gordon, a cigarette from a Georgian tea caddy or some snuff from a gold snuff box engraved 'Good at a Pinch', there would be a demonstration of the pedal-powered pianola that was one of the first in London. When his repertoire was exhausted Marshall regaled his fascinated visitors with anecdote and reminiscence. The Sheraton chest of drawers had stood unappreciated in his nursery housing his infantile boots; the engravings had been picked up for a song when he was an undergraduate; that watercolour, he assured them (contrary to all the evidence), was a Turner; Wright of Derby had painted the picture of his paternal grandparents; that watch had belonged to Robespierre; the ink stand was Sèvres; the cupboard was full of antique golf clubs; that curious object was a die used to impress silver with patterns, which he had been given by a rogue of a forger he had represented and then befriended; the silver dagger came out of a harem.

Hetty soon provided the only thing missing in this large family house: Elna (named after the heroine in the last play her parents saw before she was born) Muriella (after her godmother the Countess De La Warr) Victoria (after the Queen) was born in March 1897, five months after the marriage. Marshall adored her, 'Baba' to his 'Gaga' or 'Gaggie'. He provided her with a charming nursery and a devoted nanny, Mrs Sanders, who quickly became part of the family. When Elna was a tiny baby she had her first letter from her father: 'I trust that you are doing your duty to your mother and allowing both her and your dear friend Mrs Sanders to get some small amount of sleep at night.'[7] And he continued to write to her charming, whimsical letters throughout her girlhood:

— From assize towns: 'Gaggie … has got to work work work … he is so angry and is stumping about saying such dreadful naughty words like Baba does when she is angry … but it is all no use, the naughty judges won't make haste and so Gaggie will be kept here …'[8]

— On country house shooting weekends: 'The birds were in such a hurry they forgot to stop when I shot at them …'[9]

— From London when she was on the continent with her mother and nanny: 'I wonder what you think of Switzerland and the bears. You would find it much too hot if they squeezed you … bears do squeeze so hard … and they won't leave off when they are told.'[10]

— And in thanks for presents: 'Thank you so much for that lovely red apple. Gaga ate it for breakfast this morning and enjoyed it very much indeed.'[11]

She was introduced with pride to all his friends and the letters are full of news of them: 'Gaga went to lunch with Mr and Mrs Woofus Isaacs and Mrs Woofus asked after Baba and sent her best love …'[12]

As soon as Elna was old enough to toddle a donkey joined the carriage horses in the mews and as soon as she could talk a governess was instructed to teach her the German that was her mother's native tongue as well as the French beloved of her father. She was soon fluent in both. Marshall kept a large photograph of her prominent on his desk in chambers, lavished on her elaborate outfits and baskets of puppies and showed her off proudly in company. But, as with Hetty and the Aberdeen terrier, the unspoken price he demanded was complete and uncritical devotion to him. Until she was about fifteen Elna provided it in full measure; no one was as wonderful as tall, handsome, funny Gaggie with his loving letters when he was (frequently) away and his teasing and stories and presents when he came home.

Dr Alfred Hall, Marshall's
much loved father, in his
consulting rooms

Julia Hall, Marshall's much
loved mother

Ada Labouchere, Marshall's
favourite sister

Marshall as a schoolboy

House Eleven. IIIrd House.
July 1876.

Marshall in his house cricket team at Rugby: seated middle row, far right

Marshall whilst working at a tea
merchants in the City of London

Marshall on his call to the Bar
in 1883

Marshall as a young man, the
matinee idol looks becoming
apparent

Count Raoul de Vismes et
de Ponthieu, Marshall's first
wife Ethel's lover

Hetty, Marshall's second wife, with their new-born daughter, Elna, always
known as 'Baba'

Marshall at various stages in his life; universally said to be
the handsomest man at the Bar – and frequently the
handsomest in England

Marshall, Hetty, Elna and the chauffeur
in the 1906 Vulcan motor car adorned
with electioneering ribbons

Marshall's electioneering photograph
for the 1910 election

UNMAILED MISSIVES.

No 54.

THE HOPE OF EAST TOXTETH.

Marshall on the campaign trail

A 1907 portrait of Marshall painted by Robert Wood, the accused in the Camden Town murder

The photograph of Marguerite Fahmy which she sent to Marshall after the trial. It joined all the other trophies of his triumphs that hung on his chambers wall

Edward Marshall Hall KC

The whole set-up had to be paid for, of course, but Marshall only ever worried about money when he ran out of it. Work was anyway picking up. One of his greatest talents was an unerring identification of the publicity value of a case and he assiduously courted the contacts which gained him briefs in them.

The first, provided again by Arthur Newton, faithful since the triumph of the Hermann trial, was the criminal libel case brought in 1897 by the second Earl Russell (brother of Bertrand and grandson of the first Earl Russell, Prime Minister in the mid-nineteenth century) against his ex-mother in law. When a handsome young undergraduate, Lord Russell had met Lady Scott and her daughter whilst he was yachting on the Thames. Lady Scott originally seems to have taken rather a fancy to the young Lord Russell herself, which may have been part of her problem since he eventually married the daughter, Mabel. The marriage quickly broke down and Mabel accused her young husband of having homosexual affairs. There was a series of public and embarrassing court proceedings which culminated in the legal separation that Russell sought and his wife objected to. Lady Scott then embarked on an extraordinary vendetta against her former son in law, with the assistance of private detectives who managed to track down three members of the crew who had sailed with him in his yacht and now signed statements telling dark tales of the young lord's misdeeds with the cabin boy. These statements Lady Scott then circulated around London society.

Oscar Wilde's recent fate as a result of his ill-judged libel case must have been fresh in Lord Russell's mind and it required considerable courage to take the same course. Nonetheless he did so and Lady Scott and the three crew members duly stood their trial for criminal libel. The prosecution was represented by Sir Frank Lockwood QC, who had been leading counsel for the prosecution in the 1895 Wilde trial and who had a reputation for wit almost equalling Wilde's. Lady Scott was represented by John Lawson Walton, then a very well-known Liberal MP. Marshall represented the three crew members. The trial was to be heard by Mr Justice Hawkins, the judge who had sentenced Thomas Orrock to death twelve years previously and one of the bears Marshall was particularly fond of baiting.

The public and press sat back and waited for entertainment. Predictably bail was granted to Lady Scott but not to Marshall's clients, and predictably he made no secret of his contempt for such socially motivated bias. Once the trial began Marshall ensured maximum attention by wrangling with the famously amiable Lockwood at every available opportunity, extracting from the unexpected death of one of his clients mid-trial hours of diversionary tactics and standing up to Mr Justice Hawkins in a series of defiant exchanges from which he emerged, in the jury's eyes at least, the victor. These at last led the judge, goaded past endurance, to observe that he 'did not believe' a factual (and correct) statement made by Marshall. This was an unimaginable insult (then and now) to any barrister; professional integrity is fundamental to their duty to the court. Marshall, exploiting the moral high ground, immediately gathered up his papers and announced his intention of leaving the trial. The intimidated judge apologised. It says much for the generosity of Mr Justice Hawkins that he later publicly acknowledged the excellence of the defence although he may have derived some comfort from the fact that all the defendants were found guilty. Most importantly for Marshall, his reputation amongst the public for fearless (in the view of many of his colleagues, suicidal) advocacy was now second to none.

His name was kept in the public eye with a subsequent junior brief involving many of his closest and most famous friends. W S Gilbert, notoriously touchy, sued a theatrical newspaper, *The Era*, for libel. After one of Gilbert's characteristic tirades against all the actors, playwrights and critics who had crossed his path the magazine had observed pithily that 'Mr Gilbert's self-esteem has with advancing years developed into a malady'. Gilbert sued them, in a trial which quickly degenerated into farce. The court was regaled with his feuds with Sullivan, D'Oyly Carte and the famous actor John Hare. Henry Irving was a witness, Gilbert fell out with the judge, Edward Carson, representing *The Era*, recited chunks of Rosencrantz and Guildenstern, and a bedazzled jury announced that they liked everyone so much they could not reach a verdict.

It was Marshall's last significant and appropriately frivolous case as a junior barrister. In June 1898 he was appointed Queen's Counsel, an honour awarded to those whose advocacy was recognised as exceptional and which enabled a junior barrister to exchange his gown made of 'stuff' (a thick woven material) for a silk one and abandon the drudgery of document drafting and legal research to the junior Bar.[13] A successful leader could double his fees; the respect and prestige accorded to him by judiciary and public was vastly increased, his social standing was considerably elevated and usually a knighthood followed. The rank of QC was, unsurprisingly, much sought after, hard won and extremely exclusive. Only seven juniors took silk the same year as Marshall, amongst them one of his close friends Rufus Isaacs. In contrast in 2015 there were ninety-three appointments and the glamour (and money) attaching to the appointment has dwindled commensurately.

For Marshall the gamble of abandoning his junior practice and relying solely on his reputation as a stellar advocate was less than for many. Some barrister's practices sink without trace when they 'take silk' but Marshall already had the reputation of being a reluctant backroom boy and a born orator. In responding to a congratulatory letter he described the transition as being 'my retirement from guinea grafting into comparative obscurity';[14] but he did not really believe that and nor did anyone else. He slid with consummate ease into the new role. Silk brought with it authority. Marshall's defence speeches, irresistible in their pathos, were now to become imbued with social comment as compelling as that of Dickens fifty years before. Crimes that had caused personal tragedy for victim and defendant he now began to use as more general exemplars of the greater social evils that had led to them. Principal amongst those evils were moral hypocrisy and drunkenness, each put in the spotlight in the two murder trials in which he was instructed in his first year in silk.

The first trial concerned the all-too-familiar tragedy of the woman in humble social circumstances seduced by her social superior. Shame, an illicit birth and the death of the baby followed swiftly. Annie Dyer was a respectable ladies' maid and the strong though unexpressed sub-text was that she was seduced by her employer. She was dismissed when she became pregnant, moved into lodgings and there had a baby who died thirteen days later and was found concealed in a box. The charge was murder and the defence one of accidental overlaying, in itself a by-product of the poverty and secrecy that arose from illegitimacy: the inadequate cold lodgings, the mother desperate for comfort and warmth, the bed shared with the baby because there was nowhere else. Marshall was instructed for the defence with his young nephew Max Labouchere, Ada's son, as his junior. Max was newly called to the Bar and had recently joined 3 Temple Gardens. Their strategy in this trial was the sort of emotional plea Marshall did best.

The crucial evidence against Annie Dyer lay in two reported remarks she had made. The first had been to the visiting monthly nurse: 'How can anyone get rid of a baby?' The prosecution relied on this as evidence of an intention to kill. Could it be, Marshall asked the nurse in cross-examination, that Annie had placed emphasis on the word 'can', thereby changing the sense to one of wonderment at the iniquity of others? The nurse agreed that this was possible. Coupled with her evidence that Annie was suckling the baby as she spoke, the complexion of the case began to change. The second, even more damaging, statement had been made to a police officer: 'I killed it, I did not know what to do with it, I put it in a box.' What if she had said 'I killed it. I did not know what to do with it, I put it in a box', asked Marshall. Then the statement was not an admission of guilt but consistent with her story. Building his emotional defence, Marshall made much of the love observed between mother and child and even more of the history behind the bald facts:

'The laws of nature press unfairly on a woman in matters of this kind. The act was the act of both, the punishment the punishment of one.' He knew all about shame, after all, and about hypocrisy; Ethel had died of shame, and her aristocratic lover had paid no price. He could have compelled Annie's seducer to give evidence, he told the jury; but he had not done so, to spare his blameless wife.

Annie Dyer was acquitted by the (then mandatory) all-male jury to loud applause from a public gallery made up almost exclusively of women. The judge was incensed by this display of public support; there was after all the little matter of a body hidden in a box and panic concealment is never a very attractive defence. The courts were not there, as he sourly pointed out, to provide theatrical entertainment and he had a good mind to send these women in the public gallery to prison. He did not add, as he might have done, that the trial is not the place for social reform either; the law must be administered as it stands. But Marshall, as he always said, did not regard himself simply as a lawyer; whether entitled or not, he had a wider agenda and he regarded the law at that time as iniquitous. In cases where a mother had killed a young baby the charge was murder and in the event of a conviction the death sentence had to be passed. In these cases the sentence was not by this time actually carried out,[15] though long prison sentences were usually substituted for it. In vain Marshall campaigned against the inhumanity of subjecting a woman to hearing the death sentence passed upon her;[16] the practice continued until 1922 when an Act was passed creating the special defence of infanticide. It was only then that the killing of a new-born baby[17] by its mother whilst the balance of her mind was still disturbed by the birth was no longer classed as a capital crime but was treated instead as the equivalent of manslaughter.

The second trial, in which Marshall shone a spotlight on the evils of drink, did not have the same personal resonances but nonetheless the degradation caused by the gin bottle was well known to him; no young barrister practising in the late nineteenth century could have been unaware of the major role it played in crime. On his home territory at Lewes Assizes Marshall was instructed to defend a Brighton publican on a murder charge. Easy access to drink had dominated the lives of both him and his wife. Together they had lurched from drunken brawl to reconciliation and back again. Their noisy violent quarrels had become so well known that on the night in question two policemen passing the door of their public house, the Marlborough, ignored the sounds of a struggle from within as did the barman at the Marlborough who, on his way to bed at 11pm, saw what he described as a usual occurrence, the wife senseless on the hall floor and the husband, blind drunk, standing over her. It was only when the same barman got up at 4am and saw that she was now lying on the floor in the bar, battered with bruises, with her husband, covered in cuts and incoherent with drink, vainly trying to rouse her, that he called a doctor. She was pronounced dead from a violent fall or blow to the head.

Marshall painted one of his pictures of this awful married life of drink and blows that must, he told the jury, make their hearts ache. He reconstructed what he suggested had been a fall in the hall, the hopelessly drunken woman dragged through the swing doors to the bar, sustaining her bruising on the way. The jury would surely not convict a man merely because he was a drunkard or had the terrible misfortune to be married to a drunkard?

The judge was Mr Justice Mathew, whose contempt for Marshall's populist tactics was becoming well known.[18] He summed up strongly for a conviction; he was having no truck with swing doors or drunken attempts to lift the victim. Given the multiplicity of bruises, he said there seemed no doubt her death was due to the violence of her husband. Grudgingly he instructed the jury on the law as he was bound to; if an assault was drunkenly meted out without intention to kill or cause grievous bodily harm, it might be manslaughter.

The jury jumped at the let out and gave a verdict of manslaughter with a strong recommendation for mercy. The judge, unable to pass the long term of penal servitude he said he had had in mind, imposed instead a mere four years. Like many of Marshall's great trials, its memory lingers on. It seems appropriate enough that poor Lucy Packham's legacy is also alcohol: the pub, now the Marlborough Pub and Theatre, still serves a cocktail named after her, a potent mix of rum, pineapple juice and a splash of suitably blood-coloured Chambord. And Marshall would have been the first to appreciate drama reflecting life when in 1979 the crime was re-enacted in the pub, with the murder in the bar and the trial in the theatre upstairs.[19]

Two murder trials in Marshall's first year in silk; in each a jury showing an unprecedented compassion and a collective social conscience in circumstances when it was generally thought the evidence pointed to a murder conviction; in each case the gallows cheated. The legend surrounding Marshall as an invincible defender was growing. Only one thing was lacking to complete the picture of the successful QC; a seat in Parliament. Marshall had not exhibited much interest in politics save for a bit of canvassing for his early mentor Forrest Fulton. But lack of interest was not regarded as much of an impediment. A successful career at the Bar generally counted as a qualification in itself and by now one fifth of all MPs were barristers.

The 1900 general election was the first 'khaki' election, fought on the back of the dominating and ongoing Boer War. Many had expected it to be over in months and in the summer of 1900, with the British apparently in control of both Boer republics, it was believed that it was all but over. In fact another two years of bloody conflict was to follow but the Tories under the leadership of Lord Salisbury were riding high; triumphant victory was expected not only in the war but also in the election.

Nevertheless the Liberal MP for Southport was not too worried about his seat. Sir George Pilkington was a cuddly, friendly man who kept bees. He had lived in Southport for thirty years and married a local girl, had been a doctor at the Southport infirmary, and was honorary colonel of the Liverpool Volunteer Regiment and a knight of the realm. Conscientious and kind with a strong sense of duty, he was locally loved; his seat seemed unassailable.

The Southport Unionists were looking for a candidate. The last time they had won the seat, some fourteen years before, George Curzon had been elected: handsome, aristocratic, a brilliant (if almost too self-assured) orator. On Curzon's appointment as Viceroy of India in 1898 a by-election had resulted in a Liberal gain. Various names were now mooted as potential candidates who might replicate Curzon's authority and charisma and regain the seat for the Conservative and Unionist Party. The possibilities ranged from Sir Edward Clarke KC, an immensely distinguished and senior member of the Bar, to the twenty-six-year-old Winston Churchill who, having had a misunderstanding with Southport in relation to his electioneering expenses, ultimately stood for Oldham.

Marshall had his summer vacation mapped out that year. He had taken Ellen Terry's cottage in Winchelsea, near Rye, and Hetty and Elna were to spend their summer at the charming low-lying little house with its picturesque chaotic garden. It was whilst he was there with them that he was summoned to London and invited to contest Southport. His instinct was to decline. He was absorbed in the building of his career; and more to the point it was only the beginning of the protracted summer vacation, which he had always regarded as one of the perks of his job. When the summer days in the Sussex garden with his little daughter and domesticity with Hetty palled, as he knew they would, he had planned a holiday in Norway followed by fashionable Marienbad, in Bohemia, with Charles Gill. The Prince of Wales (very shortly to become Edward VII) visited Marienbad every August to take part in the ritual dieting of the overweight aristocracy of England and around him collected a coterie of favoured (and preferably fat) friends to keep him amused. Amongst them, valued for his loyal friendship despite his trim figure, was Gill, and on occasions Marshall spent part of his summer there, the casino, balls, high-society gossip and goings on a sharp and welcome contrast to family life. It was all a more attractive prospect than Southport.

Furthermore he would miss all the August shooting parties. He cancelled Marienbad; but a preliminary visit to Southport did not convince him and he refused the offer. Setting off on his first weekend of shooting, his strong superstitious instincts prevailed when glancing out of the train at the start of his trip. The name emblazoned on the engine of a goods train running parallel to his own caught his eye: *Southport*. It was an omen.

There were others as well: Southport bore a strong resemblance to a smaller version of the Brighton he knew so well; it was not only the pier and the military bands, the illuminations and the influx of summer visitors; it was also the burgeoning commercial class of traders and shopkeepers and the substantial wealthy permanent residential population from backgrounds like his own. He could know these people, he could tap into their fears, he shared their aspirations. Accompanied by the faithful R E Moore to act as campaign manager (and to correct the grammar in his speeches), he set out to conquer the bellicose, chapel-going, temperance-loving electorate of Southport.

His arrival on Southport's political scene was boycotted by the strongly Liberal local press, who collectively expressed their opinion that they would reserve their energies for the goodbyes which would speedily follow on. When he made his first public appearance, however, there was a certain unease. He was even handsomer than George, now Lord, Curzon. With his first speech the unease grew; it was fluent and graceful, appropriately and simultaneously humble and confident; Curzon without the stiff arrogance which had repelled his critics.[20] Marshall's message was simple in relation to the three preoccupations of the electorate. The war was paramount; he supported Lord Salisbury's policy with regard to this just and necessary war whilst emphasising the need for a longer-term aim of pacification. He opposed the current pressure for disestablishment of the Church whilst advocating the utmost tolerance towards ideological differences. He supported temperance in the true meaning of the word, not complete abstinence. As always the content of his speech was almost subsumed by the delivery, the jokes, the quickfire witticisms exchanged with hecklers, the personal anecdote and the bravura. It was a long time before the carefully non-controversial approach he described as 'progressive Conservatism' was recognised for what it in fact was, an attempt to please all of the people all of the time. The style was so overwhelming that the lack of substance went unnoticed. In a few short days, like a 60,000-strong jury, Southport fell in love.

Every time Marshall spoke the crowds grew. When he addressed the ladies' branch of the Primrose League (dedicated to upholding God, Queen and Country and the Conservative cause) 600 had to be turned away. The packed audience did not have votes, of course, but they had husbands and brothers and fathers and sons who did. And here, furthermore, was a man who wholeheartedly said he supported women's suffrage. And he was so dreadfully handsome. The word spread.

A besotted local florist provided Marshall with a fresh flower for his buttonhole every day. Thirteen thousand engravings of his much-admired manly face were distributed amongst the electorate. A huge picture of him illuminated in the window of the Conservative Club by a magic lantern drew fascinated crowds. Overflow meetings were organised. Hetty and Elna did their bit; at the Pierrot Ball Hetty, in pale pink chiffon with a diamond tiara, made a pretty picture dancing with her handsome husband. Four-year-old Elna brought the house down when she toddled onto a platform wearing a placard: 'I'm a Conservative not very tall; vote for my daddy, Marshall Hall.'

Hecklers were charmed. Those suspicious of his profession succumbed to his lyrical defence of his job: barristers consider the great questions of life, he told them. Publicly he went from strength to strength. Sir George Pilkington, despite his worthy interest in the plights of his constituents, began to lose his solid ground. Privately, however, used to the perpetual conflict of the courts Marshall was beginning to find oratory difficult to sustain when everyone was on his side and fighting talk was not required. His specialism was persuasion; he found he scarcely needed any.

Marshall gained this supposedly safe Liberal stronghold, transforming a previous Liberal majority of 583 into a Conservative majority of 209 in what was acknowledged to be one of the most notable personal successes of the general election. Poor Sir George Pilkington went on a long holiday to Ceylon and the Southport electorate settled down to a prolonged period of hero worship. One of the railway porters on Southport station summed it up in the poem he composed and then proudly recited as Marshall waited for a train back to London:

> Good old Marshall Hall!
> He does not care at all.
> They took him for a simpleton.
> He's beaten Dr Pilkington.
> Good old Marshall Hall!

The porter, overcome with adulation, then burst into tears.

CHAPTER 8

'Outrageous gutter rags'

Τhe electorate of Southport had scarcely become accustomed to the new-found glamour of its political scene than the man responsible brought it national exposure when he was briefed for the defence in a murder case in Great Yarmouth. At first glance it was just a sordid sexual encounter on a beach. But it became one of the great trials of the twentieth century, challenging the unscrupulous practices of the gutter press and heralding a new culture which, for all its failings, at least made some basic acknowledgement of the defendant's right to a fair trial in a court of law unsullied by previous trial and conviction by the media.

The excesses of the press which triggered the Leveson inquiry in 2011–12 were nothing compared to those of the second half of the nineteenth century. The rules were even then clear enough; whipping up prejudice against the accused before trial was a contempt of court just as much then as it is now. The law officers whilst denouncing the practice were reluctant to prosecute offenders and the enforcement proceedings open to them were seldom instituted. The consequence was that in some quarters an emboldened press became increasingly unscrupulous. Once they had a victim in their sights he became fair game, the subject of ill-informed opinion and scurrilous rumour, with his character and previous history put under a journalistic microscope. Articles commented freely on the anticipated evidence and in areas local to the crime pamphlets and cartoons were distributed amongst the public from whom the jury was ultimately to be chosen.

Until the Yarmouth murders, however, the English press did just about stop short of the extraordinary practices then taking place in the United States as a result of the new phenomenon known as yellow journalism. Circulation battles between two big New York newspapers had led to ever-increasing sensationalism at the expense of properly researched reporting or any considerations of ethical practice. What had started as the reporting of news in an exaggerated way had quickly degenerated into stories which had the kernel of reality at their heart obscured by layers of gossip, scandal, fake pictures, interviews and pseudo-scientific mumbo-jumbo. Although the so called halfpenny newspapers[1] in London had not previously sunk to quite such tactics, Herbert Bennett was to prove the catalyst. It would be impossible to find a more flagrant campaign than the one to which he was subjected after his wife Mary Jane was found strangled on Yarmouth beach in September 1900.

Bennett,[2] aged twenty-one, was a clever, cool petty criminal and a precocious con man from an early age. When he was seventeen he seduced Mary Jane Clarke, a young woman of twenty, and married her after telling her he was twenty-one. Dazzled by his promises of huge inheritances and glamorous jobs just around the corner she joined him in various seedy though rather successful confidence tricks and in this way, now with a baby daughter, they eventually amassed savings that enabled Bennett to buy a grocer's business. Shortly afterwards the shop was burned out in a fire which occurred in very suspicious circumstances in the family's absence, resulting in a large payment from an insurance company unable to prove what it strongly suspected. Now in pocket the Bennetts told their family that they intended to go to the United States. In fact despite the smouldering Boer War they booked passages to South Africa under fictitious names, Mr and Mrs Hood. Mysteriously they stayed only four days in South Africa before starting the journey home.[3]

Settled back in England the Bennetts' relationship became unhappy though they remained nominally together, bound in an uneasy dependency, each threatening the other with exposure of their joint crimes. Eventually they obtained separate lodgings, though still maintaining an on–off relationship. During this time Bennett met a parlour maid called Alice Meadows. He courted her as a single man, met her family and charmed them as he had charmed Mary Jane and her family with promises of a prosperous future. They became engaged, Alice quite unaware of the wife and child living at 1 Glencoe Villas, Bexleyheath, Kent.

Mary Jane, equally, was unsuspicious when Bennett visited her in Bexleyheath and offered to pay for her to have a short break in lodgings in Great Yarmouth. He even suggested a suitable lodging house situated in one of the Rows, the tiny lanes with which Yarmouth was then riddled. It was mid-September, the end of the summer season and just the time for a quiet holiday with baby by the sea. Upon arrival Mary Jane, again using the fictitious name Hood, booked into the lodgings Bennett had suggested to her. On that first evening she went out, asking the landlady to mind the baby; she was meeting a friend, she said, and when she returned from a fish supper and what had obviously been a good few drinks she mysteriously referred to the friend as her brother in law. In fact, Bennett himself had been in Great Yarmouth that evening, booking into the Crown and Anchor hotel and leaving early the next morning.

In London, he met a friend whom he had not seen for a while and who now enquired after his wife and baby. They had died of fever in South Africa Bennett, said. 'Don't say much about it,' he asked the friend pathetically, 'I feel it very much. She was my right hand.' Whether he knew it or not he had anticipated the loss of his right hand by only three days. On returning to his lodgings in Woolwich he wrote to the faithful Alice Meadows, telling her he would be away for a few days (he invented a dying grandfather as his excuse).

The next day a letter arrived in Yarmouth addressed to Mary Jane (as Mrs Hood) with a Woolwich post mark. That evening Mary Jane went out in her best dress, her hair carefully plaited and pinned up and a long gold chain, her prized possession, inherited from her grandmother, around her neck. It was her second mysterious date since her arrival in Yarmouth. She was seen that evening in the snug of a pub with a man who was later somewhat tentatively identified by the publican as Bennett. There is no doubt, however, that Bennett was in Great Yarmouth that night; he booked into the Crown and Anchor at midnight and was seen the next morning to leave on the early London train.

The next time anyone saw Mary Jane she was lying on South Beach, a popular place for courting couples. Her gold chain was no longer around her plump neck; instead there was a bootlace eight and a half inches long, biting in so deeply it had strangled her. She was on her back, scratched and bruised, the neatly plaited hair now loose, the best dress and the petticoat under it pulled up well above her knees; the implications were obvious. What was not obvious was who she was, and she had not assisted the subsequent attempts at identification by staying in Yarmouth under an assumed name. She was traced to her lodgings, where the baby was still in the care of the landlady, but her belongings gave no clue to her identity. There was only a photograph taken a day or two before of her playing on the beach with her child, her gold chain around her neck. At the inquest all the coroner could conclude was that a woman unknown had been murdered by a man unknown.

The police did not give up, however. There is a book to be written about the enormous contribution of laundry marks to the detection of Victorian crime; in this case the mark '599' on the dead woman's underwear, originally missed, led at last, after an exhaustive and fruitless attempt to link it to the name Hood, to a Bexleyheath laundry and from there to 1 Glencoe Villas and Mary Jane Bennett. It was now more than six weeks since her body had been found.

Herbert Bennett meanwhile had called at Glencoe Villas himself. Telling the neighbours his wife was ill in Yorkshire and needed some of her belongings, he broke in and removed items of jewellery and clothing which he gave to the unsuspecting Alice, still happily anticipating her Christmas wedding. Later he wrote to the landlord, terminating the tenancy on the property, and began to look for houses with Alice.

The police on discovering these activities arrested him. Bennett denied ever going to Yarmouth or having seen his wife for the best part of a year. No really reliable evidence put Bennett and Mary Jane together in Yarmouth. The police could prove, however, that Bennett, clandestinely engaged to another woman, had gone to Great Yarmouth on the very day that Mary Jane had booked in to the lodging house he had suggested to her and that he had stayed that night in the Crown and Anchor. They could prove that a letter had arrived for Mary Jane from Bennett on her last day and that he had stayed again in the Crown and Anchor on the night of her death. Furthermore he had retrieved her belongings and told lies about her whereabouts. Circumstantial it might be but it was all highly suspicious. Then they had a breakthrough; on searching Bennett's lodgings they found in his belongings a long gold chain which was identified by the Yarmouth landlady as the one in which Mary Jane had gone out to her death. The case now looked open and shut.

The press, feeding a public already ablaze with prurient curiosity about the case, the horrid murder, the hint of sex, the baby left behind and the long quest to identify the victim, now went to town and two newspapers in particular lost all restraint. Alfred Harmsworth's *Daily Mail* and *Evening News*, the latter recently bought by him, were already beginning to attract enormous readerships. It was the beginning of the monopoly that came to dominate the press, to shape public opinion to an unprecedented degree, to bring down governments and even, some said, thanks to its virulent anti-German sentiments, to help bring about the First World War. Hell bent at this time on empire building, Harmsworth had looked to the press barons of the United States for inspiration and had imported an American journalist named Saqui Smith who represented a new breed, the so-called news investigator. Smith was an experienced New York crime reporter and he employed tactics more blatant than had previously been seen in England. He visited the prospective witnesses, told them that there was not a particle of doubt that

Bennett was the killer, interviewed them all and published their 'evidence' in advance of the trial. Many of them were paid for their stories. Any rumour, however scurrilous, about Bennett's character and behaviour was prominently published before his trial. Every detail of the case against him was blazoned across the front pages, as was any theory, however unlikely or however plain the motive for fabrication and malice.

Publishers local to the crime followed the newspapers' lead with malicious pamphlets anticipating the entire course of the trial. When word got out that the murderer had had a luxuriant moustache, one was superimposed on a picture of Bennett which was then widely circulated. A trial in Norwich, the nearest assize town to Great Yarmouth, was impossible; local hostility had reached fever pitch. A successful application was made to move the case to the Old Bailey and the Lord Chief Justice, Lord Alverstone, who had been due to hear it at Norwich Assizes, returned to London especially.

Marshall was briefed for the defence by a solicitor, Edward Elvy Robb, who later said that his ambition long before as an articled clerk in Tunbridge Wells in the 1880s had been to instruct in a murder the astonishingly charismatic young Marshall Hall. Now, with the trial of the decade, his dream had come true. For Marshall the icing on the cake was the news that the Solicitor General, Sir Edward Carson, originally briefed for the prosecution was unavailable and Charles Gill, Marshall's greatest friend at the Bar, had been briefed in substitution for him. The forthcoming trial gripped the nation.

Huge crowds congregated in the street outside the Old Bailey on the first day, 25 February 1901. Horrified at the number of women desperate for admission to a trial he thought utterly unsuitable for their ears, the Lord Chief Justice took the unprecedented move of ruling that no women were to be allowed into the courtroom. They queued up nonetheless, society women in smart clothes shamelessly begged for seats, and were turned away at the door. By 11 am the floor of the court was packed with newspaper reporters from all over the world and the public gallery filled to capacity. The corridor outside the room of the under-sheriff in charge of allocating seats was like 'the vestibule to a theatre on the occasion of a fashionable matinee'.[4] No one else, regardless of their sex, could squeeze in.

The scene was set; Herbert Bennett stood in the dock 'nonchalantly', the press reported, whilst 'a delicately flushed' Alice Meadows sat nearby. Charles Gill QC[5] for the prosecution, along with two junior barristers, and Marshall Hall QC for the defence, also with two juniors, took their places. Queen Victoria had died four weeks before and the country was in mourning. The waiting barristers, immaculate in wigs, gowns and stiff collars, wore as always the pristine white linen tabs known as 'bands' at their throats. Today the bands had neat double pleats down the middle, the obligatory markers of mourning when the monarch died. Lord Alverstone presided in his new red robe trimmed with ermine, as spick and span as any schoolboy on his first day at school. He had been appointed Lord Chief Justice only four months before and this was his first murder trial. He was only too well aware, since the days of the Liberator trial, of the effectiveness of Marshall's advocacy and a Marshall aflame with rage at the press and revving up for a fight was going to be hard for even the most experienced judge to handle.

But Marshall's sense of showmanship kept him dead quiet for Gill's precise, fair opening of the case. It was only at the end of it with a consequent and designed watering down of its impact that he got to his feet to hand to the judge what he could just as well have produced at the outset of the trial, the grossly prejudicial pamphlet bought on the streets a few days previously holding Bennett up as a murderer. What chance, he demanded, did Bennett have of a fair trial? The pamphlet was highly improper, Lord Alverstone agreed meekly. The jury looked disapproving. It was the beginning of Marshall's strategy.

The utterly damning evidence relating to the necklace was the first thing to grapple with, however. Marshall relied on his own by now renowned knowledge of jewellery as well as expert evidence from his friend Howard Welby, proprietor of the Garrick Street jewellers to which he was a frequent visitor. The defence they advanced was that the chain in the photograph, undoubtedly worn on the night of the murder, was not the same chain as the one found in Bennett's possession later. The former, Marshall pronounced after much flourishing of an eye glass, was a link pattern, the latter a rope pattern. The blurry quality of the photograph of Mary Jane on the beach made it difficult to dismiss this argument.

As the factual evidence unfolded, Marshall exploited every opportunity to plant the possibilities of mythical murderers in the jury's mind. The mysterious brother in law; a robber bent on snatching Mary Jane's jewellery; some passing madman. He sprung a surprise alibi witness, kept secret, he said to protect him from the hungry press.[6] This man, produced like a rabbit out of a hat, insisted that he had had an encounter with Bennett whilst out on a walk in Eltham, near Bexleyheath, on the very evening of the murder.[7]

A reasonable doubt was quivering tentatively into being. The trial, originally predicted to last a day, now looked as though it was going to be much longer. The jury were hanging onto Marshall's every word. Lord Alverstone and Gill, who had both regarded the result as a foregone conclusion, were becoming increasingly uneasy.

All the same it was a very thin defence and Marshall knew it. The one thing he dared not do, though the law for the last two years had, for the first time, permitted it, was to call Bennett in his own defence. Bennett had never mentioned the alibi of the encounter in Eltham to anyone and to Marshall's frustration was insisting, in the face of the cast-iron evidence from the Crown and Anchor, that he had never been to Yarmouth. Given the chance, Gill would have made mincemeat of him in cross-examination.

With a typical disregard for the consequences to his own career Marshall turned on the press. He had been the newspaper reporters' dream counsel, guaranteed to come up with all the drama and headlines they could wish for. They had made his career. Now, it seemed to them, he was biting the hands that had fed him. Witness after witness, called to give factual evidence of all the little details central to the prosecution case, were forced to tell sorry stories of their involvement with the newspapers; accounts they had given to reporters were scrutinised in comparison with the evidence they gave in court; witnesses with their backs against the wall were forced either to confess to lies or to accuse the press of complete fabrication. Marshall's questions were hurled like stones:

- 'Knowing that this man had been arrested on a charge of murder, you were gossiping about this case to a newspaperman?'

- 'How dare you pose to [the newspapers] as an important witness?'

- 'I have here a report of your today's evidence, printed before you were called.'

- 'Did [the *Evening News*] pay you money?'

The listening reporters writhed. Things got worse during the defence speech, in which Marshall hurled abuse at the papers, describing them as 'outrageous gutter rags which circulated at night time under the guise of halfpenny newspapers. Sensational journalism imported from America and a disgrace to America seemed as if it would deprive England in time of its proudest boast that it was the one country in the world where one could get absolute justice.' Only Marshall could have turned evening newspapers into nocturnal predators. He could hardly bring himself to speak, he said, of Mr Saqui Smith of the *Evening News*. But then he managed to do so. Mr Smith thrived on blood and sensation. He was a *ghoul*. And Marshall obligingly spelled the word so no reporter should miss it.

And so he continued his impassioned submissions: doubts cast over the case by the equivocal evidence as to the necklace, by all the candidates for the role of murderer, by the apparent sexual motive of the crime and the stupid mistakes so uncharacteristic of wily Bennett, but above all by the press contamination of the evidence. The only person who did not appear to be carried away by Marshall's eloquence seems to have been Bennett himself. In the very middle of the speech that transfixed the entire court, Bennett suddenly leaned over the dock and tapped Marshall's shoulder. 'May I have the window shut?' he asked. 'I feel a draught.' That became one of Marshall's best stories, recounted with the aggrieved charm that his listeners always found so irresistible. But at the time it was clear to all in court that the jury were wavering. The prosecution were feeling a draught as well; the cast iron case was slipping away.

Gill did his stolid but effective best to get them back on track. There was no great mystery about the case, he said prosaically, now they knew all the facts. In the end this was just a man who had every reason to want to get rid of his wife, and the cumulative force of the evidence was surely compelling. Lord Alverstone supported him in a summing up later said by many to be too heavily biased towards conviction.

And ultimately the jury did convict. Lord Alverstone paid tribute to the conduct of the defence, expressed his own conviction that Bennett had killed his wife, passed his first death sentence and then retired to bed for several days to get over the stress of it all.

Reverberations from the trial could be felt everywhere. Saqui Smith, smarting from what he described as the public obloquy to which his name had been subjected by Marshall, wrote an indignant tirade exonerating himself, though it was noted that his own newspaper was uncharacteristically silent. The more respectable broadsheets, firmly parked despite their own dubious practices on the moral high ground, objected to being lumped together with Harmsworth's newspapers as 'the press' and universally condemned his practices. But notwithstanding their collective resentment they were unanimous in their praise of Marshall's defence. They recognised what he had been up to: 'Little discrepancies exaggerated, some obscure points not very material made much of ... the existence of a prejudice against [the prisoner] used as a basis of appeals in his favour – all these topics might for a moment distract the attention of a jury from the cogency of the case for the prosecution,' said *The Times*.[8] It was not a criticism, however; the press and public acknowledged the magnificence of a fight in a lost cause in the heroic tradition.

Yarmouth was less impressed; it could not forgive Marshall's creation of alternative candidates for the murderer, which had included a reference to 'the lust and greed for gold of some prowling brutes who haunt the shores of Yarmouth'. The tourist trade had been done irreparable damage, it was said; holidaymakers were put off by Marshall's entirely fictitious 'prowling brutes' whom they now feared to meet on its peaceful beaches.

His exposure of press practices, however, had happier lasting consequences; the Institute of Journalists, stung at last into action, condemned the gross interference with the administration of justice. Shortly after the trial Marshall in Parliament asked the Home Secretary, Charles Ritchie, to introduce measures making it a criminal offence to publish comments in the press on charges whilst trials were pending.[9] The practice could not be too strongly condemned, said Ritchie, and on consultation with the law officers the Attorney General said the whole subject of contempt should be revisited and the existing powers of the criminal law were now to be invoked wherever necessary.

In fact Marshall betrayed his relative inexperience in his defence of Bennett and it says much for his popularity at the time that he was forgiven for a lot of high-handed bullying during the trial; it was all very well to make the Lord Chief Justice take to his bed but treating the humble Yarmouth witnesses with contempt was something else. Several of the women he cross-examined burst into tears: 'That is the common refuge of your sex,' he told one sobbing girl. That comment did raise an eyebrow or two in the Southport press; the Conservative ladies of the Primrose League had been dismayed by their hero's lack of chivalry. But on the whole the rudeness to witnesses was put down to the stress of a capital trial.

The measure of that stress is apparent from the fact that for weeks after his professional involvement had ended, Marshall continued his defence of Bennett almost frantically; but letters to Lord Alverstone and to Ritchie reiterating the circumstantial nature of the evidence and the discrepancies in it were to no avail. Ultimately he wrote to Bennett himself:

> I have felt it my duty to see both the Home Secretary and the Lord Chief Justice … as you have been informed there is no hope for you and the sentence of the law is to be carried out. If there is anything … that you would desire done after your death, write me a few lines and any reasonable request you may make I will endeavour to carry out. May God in his great mercy grant you peace in the world to come.[10]

It was far beyond his professional duty and it was gestures of this kind that in the end made him so loved.

On 7 March 1901 Bennett was taken by hansom cab to Liverpool Street station and with his escort caught the 5.10 am train to Norwich.[11] There, on a sunny morning two weeks later, he was hanged. When the black flag was raised to announce his death the flag pole fell with a clatter. It was an omen, said the press; though of what, they did not say. Bennett's last moments were reported in great detail by the newspapermen present at the execution: the shaking steps as he was assisted to the scaffold; the lifting of his neck to assist the hangman in getting the bag over his head; the height of the drop; the twitching of the hanging body.[12] Here, away from the merciful anaesthetising of court ritual, defence counsel felt the reality of losing a capital trial. For Marshall it was the first of many times when he retreated for days into silent grief, reliving the trial, analysing where he might have gone wrong, reproaching himself bitterly despite the noisy acclaim of his public.

Eleven years later there was a curious postscript to the Yarmouth murder. On 10 October 1912 an eighteen-year-old girl called Dora Grey was found lying on South Beach. She had been strangled with a bootlace. Her killer was never found. The significance of the crime was not lost on the press, which had a long memory.

The longest memory of all, however, was that of Alfred Harmsworth, whose newspapers were particularly targeted by Marshall for criticism during the trial. Harmsworth's massive wealth, influence and megalomania were all rapidly increasing. He could afford to wait to settle his score.

Unsuspecting, Marshall returned to his parliamentary duties and made his maiden speech in the House of Commons on the day Bennett hanged. He chose to speak on the second reading of a Bill that imposed penalties on publicans who sold or delivered alcohol to children under sixteen. This worthy if unglamorous topic had come to his notice when Cissy Silversides, aged twelve, the child of one of his constituents, had written to him begging for his support. Cissy's touching little letter and Marshall's equally touching response ('Dear little Cissy ... no one can be fonder of children than I am and I will do anything I can for them ....'[13]) had already been published in the Southport newspapers with gushing approval. The Bill was designed to discourage the practice of parents sending young children to 'fetch a jug of beer', thereby exposing them to not only the unsuitable sights and sounds of rowdy public houses but also the temptations of alcohol. The debate was an impassioned one, the issue dividing those who invoked the image of the country labourer who in a centuries-old practice sent his boy for a jug of beer from a friendly village innkeeper and those who pointed to the drunkard father who exposed his frightened child to the gin-soaked vice of urban pubs, the evil to which the Bill was really addressed. A legend has arisen that

Marshall's speech was a disaster, and that open mockery by the House resulted in his failure ever to make his mark in politics.[14] It is true that his suggestion that beer could be delivered house to house like milk was greeted with loud laughter; but he dealt with it coolly enough, vowing to take no notice of the ridicule and completing the rest of a long speech apparently unflustered. The newspapers made no reference to any undue degree of mockery by the House nor to any particular reaction by Marshall. On the whole they reported favourably if, by the standards Marshall was accustomed to, moderately.[15]

It is nonetheless true that Marshall's political career was unimpressive. Other than a few contributions to the Temperance Bill, his early utterances in the House were confined to brief questions relating to narrow domestic issues affecting his constituents (school holidays during the Coronation; safety on the Lancashire railways after a signalman was killed), or to matters of naked self-interest (the lifting of restrictions relating to the use of Hyde Park at night, the most direct route home from Westminster to Cambridge Terrace; tax concessions for the self-employed professional). He found what he perceived as the time wasting in the House of Commons intolerable. Even when his head was in Westminster, his heart was in the Temple. His priorities at the end of his first year were apparent: of the 482 divisions in the House of Commons he took part in only 120 and his only major speech had been his maiden speech. The bald fact was that he was not interested in politics but only in the challenge of persuasive oratory. The prize was the gaining of popularity and an admiring audience of thousands on a larger stage than that of a court of law. Victory had been sweet; the work that went with it was not to his taste.

This does not mean he went unnoticed in Westminster by any means; excellence in the parliamentary golf team, letters to *The Times* and the occasional publicity stunt[16] saw to that. And in Southport he went from strength to strength. He was far more comfortable with the personal touch than with abstract altruism. 'Is there anything I can do for the widow?' he wrote anxiously after the death of the signalman at Southport station. And he was always ready to provide his constituents, basking in his charm, with entertainment. At the Formby village fair and the Freshfield Bazaar he gave spontaneous displays of his rifle shooting: not content with carrying off the first prize of a box of Havana cigars from the shooting booth, he then positioned a fearless Hetty with a playing card held between her teeth and shot out the pips unerringly. He was a wonderful raconteur and a hilarious mimic and he told easily appreciated jokes ('When is a judge not a judge? When he is awake!'). His golf handicap at Formby was a six. He would like to learn farming, he told the Farming Society. And he had enjoyed fisticuffs in his youth, he said, and was not afraid to give his detractors a black eye or a bloody nose (how they all cheered at that). 'Southport's darling is the Apollo of the House of Commons,' said an article entitled 'Best dressed MPs'.[17] Marshall Hall was the handsomest man at the Bar, said the Candid Friend; 'his profile is as perfect as is compatible with the existence of brain power behind it'.[18] His constituents, basking in reflected glory, loved it all.

CHAPTER 9

'Disgraceful conduct'

T he fall after the pride was a heavy one. It was gradual in coming and resulted from a number of different events. They were minor things; some were only the everyday reverses of a barrister's life: the error of judgement in the conduct of a case, the irritation of a judge, the unfavourable verdict. Some were due to the lack of experience of a young politician: the injudicious remark, the espousal of an unpopular cause, the indifferent speech. Some were the result of Marshall's self-destructive personality. All were now occurring in a spotlight created by his reputation as an electrifying speaker and the expectations of an adoring electorate; but outside it, in the penumbra, lurked an increasingly vengeful press.

The first storm broke in July 1901 when he was instructed in a case which looked at first glance right up his street with its theatrical background and publicity potential. Miss Hettie Chattell, leading lady in the current wildly popular show at the Hippodrome, sued the proprietor of the *Daily Mail*, Alfred Harmsworth, for libel. Marshall was instructed to represent her. In an article entitled 'Greenroom gossip' the *Daily Mail* referred to an actress called Miss Rosie Boote who had recently become engaged to a member of the aristocracy. 'Miss Rosie Boote', said the item, 'is the daughter of Miss Hettie Chattell, the principal boy in the Hippodrome summer pantomime.' Miss Chattell, who was only twenty-eight, took instant and understandable exception to this and issued a writ for libel forthwith. The newspaper issued an apology: 'The many friends and admirers of Miss Chattell are aware that Miss Chattell is an unmarried lady…' Whether deliberate or inadvertent, no mention was made of what Miss Chattell regarded as the real insult, the implication that she was far older than she really was. She refused to accept the apology and pursued her action. The newspaper asked the court for three weeks in order to prepare its defence but three weeks later, no defence having been filed, the case went before a court for the damages now due to Miss Chattell to be assessed. Miss Chattell had asked for £1,000. Marshall, instructed on her behalf, hurled himself chivalrously to her defence. It was a dastardly attack, he said, that pandered to the tastes of gossips anxious to hear the least bit of scandal about the private lives of individuals in whom they could not possibly have the slightest interest. That was a bit rich coming from Marshall, who himself relied on those very tastes, but the jury lapped it up and Marshall, who had a habit of underestimating his own powers of persuasion, won for her the ludicrously high award of £2,500 (over £280,000 by today's standards). In doing so he brought about his own ruin.

During the course of his impassioned representations on Miss Chattell's behalf he once more offended Harmsworth, who was still smarting from the Bennett case, on two counts. Professionally Harmsworth was insulted by the suggestion that the three-week adjournment had been sought whilst the newspaper searched for any dirt they could use to besmirch Miss Chattell's name and that only on finding nothing did they decide not to defend the action. Personally he took exception to a throwaway remark to the jury intended to neutralise any disapproval of Miss Chattell's chosen profession: 'My client may have to work for her living but is entitled to the same consideration as any other lady in the land – including Mrs Alfred Harmsworth,' Marshall said.

Harmsworth, waiting for revenge, was now stung by what he chose to interpret as a deliberate insult. Incensed by the adverse publicity the case had attracted, he appealed. He briefed a team of no fewer than five counsel headed by the immensely senior establishment figure Sir Edward Clarke KC, an enterprise likely to have cost very substantially in excess of the amount of damages he had been ordered to pay. The case began to assume huge significance.

In the Court of Appeal the Master of the Rolls sat with two Lords Justice. One of them was Sir James Mathew, whose violent dislike of Marshall was so well known that it was frequently commented on by the press.[1] The reasons and origin were obscure, but it was by this time of long standing. As a young barrister, Marshall openly complained that he could not win a case in front of Mathew; on one occasion he held twelve small briefs in an assize court in which Mathew was presiding and lost every one. He had retaliated by being as fearlessly rude as only Marshall could be. 'Sit down,' Mathew said after one particular bit of impudence. Marshall cast a look at the public gallery and remained standing, continuing with his speech. 'Sit down, Mr Hall,' bawled the judge. 'Oh, Your Lordship is addressing me,' said Marshall sweetly. 'I thought you were addressing a lady at the back of the court. Of course if Your Lordship would prefer me to address you sitting down I will do so.' In those days when extreme deference to the Bench was the norm, it was incendiary. Never one to bear a grudge, Marshall afterwards sought to apologise through an intermediary. The two barristers tracked Mathew down at his club, the Athenaeum, and whilst Marshall waited hopefully outside like a chastened dog, his friend went to effect a reconciliation. 'It's no use, Marshall,' he reported moments later, 'the judge says he hates you.' Marshall thought it was funny at the time; but he was fast to learn his mistake. The Bench, and the Bar from which it was selected, made up a very small world in the late nineteenth and early twentieth centuries. There were only seven judges sitting in the Court of Appeal in Marshall's day (now there are thirty-eight) and only twenty-one sitting in the High Court (now there are 109). Enemies once made were hard to avoid and Mathew became an implacable one.

It does not require very sophisticated psychology to analyse the reason for Mathew's dislike. He had not himself had an easy start at the Bar though eventually he had built up a huge practice with an emphasis on preparatory paperwork in commercial cases. He never took silk; he was a plain-featured, stolid-looking man and his voice, weak in volume and harsh in tone, was thought by some to have held him back. His elevation to the High Court Bench as a junior barrister who had never become a QC was exceptional and a tribute to his intellectual abilities. Marshall's nationwide popularity, film star looks and beautiful voice, constantly remarked upon, combined with an intellect which many at the Bar regarded as lightweight must have been an unbearably irritating combination to Mathew. Both the judge and Marshall had reputations for their courtroom exchanges; but where Marshall was warm and amusing, Mathew had a bitter sarcastic wit. Marshall's irrepressible personality and populist advocacy were red rags to Mathew's incisive intolerant intellect. And then to cap it all there were the politics. Mathew was an Irishman steeped in Nationalist philosophy and an ardent supporter of home rule. Marshall, as a Unionist, had been vocal in his support of Lord Salisbury's anti-home rule policy.[2] No two men could have been more diametrically opposed in every way; but Mathew, as a result of his appointment to the Court of Appeal only a month before Marshall's case was due to be heard, now held all the cards. Given the strength of his own dislike it was generally thought that Mathew should never have agreed to sit in this case, in which Marshall's entire reputation was at stake. But, far from acknowledging how inappropriate his role was, Mathew seems to have relished it. Those witnessing his tirade in court were struck by its personal nature; he seemed hell bent on humiliation. Lord Birkenhead,[3] writing nearly thirty years later, summed up the views of the legal profession: the censures of Marshall's behaviour and advocacy were ludicrously severe, he said, the severest being expressed by a judge known to have a private agenda; the court had been guilty of a great injustice.[4]

In the Court of Appeal the very style of Marshall's oratory came under fire; the disproportionate amount of damages had arisen, said Sir Edward Clarke, because Marshall's speech had been inflammatory both in content and delivery. It was probably the first time a barrister had been accused of being too persuasive. The Court of Appeal agreed with him. A verdict obtained by such means could not stand, it ruled, and ordered Hettie Chattell either to accept the reduction of her damages to the £1,000 she had originally asked for, or submit to a retrial of the whole case. The court's view of Marshall's conduct in the original trial was stated in terms which made newspaper headlines without any creativity on the part of the reporters. Lord Justice Mathew's epithets could not be bettered: 'shocking advocacy' and 'disgraceful conduct', quoted the popular newspapers with relish. *The Times* devoted a leader to the subject. The great licence accorded to the Bar, a profession relied upon to act as gentlemen, had been abused, it reported. Zeal for the client had traditionally been tempered by more important considerations, those of the public interest in restraint and courtesy. This was a new form of advocacy and a new laxity. Perhaps most serious of all was the opinion of the *Law Times*, the professional journal read by most of the solicitors upon whom the Bar relied for its work. Marshall Hall had tarnished the honour of the Bar, it said.

It seemed, having never been able to do wrong in the eyes of press and public, that Marshall could now never do right. In 1903, his tactics were once again the subject of fierce criticism in a libel trial remarkable only for the pettiness of the protagonists and the sordidness of their dispute. Lady Cook was the American-born widow of an English baronet, Sir Francis Cook. During her husband's lifetime, convinced he was having an affair, she enlisted the aid of his secretary, Wallace, to spy on him on her behalf. Wallace was subsequently sacked and shortly after Sir Francis died. Wallace then emerged from obscurity to claim that Lady Cook had never paid him for his services as a private detective. Lady Cook alleged that when demanding his dues from her, Wallace had threatened to expose her as having been implicated in her husband's death. She then put a notice in the *Evening News* and the *Daily Mail* saying that Wallace had subjected her to blackmail. Wallace sued for libel and his unpaid fees.

Marshall represented Wallace against Sir Edward Clarke KC with whom he had crossed swords in the Chattell case. During the course of his opening speech on behalf of Wallace, Marshall, in emphasising the malice of Lady Cook's allegations, told the jury that Lady Cook had herself been implicated as a blackmailer in a previous unrelated case in America. He could not, at the time he said this, prove it and was relying on extracting an admission from Lady Cook when he ultimately cross-examined her. Technically he should not have referred in his opening speech to matters on which he had no proof, and Clarke then pulled the rug from under his feet by vigorously cross-examining Wallace and then announcing he was calling no evidence himself and therefore no Lady Cook to be cross-examined by Marshall. He then made a speech, all righteous indignation at Marshall's unsupported allegations. Despite these criticisms, in what was now an emerging pattern Marshall won over the jury and the case almost in spite of himself. Lord Alverstone, the Lord Chief Justice, who heard the case, had a soft spot for Marshall and, anticipating trouble, sought to exonerate him. No doubt, he said, Marshall had mistakenly relied on the not unreasonable expectation that Lady Cook would go into the witness box. But Lady Cook promptly went to the Court of Appeal demanding a new trial.

The Court of Appeal again included Lord Justice Mathew. Marshall's conduct had now passed all bounds of acceptable advocacy, he ruled. It was all very technical and today would have been of interest to no one but the legal profession. But the combination of a hostile Lord Justice of Appeal and a vengeful press baron is a potent one. The *Daily Mail*, with an axe to grind, reported it all with high glee.[5] Inconceivable today, the finer points of ethical practice in advocacy became the subject of public debate and Marshall's name and perceived misdemeanours served as a symbol for the controversy surrounding a series of cases. Sir Edward Clarke as one of the greatest advocates of the previous generation had always been one of Marshall's heroes. After the Cook case, crushed by the criticism, he wrote to him with an uncharacteristic humility; only the last few words, an obvious jibe at Mathew, betray his resentment.

> There was a time not so very long ago, when I had begun to hope that some day I might attain some of the measure of success which you have achieved as an advocate, but I fear those hopes have had to be abandoned. It may be to some extent my own fault that I have missed my chance, but I cannot help thinking that there is now no such scope for advocacy as there was a little time ago and I am quite sure that some of the judges never having been advocates themselves cannot appreciate the difficulties ...[6]

The Times ran another leader on the subject, whilst the tabloids contented themselves with headlines: 'English Bar's honour', 'Strong rebuke by the Master of the Rolls' or just 'Mr Marshall Hall again'.

Within a few months he did do it again, this time in a divorce case[7] when he made a throwaway remark that 'column after column of filthy details of the case' had been published in the newspapers. The press, collectively priding itself on its restraint in respect of some of the more salacious medical evidence in the trial, reacted with fury. 'A counsel's remarks in Court are privileged and if he oversteps the bounds of truth and decency in pleading the cause of a client the only consolation which the victims of his "eloquence" can take to themselves is the reflection that he does little good to himself or his reputation by the employment of such methods' was the acid comment in the *Evening News*.[8]

Soon he did not have to do anything wrong at all to attract adverse headlines; in a fraud case in the Old Bailey a minor dispute with the judge, expressly acknowledged in open court by the judge to have been a misunderstanding by him, attracted an enormous drawing in the press of a towering judge on the bench and Marshall Hall standing abject in the well of the court under the title 'Judge reproves Mr Marshall Hall'. By 1904 it had reached the stage where a minor local case devoid of interest to anyone other than the protagonists was very briefly reported under the prominent headline 'Mr Marshall Hall's client loses his case'.[9] On occasions when it was unavoidable to report that he had won, Marshall unhappily noted, he was referred to simply as 'Mr Hall'. Devastated by the attacks Marshall was nonetheless unrepentant; 'I was absolutely right and the judge and the newspapers were wrong,' he wrote to Hetty.[10] That was the general view of the Bar even amongst the many who thought Marshall deserved the fall after the hubris. The ferocity of the attacks, masterminded by Lord Justice Matthew and a press with a score to settle, was felt to be unmerited. But by now the sympathy for him scarcely mattered. The damage was done.

In those few years Marshall's income had halved and then dwindled almost altogether. The dealing, an amusing hobby, became a lifeline. He was shameless in touting for business amongst his friends at the Bar, becoming dealer, interior decorator and stylist all in one. The long-suffering Charles Gill was particularly targeted. On one occasion Marshall wrote to him: 'Having had alas nothing to do in the past ten days I have hunted up a few blue plates – I got twenty altogether, genuine of course but not very fine at a cost of a little over 5/- each … Times are bad so that I must stick my cabs on that so suppose we say seven pounds for the lot – I know your wife will like them and they will do the Hall beautifully …',[11] and in another letter:

'I wanted to see you to ask if you would care to buy one of my … pearl pins … I am sure it would lend character to the whole get up …'[12]

Others also became the recipients of offers solicited and unsolicited and, aware of his difficulties, were too generous to refuse. Travers Humphreys commissioned cigars off Marshall until he pleaded that doctor's advice prevented him from doing so any longer. Rufus Isaacs, a close friend who took silk at the same time as Marshall and was now going from strength to strength, refused to purchase a pearl tie pin from him, offering him instead a loan with the pin as security. Marshall promptly turned down the loan. He was willing to haggle cheerfully with his friends but regarded borrowing as humiliating.

Eventually the wonderful collections of silver accumulating in Cambridge Terrace went under the hammer at Christie's. 'The Collection of Mr Marshall Hall Esq KC of 3 Temple Gardens EC' caused quite a stir amongst the dealers and private collectors. Marshall was devastated by the loss of the collection, which contained inherited items from his Cressy Hall ancestors as well as the many testimonies to his own unerring eye as a collector. He had always felt defined by his possessions, revealing them hedged around by anecdote and romance to an admiring audience. Now he lost 128 lots of early eighteenth-century lemon strainers, muffineers, porringers, Queen Anne mugs and coffee pots, cutlery and pin cushions, and his prized collection of thirty-eight early English spoons. The collection realised nearly £4,000, which kept his lifestyle afloat and typically, despite a resolution at the time to buy no more snuff boxes, almost at once helped to fund a new collection, this one not sold until after his death twenty years later.

The adulation of the electorate of Southport was beginning to diminish. For a short while the town continued to be impressed with the bravura of its new MP. Then gradually it began to dawn that his health was uncertain, periods of frequent illness[13] resulting in cancelled engagements; that his time was limited, his demanding work being five hours away in London; and furthermore that there might not be much substance behind the style. 'The froth has disappeared; the sparkle has gone from the champagne and the residue is disappointing,' said the *Southport Guardian* in 1901. Even his profession became the subject of suspicion: 'To play on the feelings of the populace by the aid of that versatile personality was the easiest thing in the world for a successful lawyer.'[14] More significantly the lucrative work pouring in for the successful barrister began to look fatal to the successful politician. The chapel-going Southport electorate had voted Marshall in on his manifesto pledging temperance reform. His fellow Garrick Club members would have been amused, if not surprised, at the passionate eloquence with which he supported the temperance cause. Now, however, he began to accept briefs at fees too enormous to resist, to represent the local licensed victuallers in licensing applications. Cartoons depicting him as a little Jack Horner figure with fingers in two pies began to appear in the Press. And then there was the disquieting change in the reporting of his cases; could the idol have feet of clay after all?

When the next general election was called for February 1906 Marshall, disillusioned with politics, reluctantly embarked on a campaign of flourish and flamboyance, not to mention courage given the hostility with which he was now met in some quarters. There was a new political climate everywhere and the sense of a new era; in July 1902 Arthur Balfour had succeeded Lord Salisbury as Prime Minister, coinciding with the coronation of Edward VII and Queen Alexandra and the end at last of the Boer War. By the time of the 1906 election the residuum of Salisbury's Victorian values, imperialist foreign policy and support for tariff reform to protect British industry from foreign competition had lost popularity. The electorate were attracted to Henry Campbell-Bannerman and his Liberal reforms, and fearing food shortages, to the free trade the Liberals supported.

In Southport a new Liberal candidate, John Astbury, also a barrister, born in Lancashire and practising in his junior years from the Manchester Bar, now arrived on the scene. Marshall campaigned valiantly, blue cineraria in his buttonhole, chauffeur driven in a motor car, amongst the first produced by Southport's very own engineering firm, Vulcan. This caused little short of a sensation. The fourteen-horsepower car could carry five, open at the front with a steering wheel on a stick and deep running boards, but closable at the back for privacy. Specially commissioned, Vulcan provided the chauffeur and the car was produced in the Conservative Party colours: royal blue with lighter blue lines and blue leather upholstery. It was love at first sight for Marshall and the beginning of the end for the inhabitants of the Cambridge Terrace mews. In those early days motor cars were regarded as an indulgence rather than a method of transport and their drivers as rich and eccentric public nuisances. The constant repairs, the replacement tyres, the motoring coats, gloves and goggles and most importantly of all the chauffeurs all added to the exorbitant cost. But Marshall was now addicted to this new form of speed.[15]

Over the next decade in a series of motor cars he pushed the new technology to its limits, incurring, usually vicariously through his chauffeurs, a series of speeding summonses. Prosecutors had no knowledge of the technicalities. In the first cases speeding convictions followed the evidence of bucolic policemen that a car had been seen 'tearing past like the wind'. But they reckoned without Marshall. Magistrates in country courts must have been astonished at the impassioned defences advanced by him and even the more sophisticated of policemen, who insisted on the accuracy of speeds timed with their wrist watches, were shaken by the rapier cross-examinations to which they were subjected.

It was in London, however, that he really hit the headlines, when the chauffeur, Marshall by his side egging him on, was alleged to have 'scorched' (the new term for excessive speeding) down Constitution Hill. Marshall had treated authority, in the shape of a park keeper, with a predictable loss of temper. He had been doing eighteen miles an hour, the park keeper said. The keeper was a damned liar, said Marshall; he had only been doing twelve; and furthermore, he ranted, he had been overtaken by a horse-drawn carriage; the park keeper turned a blind eye to speeding horses and discriminated against motor cars. Since the speed limit was ten miles per hour Marshall was fined anyway, two pounds and two shillings costs, and told off by the magistrate for swearing at the park keeper. 'I regret the epithet,' he said in court. The newspaper reports with huge headlines ('The well-known barrister and the park keeper') took up five pages of his press cuttings album and led to his becoming counsel of choice for the Automobile Association and the *Motor Car Journal* in the new rash of motoring cases. And after a series of chauffeurs Marshall managed to find one who, in an Edwardian take on personalised number plates, a concept he would have loved, was appropriately called Innocent.

The motor car was not the only thing to give Marshall's 1906 electoral campaign Mr Toad characteristics. He flung himself into it with bluster and bravura. But his enthusiastic rhetoric was not enough to sway voters, who were not only attracted to the new Liberal policies but were also disillusioned with the commitment of their Member of Parliament.

On polling day thousands gathered in Lord Street, Southport's show street with its colonnaded shops and ornate ironwork balconies, to watch Marshall's carefully choreographed last push. Pantomime props had been borrowed from the Southport Opera House and in lashing wind and rain Elna rode proudly by in Cinderella's carriage followed by Marshall and Hetty in an open-topped barouche, a pug dog in attendance as a page dressed in a white coat with buttons bearing Marshall's portrait.

Marshall lost his seat, by 240 votes, to Astbury. Half the other Conservative members countrywide also lost theirs, amongst them Balfour, the outgoing Prime Minister, in a massive Liberal landslide. In the crowd in Southport Conservative Club watching the election results come in was a little boy taken by his father. He grew up to be a journalist and more than forty years later wrote an article describing the scene he had never forgotten:

> Balfour out! Everybody seemed to be out. But our man would surely be in. It seemed incredible that so handsome, so gallant, so gay, so irresistible a Member, could be replaced by a dry little lawyer like Astbury. But replaced he was. He came shouldering his way into the room, a head taller than anybody else there, looking like some Roman Conqueror rather than an unseated politician. As he pressed through the throng he thrust a hand each side of him into the press. An excited small boy spilling his fifth lemonade found himself grasping one of them. It was a memorable moment.[16]

The Roman Conqueror, graceful in defeat, was given a splendid send off from Southport railway station and as the train steamed out he waved his blue scarf from the window and called: 'Keep the flag flying!' Back in London he wrote a farewell letter to his constituents. The calls on his professional life, he said, made it imperative that he should retire from political life and, should he ever stand again, seek a constituency nearer to London. His sigh of relief is almost audible.

In fact the calls on his time by his professional life had so dramatically diminished that he could no longer be confident of his ability to keep his family and fund his lifestyle. Within two years his income had dropped from £16,000 a year to £2,000. At heart he was sick with disappointment and humiliation.

At last he swallowed his pride and sought to rebuild his relationship with the Press. Harmsworth had proved his point and his power by making him and by ruining him. As was so often the case with gentlemanly disputes of the period it was membership of the same club that ultimately brought about a reconciliation. Thomas Marlowe, editor of the *Daily Mail*, was a member of the Garrick Club, and this was a bond with invisible ties. He was also a close friend and admirer of Lord Harmsworth, the proprietor of the *Daily Mail*.[17] To Marshall Harmsworth seemed now an implacable enemy but Marlowe might be the way back into his good books. In the leather armchairs of the Garrick amidst the whisky-and-sodas and the cigar smoke many differences have been mended. Harmsworth's continuing grievance arose from Marshall's throwaway remark in the Chattell case, Marlowe told him. Harmsworth notoriously prickly and sensitive had taken the remark 'My client may have to work for her living but is entitled to the same consideration as any other lady in the land – including Mrs Alfred Harmsworth' as a deliberate personal insult. A disarming apology from Marshall to Harmsworth followed and was accepted. But the reputation Harmsworth had smashed now needed a boost to rebuild it.

It was a difficult time personally for Marshall; in 1905 his sister Ada, the comfort to whom he had always turned, died. Hetty's gentle support was soothing but no substitute. Her own world to her seemed unassailable; the joy of companionship with Baba, now ten, the frequent trips to Hamburg to see her mother, the outwardly unaffected grandeur of Cambridge Terrace and the continuing social endorsements such as the invitation to the coronation of Edward VII and Queen Alexandra were all reassuring and furthermore she had an unwavering belief in Marshall. But success at the Bar has always depended principally on self-belief. Fundamentally insecure, always heavily reliant on public adulation, he had now lost this vital ingredient though never his optimism. In Marshall's philosophy there was nowhere to go but up. And in 1907 up he went.

PART III

ASCENDANCY

CHAPTER 10

'A simple matter of a moment'

The Camden Town murder, with which this book began, took place in the early hours of Thursday 12 September 1907. Not only did it end one life in the most horrible of circumstances, it changed many others, caused fear throughout London, became associated with some great art, resulted in one of the most sensational (and legally ground-breaking) trials England had ever seen and established Marshall Hall in all his celebrity and wealth. The trial has been shrouded, almost since the day it was committed, in layers of speculation, myth and obscure associations. They have become part of its story, the facts entwined with the growing legend.

A prostitute was killed by an unknown client. It was as simple and commonplace as that; but not many murders are characterised by the artistry of the death, and in the end it was the death itself that made the Camden Town murder[1] so resonant for so many reasons.

Emily Dimmock, twenty-three years old, pretty and fascinating, was in a stable relationship with Robert Shaw, a cook on one of the restaurant cars of the Midland Railway, and lived with him at 29 St Paul's Road, Camden Town.[2] He worked nights; and so, unbeknown to him, did Emily (who sometimes called herself Phyllis), walking the streets and frequenting the shadier pubs of her neighbourhood. It was Robert who found her on his return from work on that Thursday morning. She was lying in their bedroom on the iron bedstead amidst the crumpled white bedlinen. The window shutters had been left ajar, filtering a dim light across the scene, a conversation piece of a sleeping girl. She was on her left side, her slim body curved, her legs slightly drawn up, her left arm across her back, her right across the pillow. Her rippling hair, pinned up at the front, fell in picturesque disarray down her back. She was naked, half concealed by the gentle folds of the sheets. Her face was utterly peaceful.

It was only on drawing closer that the massive, clean incision across her throat from ear to ear became apparent. The carotid artery, windpipe, jugular vein, pharynx and spine had been severed so that her head remained attached to her body only by a few muscles. The blood had drained through the bedclothes and mattress, gently pooling on the uneven floor and trickling towards the skirting board. In a bowl nearby the murderer had washed his hands and dried them on Emily's petticoat, which he had left neatly folded over the back of a wooden chair. The cut must have been administered whilst Emily lay in trusting post-coital sleep, said the police surgeon. It had been inflicted by an extremely sharp knife wielded with determination and force. Her head had been gently lifted, he said, and then it was only 'a simple matter of a moment'. Here was no lingering sadistic torture; she had, it seemed, been killed with the inexplicable tenderness of a very sick mind.

That scene triggered a maelstrom of emotion across the country. First of all there was fear. All the terror of the crimes of Jack the Ripper, nineteen years before, was reignited. This body was very different to those the Ripper had disembowelled and discarded unaesthetically in back alleys.[3] Nonetheless, theories that the Ripper was the perpetrator of this crime and indeed a man of power and influence bubbled once again to the surface in the popular press, and candidates' names were whispered in political and society circles.

In artistic circles too there were resonances; lush, half-dressed, willing women, their reality only then to be found amongst prostitutes, had become an artistic preoccupation in the late nineteenth century. The Jenny of Dante Gabriel Rossetti's poem thirty years earlier with its horrid mix of sentimentality and contempt ('Lazy laughing languid Jenny, | Fond of a kiss and fond of a guinea') was now reflected in the swirls and curves of Art Nouveau, with its celebration of the female form in decorative visual orgies. In his studio a mile away from the murder scene, in a reaction against these arty images, Walter Sickert, already preoccupied with sexual violence and the Ripper, produced four paintings later jointly titled *The Camden Town Murder*, depicting naked women on iron beds with men standing over them or sitting beside them in attitudes ranging from threatening to despairing. Theories as to whether Sickert, the Ripper and the Camden Town Murderer were one and the same man abound,[4] but have never been proved; what is clear is that Sickert sought in the pictures to portray not the murder itself but the world it represented of impoverished lodgings, amateur prostitution to pay the rent and the evocative domestic paraphernalia of working-class lives behind dingy curtains. A striking number of novels and plays have since evoked the same images inspired by the trial and Sickert's paintings.[5] Symbolic iron beds and splayed bodies have gone on featuring in dramatic representations of the murder right up to 2012 when a ballet, *Sweet Violets*, was based on it.

Excitement at the time reached fever pitch when a young artist was arrested and charged with the murder. Robert Wood came from a middle-class family and lived with his widowed father in Frederick Street, off Gray's Inn Road. A sensitive foppish aesthete, his considerable talent had landed him praise from none other than the great William Morris and a job with the Sand and Blast Manufacturing Company, drawing designs to be engraved on glassware. The company had become successful and Wood's swirling Art Nouveau designs were central to that success. The firm valued him highly and his colleagues spoke unanimously of his popularity. He was gentle, kind and decent, they said, and they would not hear a word against him.

For the preceding three years Wood had had a girlfriend, Ruby Young, who described herself as an artists' model but had drifted into prostitution, a fact of which Wood had become aware and which, significantly, seemed to have enhanced rather than detracted from her appeal to him. On 29 September, seventeen days after the murder, Ruby saw in a newspaper an appeal for information with a £100 reward. The police had found in the victim's room a postcard depicting on one side a classical picture of mother and child and on the other a manuscript message: 'Phillis [*sic*] darling; if it pleases you meet me at 8.15 at the [sketch of a rising sun] – yours to a cinder Alice.' Ruby instantly recognised both the handwriting and the style of sketch as being those of Wood. So did one of Wood's colleagues, John Tinkham. On being confronted Wood gave to each the same explanation which he later gave in the witness box. It was far more plausible in 1907 at the height of the postcard craze than it would be now. He had dropped into the Rising Sun for a drink, he said, on 6 September, the Friday prior to the murder, and there had a casual encounter with Emily, whom he had never met before. He bought her a drink at her request and whilst they sat together a man had come in selling cheap postcards. Emily collected postcards, she told him, and she would have bought one, but he, the artist in him aroused, prevented her. He had recently been to Bruges and there had bought some of far better quality depicting some wonderful art. He allowed her to choose one from the selection he had with him. But what she really wanted for her album were postcards sent through the post. 'Write something nice on it and send it to me,' she said and he, to humour her, had written a fictional assignation. He was about to sign it when she prevented him, asking him to put a woman's name; her husband was a jealous man, she said.

Over the next few days he had seen Emily twice, Wood admitted, again by chance; once in the street and once, on the Monday before her death, back in the Rising Sun. That was the last time he had seen her. He was concerned at any involvement, however peripheral, in such a sordid case and anxious to protect his frail father. Both Ruby and Tinkham agreed to keep silent.

In fact the relationship between Wood and Ruby had been cooling. She was quite surprised when he began to seek her company again. Invitations to drinks and the theatre followed and in the course of their outings Wood asked Ruby to tell anyone who enquired that they always met on Monday and Wednesday evenings. Ruby agreed to do so although she was uncomfortable about the request. She would have been even more uncomfortable had she known that another friend, a bookseller called Lambert, had also been asked to lie for him. Wood, in the company of a girl, had met Lambert on the Wednesday, the very night of the murder. Would Lambert now leave the girl out of any account he was asked to give of the meeting, Wood asked.

As time went on, Wood began to pester Ruby to collaborate in a more specific alibi relating to the particular Wednesday night of the murder. Increasingly anxious, she told a friend; the friend told a journalist and the journalist told the police. The net was closing.

On the evening of 4 October, Wood left his workplace, as he usually did, at half past six. Outside, unexpectedly, he encountered Ruby. She stretched out her hand and took his. It was later widely reported as a Judas kiss. Inspector Neil, the detective in charge of the case, on this sign, stepped out of his nearby concealment and asked Wood to accompany him to the police station in a waiting hansom cab. Unaware of the role played by Ruby, Wood bade her a tender farewell. At the police station he gave the same account of his involvement as he had given to Ruby but, disastrously, on being asked to account for his movements on the night of the murder, believing she would confirm his story, relied upon the alibi he had concocted with her. He was remanded in custody in Brixton prison.

From that point on, the circumstantial evidence linking Wood to Emily Dimmock grew and grew. At the murder scene, in the parlour next to the bedroom, alongside the table with the remains of a meal for two, was Emily's prized postcard album. Emily had collected postcards as she collected men. There were hundreds of them, mainly from soldiers and sailors who had remembered with pleasure their encounter with her when they were on leave and afterwards sent her postcards commemorating the event from their lonely ships and barracks in obscure corners of the world. But Wood's 'Rising Sun' postcard was not amongst them. It was found later concealed in the back of a drawer. The police concluded that there was a strong possibility that the murderer had ransacked the album looking for it. Also in the room, half burnt in the grate, was a letter. Only a few words of it were decipherable.

Then one of Emily's last clients had come forward, a ship's cook who had spent his shore money on nights with Emily in the week before her death. His evidence was highly significant. Two days before the murder, on the Monday, Emily had shown him the 'Rising Sun' postcard. On Wednesday he was with her when her post arrived. She showed him a letter she had received which he recalled as reading: 'Will you meet me at The Eagle Camden Town 8.30 tonight, Wednesday – Bert.' She then put the postcard into the drawer in which it was subsequently found by the police and burned the letter in the grate. The few half-words decipherable on the charred letter were consistent with this account and the writing identified as being the same as that on the postcard.

The working men and women, the prostitutes and their clients, who frequented the seedier pubs of Camden Town had already been interviewed and several had given statements saying that on the two or three nights preceding the murder they had seen Emily with a man whom they all described in strikingly similar terms: aged about thirty, short, thin, sunken eyes, of plainly good education. Some said that Emily had seemed uneasy; some that she had expressed fear of the man. Furthermore, a man called McCowan came forward to say that, walking past the house in St Paul's Road in the early hours of the morning after the murder, he had seen a short, slim man apparently emerging from the gateway. McCowan had noticed he walked in an unusual way, his shoulders jerking as he did so.

Now, with a suspect in their custody, the police held identification parades. A number of the witnesses identified Wood as the man they had seen with Emily and their statements contradicted much of what Wood had told Inspector Neil. Several of Emily's associates now said they had seen Wood with her on many occasions for months before the September meeting that he had insisted was their first encounter. Lambert the bookseller, as well as others, now told the police that Wood had been with Emily in the Eagle Tavern on the Wednesday, the night of her death. When the men on the identification parade were asked to walk about, McCowan unhesitatingly identified Wood by his walk as the man he had seen leaving the murder scene. The accumulating evidence, together with their knowledge of Wood's attempts to create a false alibi, led the police to charge Wood with murder.

Here were all the hallmarks of a truly sensational trial. Could this gentle young artist really be the homicidal maniac of nightmares? The evidence linking him to the crime was all circumstantial, or presumptive, in kind. Coupled with that was the complete absence of motive. Psychologists, both professional and armchair, were as fascinated as the lawyers. For the latter, the great question dominating the trial was whether any advocate instructed to defend Robert Wood would dare to put him into the witness box to tell his own story.

Marshall's timing was always consummate and it so happened that the year he took silk, 1898, coincided with the passing of a new Act of Parliament which provided for the first time that a defendant in a criminal trial was entitled to give evidence in his own defence. Nowadays a system whereby someone accused of a crime could not go into the witness box and give the jury his or her version of events is unimaginable but until 1898 that was the basic position.[6] The lawyers had been the ones who expressed most concern about the proposed change. Their objections stemmed from a belief that the innocent would be disadvantaged. The centuries-old principle that it was for the prosecution to prove guilt and for the accused to prove nothing would, it was argued, be undermined. The accused might be compelled to give evidence, since if he was entitled to do so yet chose not to, a jury might draw adverse inferences; an innocent person with a bad character which could be the subject of cross-examination if he chose to give evidence was faced with an uncomfortable choice; above all, uneducated prisoners facing skilled cross-examination might be unfairly convicted. And for the Bar, overshadowing all these concerns was its collective resistance to the idea in capital cases of cross-examining a man to his death.[7]

Ultimately, however, the basic contention in support of reform had prevailed: the system as it then was prevented juries from getting to what they believed to be the truth. Marshall, with his increasing fascination with the psychology of juries, was amongst those who believed the change must be made. Eventually the pressure for reform became irresistible. Between 1886 and 1895, nine Bills were introduced only to be rejected at one stage or another, until at last in 1898 the Criminal Evidence Bill received royal assent. There followed years of teething problems as Bench and Bar grappled with its implications. Should an accused whose evidence was disbelieved by a jury automatically be charged with perjury? Should an accused be allowed to give an account in the witness box which he had not given prior to trial? How to direct a jury when an accused chose not to avail himself of the new right?

For the first nine years that right had been exercised with extreme caution by defence counsel and often with disastrous consequences. It had never been successfully employed in a capital case and with a life at stake few had attempted it. Those who did had regretted it, though probably not as much as did their clients. In the end, the effectiveness of the accused giving evidence was going to depend not only on the astuteness of defence counsel but on that of his client. If the two were as able as each other, as Marshall was to prove time and time again, the results could be miraculous.

Wood's employers instructed Arthur Newton as his solicitor and he briefed Marshall for the defence, rightly judging him to be a risk taker with nothing now to lose. He had no fewer than three other barristers to assist him[8] and in addition Wellesley Orr, a young man recently arrived in his own chambers, not formally briefed but 'devilling'.[9] Between them Marshall and Orr devised a strategy of nerve, psychological subtlety and bravura. Central to it, however, was the calling of Wood himself to explain away, if he could, not only the edifice of evidence constructed by the prosecution, but his own predilection for prostitutes. Marshall, always generous to the young in his profession, afterwards said that Orr had guided his strategy; but the terrible decision, whether or not to advise Wood to give evidence, had ultimately to be Marshall's. Haunted by the knowledge that his decision not to call Herbert Bennett, the Yarmouth murderer, in his own defence might well have contributed to the verdict against him, Marshall agonised for days.

He visited Wood in Brixton prison. In theory educated and articulate, he was an obvious candidate for the witness box. And yet, thought Marshall, there was something unnerving about him. Could he be raving mad? He decided he dared not risk it. Orr and Newton argued strenuously against his decision, convinced Wood would hang if he did not face the jury. Then on the night before the trial Newton visited Wood alone and like Marshall was struck with an odd sense of unease. 'We cannot call him,' he wrote to Marshall that evening. 'You were perfectly right in every way.'

The next morning, Thursday 12 December, the trial was opened by Sir Charles 'Willie' Matthews, now senior prosecuting counsel at the Old Bailey. He had been knighted in a special ceremony when the new courts had opened in the February of that year. The high oak panelling was still aggressively new, the paint fresh and the judge's massive chair high above the well of the court was pristine green beneath the gleaming sword of justice.[10] It was Marshall's first murder trial in these new surroundings, so different from those against which he had railed in the Marie Hermann trial back in 1894. That trial too had been against Willie Matthews and there had been several since. They were old friends now, sparring partners who knew each other's technique. During the trial a startled Wood, peering down from the high dock, later recalled seeing Willie and Marshall, verbally at each other's throats moments before, amiably sharing a bar of chocolate.[11]

Now, Willie's deadly opening speech was listened to by a breathless audience of lawyers, celebrities,[12] pressmen and public, the tension palpable. Only the jury seemed unmoved by the array of famous spectators and the magnitude of the task in front of them. They were a dull-looking bunch; one newspaper said they looked as though they were wondering how the shop was getting on in their absence. The judge was furious at that: these men were serving their country, he said; he would not have them abused by the press. But Marshall, watching, was wondering how he could turn the solid respectability of his jury to his advantage.

The prosecution witnesses called, individually insignificant, collectively compelling, began between them to build a picture of a quite different Robert Wood: one who slid in and out of respectability, who was not always the gentle young artist that his family and friends knew, who sometimes inhabited a sordid world of prostitution, secrecy and vice in the pubs and backstreets of Camden Town. The jury woke up and began to look disapproving. Marshall had learned a lot by now; the cross-examinations which in the Yarmouth murder trial had reduced witnesses to tears were now conducted with a rapier rather than a bludgeon. This time they were generally acknowledged to be a masterpiece of forensic subtlety.

The ship's cook with his evidence of the charred letter was savagely cross-examined as to his involvement with Emily and his movements on the night of her death. Not, as many of the spectators initially thought, to implicate him in the crime but to lay the ground for the suggestion that his vulnerability had led him to invent evidence that would exculpate him. Ruby Young, on the other hand, too pathetic to attack without arousing the sympathy of the jury, was gently dealt with. Had it occurred to her, Marshall asked, that given the time of death in the early hours, the alibi she had been asked to provide was useless as an alibi for murder but a perfect one for the earlier meeting with the victim? Ruby, still in love with Wood, gratefully grasped the life belt. McCowan's identification of Wood as the man with the peculiar walk he had seen outside 29 St Paul's Road was neutralised by his uncertainty as to detail, and the witnesses' identification at the parade was weakened when it had emerged that all had attended together and had thus seen, and inferentially been influenced by, each other.

All the same, despite the skill of the cross-examination, the evidence against Wood still looked black; he had written the victim not only the postcard but also some kind of note making what looked like an assignation; he had been with her in the Eagle apparently as a result of that assignation on the very night of the murder; he had tried to set up alibis; and he had lied and lied again about his whereabouts, the length and nature of his relationship with the victim and the friendships which were not those of a respectable man. In 1907, with no forensic evidence, it was quite enough to hang him.

By the end of the third day, the Saturday,[13] the prosecution case almost completed, the entire court seemed exhausted. 'To be tried for one's life is

I think sufficient for the day and I am now weary,' wrote Wood to his brother from Brixton prison. 'I understand that there are great odds to face that may end disastrously ...'

When the court adjourned for the Sunday break, Marshall, faced with the construction of his opening speech to the jury, was only too well aware of the magnitude of the odds. The members of the jury, together in their isolation since the beginning of the trial,[14] were given the day off. Under escort, they all attended divine service in the Temple Church, walked to Victoria Embankment to watch the seagulls swirling over Blackfriars Bridge and then returned to their hotel, the Manchester in Aldersgate Street, for luncheon with wine and cigars. Cards and chess were provided for entertainment. Anyone wishing to play billiards was permitted to go to the hotel billiard room; but only provided the other eleven were willing to go with him.

On the Monday, suitably refreshed, they returned to their solemn duties and to Marshall's speech. Wood, he had now definitely decided, must give evidence; he must save himself. Marshall, under no illusions as to the horrible risks, characteristically met them head on and took the flattered jury into his confidence. It had been an agonising decision, he said. Wood was to go into the witness box tainted by all the lies he had told, by his relationship with Ruby Young, a prostitute, and by his association with the deceased. Having whetted their appetites, he kept them in suspense for two long days. It had become the custom, though not the rule, that if an accused was to give evidence, he did so first. But Marshall called Wood last, after the jury had heard from his elderly father, tremulous and loving with his evidence of a visit from his son on the night of the murder; from his two brothers, pillars of supportive respectability; and from work colleagues, unanimous in their praise of Wood's friendly disposition.

When at last Wood made his way from the dock to the witness box, Marshall had much to lose, if not as much as his client. Everyone in court knew that his practice was at a low ebb, that the ethics of his advocacy had been publicly criticised and that his technique was regarded by the Bench as unacceptably inflammatory. Now he was to embark on the novel task of examining his own client with no successful precedents to follow. It is impossible now to convey the impact of his questions. Nowadays it is not uncommon as a tactic to plunge straight into the central issue; when Marshall did it, it was revolutionary.

'Did ... you ... kill ... Emily ... Dimmock?' he asked in his beautiful resonant voice, with a short pause between each word. But his partner in the dialogue had no such sense of drama. He smiled and said nothing. 'You must answer straight,' said poor Marshall, his moment of theatre lost, driven to press his own client in a way more consistent with the cross-examination of a prosecution witness. 'It is ridiculous,' responded Wood dismissively in his light effeminate voice.

Things went from bad to worse; unlike his counsel, Wood had no common touch. His whole demeanour seemed calculated to put the jurors' backs up. Contempt for the victim, her way of life and the 'class of public house' she frequented all sounded a note that was not only unkind, but given his own tastes, hypocritical. Far from assisting Marshall, the result was that his counsel was faced with a salvage job.

Marshall's closing speech showed bravery and genius. It took a tremendous courage, with the stakes so high, to turn on his own client and genius to do it in such a way as to persuade a jury that the obvious defects of character they had seen in Wood were the very characteristics which established his innocence: 'You will have noticed ... he is a person of overweening personal vanity, a vanity that is inordinate ... [he] could not take it upon himself, by reason of that vanity, the responsibility of admitting that he had done anything which would cause people who held a high opinion of him to diminish the undivided affection and respect they had for him.'

Such a character sketch accounted for everything Wood had done, he pointed out. It was not fear of the gallows that led to the lies and deceit; it was fear of losing respectability. The stolid jurors understood all about that particular God; their own lives had been ruled by it. By the time Marshall sat down, the verdict was determined.[15] Wood was saved and Marshall had redeemed himself. 'An almost overpowering appeal to the intellect as well as the heart of his audience ... a thrilling and most honourable exhibition of forensic ability,'[16] said the press, who could be generous when it suited them and who had anyway come to regret the killing of a goose whose eggs had promised to be so golden.

The news of the acquittal was greeted by the 10,000-strong crowd outside the court in the extraordinary scenes described at the beginning of this book. Stopped by the hysterical throng, the traffic piled up along Ludgate Hill and into Fleet Street. In the theatres curtains were brought down mid-performance to announce the verdict to the audience. All over the world, newspapers gave blow-by-blow accounts of the trial and the last thrilling moments of Marshall's speech: 'You cannot hang a man on evidence such as that. I defy you to do it. I defy you. I do not merely ask for a verdict of not guilty, I demand it.'

He got it; but there is still speculation about that verdict; like the police at the time and many of today's crime writers, Marshall himself in later life said that he thought Wood was guilty. The jury might also have thought so had they known of Wood's later comments about Emily: 'She impressed me as a crushed rose that had not lost all its fragrance … she appealed in some way to my sense of the artistic,' he said. Perhaps the manner of her death also appealed to this vain, repressed young man with his double life and his conflicting passions for art and respectability. Whatever the internet may say, like the jury we are unlikely ever to be sure beyond a reasonable doubt.

Marshall was now first choice of counsel in every sensational criminal case, a position he came to regard as a mixed blessing. Then, as now, it was not where the money was usually to be had; but sensational trials were where the publicity lay, and also, for Marshall, much of the fun of the job. Whether he liked it or not his extraordinary future was mapped out. The technique developed since the Hermann trial was perfected, his style now polished, and his great fame brought with it privileges in court. Opponents and judges might frequently find him irritating but from then on they feared his overwhelming public popularity and the blaze of publicity that now accompanied his every utterance. He was indifferent to their irritation anyway; the jury was what mattered. 'Think as the jury are thinking,' he used to say. 'Become one of them. Get into the jury box with them. Make yourself the thirteenth juror.'

CHAPTER 11

'The scales of justice'

Hetty had bronchitis and digestive problems and longed to get away from the London smogs. With happy memories of Ellen Terry's cottage at Winchelsea and the seaside she favoured the exclusive prosperity of Westgate-on-Sea, on the north Kent coast. The resort had developed in the 1860s when a group of early property developers bought the land between two picturesque bays, constructed a sea wall and promenade and sold off plots on a gated development to wealthy London families. Marshall, reconciled to the plan by the proximity to West Foreland Golf Club, bought a large family flat. It proved to be the beginning of not only a geographical distancing from Hetty but an emotional one as well.

The lease on Cambridge Terrace relinquished, in 1908 Marshall bought a flat in Welbeck Street, Marylebone, for the family's London base and proceeded to divest himself of most of his domestic paraphernalia. The majority of his precious collections had of course already been auctioned and now much of the furniture was disposed of. The horses and carriages were sold, the long-suffering Charles Gill being asked if he wanted to buy the brougham, on which Marshall was quick to point out he had just fitted new tyres.[1] Places were found for the stable hands. There was no room in the new arrangements for the donkey or the governess; the former was sent to live in the country and the latter discharged. Elna, more upset about the donkey than the governess, was sent to school for the first time, originally in Westgate and then to Queen's College, Harley Street, a typically liberal choice by Marshall. He was always strongly supportive of the education of women in theory if not always in personal taste. The new arrangements were the first of a number of moves as Marshall's enthusiasm for his collections grew whilst that for his family diminished.

Along with the Garrick Club, the one constant refuge for the rest of his life was his beloved room in 3 Temple Gardens with its view over the trees in the gardens themselves towards the broad sweep of the Thames. Until relatively recent times a barrister's room was his for life, furnished at his own expense to his personal taste, warmed by a fire tended by a Temple servant and sacrosanct as a refuge, guarded by his clerk from solicitors, wives and creditors alike. Old age might eventually put a stop to work at the Bar but many barristers hung on in their chambers. Marshall's room on the south side of 3 Temple Gardens, with its charming inner alcove in one of the whimsical turrets that adorn the corners of this neo-classical building, was an intensely personal space; in it he built both the little world of things that were closest to his heart and his public showcase.

Encircling the walls was a complete set of *Vanity Fair* legal cartoons by 'Spy'; now a decorative cliché in lawyers' rooms, then immensely innovative and stylish. Here behind his leather-topped desk Marshall sat in a Hepplewhite wheelback chair. Photographs of his father, his early mentor Forrest Fulton, now Recorder of London, and Elna, winsome in bonnet and frilly dress (Hetty notably absent), stood on the mantelpiece above the glowing fire alongside the Sheraton clock and the much-valued bronze statues of Jean-Jacques Rousseau and Voltaire. Oak bookcases contained rather less valued legal textbooks. The walls beneath the 'Spy' cartoons were crammed with pictures and caricatures, many by friends and mostly of Marshall.[2] Most important of all, as the press cuttings volumes grew so too did memorabilia from his most celebrated trials, reminders of successes not past for Marshall but ever present, rich sources of anecdote and part of the carefully created legend in which he was beginning to believe as implicitly as his public. Here were sketches of the main protagonists in the Liberator fraud trial, a special case containing the gold chain featured in the Yarmouth murder trial and a collection of Robert Wood's pictures including a charming little portrait of Marshall himself.[3]

The next thing to join the collection was to be the .383 calibre 'Brute' revolver[4] with which a Wolverhampton businessman, Edward Lawrence, shot his mistress Ruth, the first of what was ultimately a fearsome armoury of guns and knives, phials of poison and daggers, all lovingly labelled and displayed. The Lawrence trial was to be heard in Stafford, the nearest assize town.[5] In the first cold week of January 1909 the clerk to a young barrister called Dorsett who practised from chambers in Birmingham was telephoned by a local solicitor. Was Dorsett free to represent Lawrence, the solicitor asked. It was not the first time Dorsett had done so. 'Don't tell me he's been biting policemen's thumbs again,' said the clerk. 'It's a bit more serious this time,' the solicitor replied. 'It's murder.' And as though that was not sensational enough Lawrence was insisting on Marshall Hall to lead the case. Special provision was made for Marshall to appear in a case off his own circuit; circuit rules, designed to discourage poaching by outsiders, required a so-called 'special' of an exorbitant 100 guineas to be charged to the client on top of the brief fee. Money was no object to Lawrence, an extremely rich brewer. He always wanted the best and now, when it came to saving a man from the gallows, Marshall was regarded as the best.

Arriving in assize towns far distant from the capital, London counsel always descended like exotic birds, the object of fascination to the local press and population. At this spring assize, Marshall was as glamorous as anyone could wish for; his brief fee was enormous, it was whispered, and he could get the devil himself off a criminal charge. Certainly Lawrence,[6] notorious for his womanising, drinking, gambling and violence, was going to be a difficult client. The victim had been shot in the head at close range and the accused, who already had a criminal record as a result of the policeman-biting episode, had called the police and ultimately made a hysterical and maudlin confession.

Marshall flung himself into what was locally regarded as a hopeless defence. The key was his attack on the character of the dead Ruth. Defence witnesses attested to Ruth's desperation at her lover's behaviour and her threatened and actual violence towards him. As the only one who could give an account of the killing at which he was admittedly present, it was essential to call Lawrence in his own defence. Intelligent and articulate, he was also an arrogant bully, brutal and dissipated in appearance. Tiptoeing through his evidence Marshall somehow managed to reveal the pathos under the bluster. Ruth had been about to shoot him, Lawrence told the jury; as he saw the hammer rising he sprang forward to save his life; he seized her wrist and they struggled. The gun fired and she dropped to the floor. In the hushed court Marshall handed Lawrence the revolver. 'Show my Lord and the jury,' he said calmly. Lawrence grasped the gun, grabbed his own right wrist and showed how the revolver jerked upwards. To the astonishment of all the judge ordered him right up onto the bench and asked him to demonstrate again, this time with the judge's own clerk holding the gun. His Lordship was plainly impressed; from that moment on, observers noticed, he referred to the accused as 'Mr Lawrence'. Until that moment he had been 'Lawrence'; the tide was turning.

All the technique Marshall had now learned he put into his closing speech. No one could take a jury into his confidence with as much charm as could Marshall nor treat them with as much intimacy. How could they be anything but flattered by his revealing the thinking (carefully edited) behind his trial strategy? It was terrible to attack poor dead Ruth's character, he said. He had had had do it. And the jury, touched by the grave contrition with which he humbled himself, quite forgot the relish with which he had approached the task and remembered only the evidence he had by this means elicited: the violent drunken jealous woman revealed. As with Robert Wood he again openly referred to his client's deficiencies of character. His orator's trick of repetitive rhythmic sentences gained him maximum impact. 'We are not trying this man for drink. We are not trying this man for immorality. We are not trying this man for error of judgement or human frailty.' It was almost hypnotic in its effect. He adopted the actor's technique employed in the Hermann trial of using his whole body to enforce his speech, levelling the revolver directly at the jury, inviting them to watch the hammer rise as he pulled the trigger, to feel the fear, as they looked straight down the barrel, that Lawrence would have felt if, as he now said, the girl had turned the gun on him.

Finally and famously he invoked, like defence counsel everywhere, the vital importance of the presumption of innocence until proved guilty beyond a reasonable doubt. The concept of the personification of justice holding the scales of truth and fairness was not new; it dated back to classical times and statues outside courthouses all over the world depict it. But Marshall's lyrical interpretation, delivered as he stood for long minutes with his arms held outstretched at shoulder height, his body the central pillar, his hands the scale pans, has never been bettered:

> It may appear that the scales of justice are first weighed on one side in favour of the prisoner and then on the other against the prisoner. As counsel on either side puts the evidence in the scales, I can call to my fancy a great statue of Justice holding the two scales with equally honest hands. As the jury watch the scales they think for a moment that one scale and then the other has fallen and then again that they are so level that they cannot make up their minds which was lower or higher. Then in one scale, in the prisoner's scale, unseen by human eye is placed that overbalancing weight, the presumption of innocence.

And his hand dropped slowly down to his side.

Lawrence was acquitted.

The papers ran out of words to describe the impact of the speech. Even the judge was moved to describe it as brilliant. For ever after Marshall built on his performance. It became known as 'Hall's scales of justice speech' by his colleagues and if there was an element of affectionate derision in the description nonetheless it was generally acknowledged that juries found it a spellbinding practical demonstration of the deciding factor that the presumption of innocence is intended to be. In his later trial of Seddon the poisoner, Marshall developed the metaphor, ever keen, whatever the law might say, to tip the balance further in favour of the accused with the addition of compassion:

> Gentlemen, I often think, when I look at the great figure of Justice which towers over all our judicial proceedings, when I see the blind figure holding the scales I often think that possibly the bandage over the eyes of Justice has a twofold meaning. Not only is it put there so that the course of justice should not be warped by prejudice or undue influence one way or the other; but sometimes I think it is put there so that those who gaze should not see the look of infinite pity which is in the eyes of Justice behind that bandage, the look of infinite mercy which must always temper justice in a just man.

In Victorian and Edwardian England it was not shooting but poisoning that was the method of choice for most domestic murder. It was regarded as a particularly wicked act, smacking as it did of the cruellest premeditation and meted out with the coldest vengeance. Until 1957 its extreme seriousness was marked by the requirement that the Attorney General, as the senior law officer of the Crown, had to appear personally to prosecute all poisoning cases that got to court. But since arsenic and strychnine were easily obtainable and highly effective, and forensic analysis was either non-existent or very unsophisticated, there was a good chance of getting away without prosecution.

Doctors' evidence had consisted mainly of reliance on their professed expertise rather than any practical or scientific demonstration of it. It was not until the turn of the century that scientific knowledge relating to the effects of poisons, to blood type[7] and to fingerprints[8] began to play a significant part in the detection of crime. At St Mary's Hospital in London, a formidable team specialising in forensic pathology was growing up, led by Dr Augustus Pepper, the pathologist in the Hermann trial, who was nearing retirement; in the wings were William Willcox and his junior assistant, Bernard Spilsbury. Invariably instructed by the Home Office on behalf of the prosecution, their evidence was usually unchallenged; even if the corresponding expertise could have been found, the cost was beyond the means of most defendants.

By this time the expansion of popular journalism had led to an ever-increasing public fascination with the detection of crime, serious scientist and frivolous sensation seeker united by a common interest in both method and motive; the more ghastly the crime, the more fevered the speculation as to the how and the why. Theories concerning both these questions were fuelled scientifically by the newly developing forensic science and artistically by the creation of fictional deductive detection. Novelists, lawyers, doctors and scientists were not only contributing their own expertise but exploring the interfaces with each other's.

At the forefront of this exercise was the Crimes Club. This gentlemen's dining club had been founded by H B ('Harry') Irving, son of Sir Henry. Harry Irving was himself an exemplar of the multi-disciplinary approach, a trained actor, a barrister and an acknowledged writer on criminology. In 1894 he had sat transfixed in the public gallery watching Marshall's extraordinary performance in the Marie Hermann trial. He, like Marshall, was fascinated by the point at which drama and real life met. The two became close friends. Later, as defence counsel in some of the greatest trials of the age, Marshall became a member of the Crimes Club along with George Sims, an author and journalist intrigued by the psychology of crime, Bernard Spilsbury, the pathologist at the forefront of the new forensics employed in its detection, and Sir Arthur Conan Doyle, who preached through his fictional detective Sherlock Holmes the new understanding of the importance of the integrity of the crime scene, of fingerprints, of ballistics, of handwriting analysis, of analytical chemistry and of toxicology. Everyone could be a detective now.

In this new creative melting pot, Marshall rather hankered after a poisoning case. He had watched with a growing disquiet and rising ambition the trend that was developing: the body exhumed at dead of night in the presence of a policeman, an undertaker and a government-instructed expert; the contents of the stomach moved to London for analysis. It is true that samples were made available to the accused but that was little help since he usually needed every penny he could raise to secure a legal team, let alone a scientific one as well. And then there was the slick confidence of an unchallenged prosecution expert and the unquestioning acceptance of a jury dazzled by his eminence and ignorant as to how uncertain in reality the supposedly certain science was. Vivid in Marshall's memory was his beloved father regaling his thirteen-year-old self with the explanation of the properties of poisons in the Brighton chocolate cream poisoner case. Furthermore there had always been a mystique about poisoning that not even the new science could dispel; criminal barristers were taught that 'of all forms of death by which human nature may be overcome the most detestable is that of poison'[9] and the insidious wickedness of it had always captivated Marshall. The year after his triumph in Lawrence he thought his moment had come.

It was 1910 and a meek little doctor who worked as a salesman and distributor of patent medicines obtained a new poison and dispatched his wife with it. The poison was hyoscine and the murderer Dr Hawley Harvey Crippen.

Of course Marshall was going to represent Crippen. Who else? The newspapers announced it at once. It was the dream case, the respectable doctor who poisoned his wife, a music hall singer, for the love of a young typist, Ethel Le Neve, cut up the body and buried it in his cellar and then boarded the SS *Montrose* bound for Canada, accompanied by Le Neve disguised as a boy. He was the first murderer ever to be captured with the aid of wireless communication, the *Montrose*'s captain having sent a telegram that read: 'Have strong suspicions that Crippen London cellar murderer and accomplice are among saloon passengers. Moustache taken off growing beard, accomplice dressed as boy. Manner and build undoubtedly a girl.' They were arrested by Chief Inspector Drew of Scotland Yard, who boarded a faster liner, arrived in Canada before the *Montrose* and came aboard her disguised as a ship's pilot as she entered the St Lawrence River. No novelist could have devised the story.

Whilst in Canada awaiting extradition Dr Crippen received an enterprising telegram from Arthur Newton, ambulance chasing Edwardian style. 'Your friends desire me to defend you and will pay all necessary expenses but you must promise and answer no questions,' it ran. The friends were fictitious but Crippen fell for the offer and Newton duly waltzed into Marshall's chambers to bestow the prized brief upon him. In fact there were no funds to pay him, he told Marshall's clerk. If Crippen was acquitted he would then sell his story; if convicted and hanged Newton would sell his confession. In later trials, Marshall was one of the first to evolve and benefit from schemes in which the accused bartered his life story for funds with which to instruct his defence barrister but these, as will be seen, were carefully formulated in order not to offend public policy. Newton's proposal was novel and speculative and with regard to the anticipation of a confession before a trial in which the accused intended to plead not guilty, ethically dodgy. In consultation with his clerk, Marshall refused to accept the brief on these terms. Newton flounced out of 3 Temple Gardens and into the nearby chambers of the almost unknown Arthur Tobin KC, to whom he offered the brief of the century and who must have thought he was dreaming. Tobin subsequently did a perfectly competent job in hopeless circumstances and did not really deserve the epithets 'dull' and 'plodding' applied to his performance by a disappointed press. He just wasn't Marshall Hall.

Marshall's views of the case were eagerly sought and without the professional constraints imposed by representation of the accused he came up with ingenious and theatrical defences, to the fascination of the public and no doubt the exasperation of those actually involved in the case.[10] Only Marshall could have quite so effectively appropriated publicity and kudos in a case in which he never actually appeared. Crippen was convicted and hanged. Newton suffered a different kind of suspension, as a solicitor, having been found guilty of professional misconduct in giving the newspapers confessional correspondence purporting to come from Crippen and in fact concocted by himself.[11] The case had been conducted largely for the purpose of making newspaper copy, said the judge. It was a narrow escape for Marshall, who was able to take the moral high ground despite his own weaknesses in that direction.

Marshall got his own great poisoning case two years later in March 1912. Few trials have been written about so much or been so notable for so many reasons as that of Mr and Mrs Seddon,[12] charged with the murder of their lodger Eliza Barrow. It was just the sort of cosy murder that particularly appealed to the Edwardian public:[13] the evidence taken as a whole providing a window into social history, compelling in its clarity and detail; the mean, cold, hypocritical lay preacher and dictatorial head of his household Frederick Seddon, his tired, put-upon wife, the five children, the striving, parsimonious middle-class household, the unattractive exploited spinster lodger; how they lived their unfulfilled lives; and the greed that bound them together.

More than that, however, the trial was said by jurists then and since to have marked a new era. The tenuous links in the chain of evidence were wholly circumstantial, concerned not with facts or actions, as Robert Wood's trial had been, but with the simple establishment of motive and opportunity. A completely novel use of scientific evidence by the prosecution purported to establish the precise and fatal amount of arsenic that must have been in the victim's blood at the time of death. Seddon had given evidence in his own defence, cold, confident, clever, ultimately unattractive. It had all contributed to his conviction and hanging. And the case was unique in that whilst Seddon was convicted, his wife, on the same evidence, was acquitted.

Miss Eliza Barrow, the victim, was a spinster of considerable means, consisting of stocks and shares, two commercial properties and, since she did not believe in banks or banknotes, a considerable hoard of gold. In many ways, both obsessed with money, she and Seddon were alike; but where Miss

Barrow was lonely, vulnerable and naive, Seddon was manipulative, clever and ruthless. During her fourteen-month stay with the Seddons, Mr Seddon, the superintendent of an insurance company, divested Miss Barrow of most of her wealth, with which he purported to buy her annuities. By September 1911 she was Seddon's pensioner, living off the small income he paid her, which he assured her would be paid for the rest of her life. She was then forty-nine years old. That month she was taken ill and within two weeks she was dead, the death being certified as due to epidemic diarrhoea. Seddon composed a verse for the death announcement ('A dear one is missing and with us no more | That voice so much loved we hear not again') and arranged for her burial in a pauper's grave, having negotiated a commission from the undertaker for introducing the business. That would have been that, had it not been for some rather inconvenient relatives who turned up asking questions about where Miss Barrow, and more to the point her money, had gone. In November, after they demanded an investigation, the body was exhumed and expert opinion sought from the examining pathologists, William Willcox and Bernard Spilsbury. She had been poisoned by arsenic, they said; and the prosecution theory was that the poison had been extracted by soaking in water the fly papers hanging around her fetid sick room and giving her the resultant deadly solution. There was no evidence to link the Seddons with the arsenic; true, they had tended her in her last illness; true, they benefited from her death. But that was all. The rest was conjecture.

Marshall got the brief this time, representing Mr Seddon, with Mrs Seddon nominally represented by a junior barrister. Rufus Isaacs, Attorney General, a formidable advocate and Marshall's old friend, was to prosecute. With grim and studious determination, quite at odds with his reputation for off-the-cuff showmanship, Marshall applied himself to the science, poring for long hours over medical textbooks and the Royal Commission report on arsenical poisoning and dredging his memory for the knowledge imparted by his father.

Willcox and Spilsbury, fresh from their Crippen triumph of concocting from the pulp that had once been Mrs Crippen both her identity and the type of poison from which she had died, had now conducted a series of experiments on the remains of Miss Barrow. Traces of arsenic in all the major organs in the body had been detected using what was known as Marsh's test, whereby a tiny part of each organ is subjected to a chemical experiment which expels the arsenic in gas form. This is in turn distilled into a measurable, if minute, deposit of arsenic. The test, though long established, was of limited value in answering the common defence in arsenic cases that the poisoning was the chronic type associated with its then recognised medicinal and cosmetic use. Willcox, correctly anticipating this defence, devised a further 'scientific' method to calculate the total amount of arsenic at the time of death, and so, given its rapid expulsion by the body, the length of time for which it was likely to have been present. This he did by analysing the microscopic amounts extracted from various organs by Marsh's test (some as tiny as a fiftieth of a milligramme), scaling them up to calculate how much arsenic there had been in each organ, and then adding those amounts together to calculate how much of the poison had been in the body at death. By this speculative method he concluded that the level of arsenic was such that it was consistent only with acute, and therefore deliberate, poisoning. A fatal quantity of 2.01 grammes of arsenic must have been present on death, he said, and given the body's rapid expulsion the dose must have been up to five grammes, administered during the last two days of life. Furthermore, the clincher, he said, was that separate tests had revealed arsenic still present in the victim's long hair.

In a cross-examination lasting for several hours Marshall all but demolished Willcox in the witness box, extracting from him acknowledgements that the amounts of arsenic were so minute that the multiplying factors had to be enormous and any tiny error thus commensurately magnified; and crucially, that Willcox had not factored into his calculations of weight the different rates of water evaporation from different body parts in the period immediately after death. With regard to the long hair, Willcox was forced to concede that the poison was found in the distal end, furthest from the body, and, given the rate of growth of the hair, was therefore consistent with arsenic having been taken several months prior to death.[14] It was, Willcox said later, quite extraordinarily clever; and never had he felt as trapped as he did then.

So tenuous was the evidence at the end of the prosecution case that both the Seddons would have been acquitted had not Mr Seddon insisted on availing himself of his right to give evidence. Marshall had advised him repeatedly not do so. Now, at the end of the prosecution case, he left his seat in counsel's row and went over to emphasise his advice to Seddon as he stood in the dock. But Seddon, with an unshakable belief in his own intellectual abilities coupled with an arrogance which made him blind to the fact that the inroads on the prosecution case made by Marshall could not be bettered and might be damaged, relished an exchange with the Attorney General.

Into the witness box went Frederick Seddon, with his cold narrow eyes, his enormous waxed moustache, his precise manner and his obsessive attention to detail. And there he proceeded to reveal himself: his vanity, his pettiness above all else, his passionate love of money. It was not that anyone managed to catch him out; he had an answer to everything and he talked like a lawyer: 'I never purchased arsenic in my life in any shape or form. I never administered arsenic. I never advised, directed or instructed the purchase of arsenic in any shape or form. I never advised, directed or instructed the administration of arsenic.' It may have been true, but the jury hated him, as Marshall had known they would, and found him guilty whilst acquitting downtrodden Mrs Seddon on the same evidence.

It was customary, prior to passing the death sentence, to ask the prisoner if he had anything to say on why such a sentence should not be passed; the most anyone normally managed was an incoherent protestation of innocence. But Seddon proceeded to make a detailed speech in his own defence culminating in a reference to the Great Architect of the Universe, a sign that he, like Mr Justice Bucknill, the judge, was a Freemason. 'We both belong to the same brotherhood and it is all the more painful for me to say what I am saying. But our brotherhood does not encourage crime; on the contrary it condemns it. I pray you to make your peace with the Great Architect of the Universe,' said the judge, struggling with emotion as he donned the black cap. The moment was captured by a covert (forbidden) press camera. It is the only photograph ever taken at the moment of the pronouncement of a death sentence.

Despite the verdict, Marshall's defence was generally said to have been faultless and his analysis of the scientific evidence technically unassailable. There had been no fireworks; it was not a case that required them. It was, said the Attorney General, his opponent, a job nobly done, a magnificent forensic effort conducted in accordance with the highest traditions of the profession. In his final speech Marshall had been unable to resist expressing his personal belief in the triumph of emotion over reason and instinct over science, and the horror of the finality of the sanction that attached to a conviction, in itself ultimately uncertain:

> Gentlemen, the great scientists who have been here have told us much of the marvels of science and of the deductions to be made from science. There is one thing that the scientists have never yet been able to discover with all their research … and that is how to replace the little vital spark that we call life. Upon your verdict here depends the life of this man. If your verdict is against him that spark will be extinguished and no science known in the world can ever replace it.

The verdict caused widespread discomfort. Within days, articles appeared in the press strongly criticising it. It was generally thought to have been gained by suspicion and conjecture built into a spurious edifice. Those in the legal profession who had predicted that the Act giving the accused the right to give evidence in his own defence would lead to an erosion of the presumption of innocence now said they were vindicated. The jury assumed the accused would explain himself, they said, and with that assumption had come an expectation that he would contribute to proving his own innocence. The public, unconcerned with the technicalities, were nonetheless uncomfortable with hanging a man against whom there was no evidence but motive and opportunity. And anyway, Marshall had by now, all by himself, achieved the status of an iconic football team; they did not like him losing. As for Marshall himself, a supporter of the 1898 Act, the verdict showed what he had always said to be the case: the psychology of the jury was the determinant, regardless of the evidence, or lack of it. In later life he met the problem of the unattractive defendant head on. 'You don't like him, members of the jury, do you? I can see that in every one of your faces,' he yelled at them on one occasion; and a sheepish jury acquitted his villainous-looking client.[15]

An appeal on Seddon's behalf to the newly established Court of Criminal Appeal and a 300,000-strong petition to the Home Secretary were to no avail. Seddon was hanged; and the last detail in this unique case is that John Ellis, the hangman, achieved a personal best and broke the record by dispatching him in twenty-five seconds.

Amidst all the furore Marshall and his opponent were both observed to be drained with stress and exhaustion. It had been Rufus Isaacs's first murder trial. He swore it would be his last: the strain was too much, the stakes too high, he told Marshall; and Marshall agreed with him. Enough was enough.

CHAPTER 12

'I have shot him – he dared me to do it'

'I don't think I'll ever take on another murder case,' Marshall told his clerk Edgar Bowker the day after the trial concluded. 'The strain is too great. It takes too much out of me.' Bowker was a highly experienced clerk, one of that faithful band of special servants who combined in an inherited tradition the loyalty and discretion of a good butler with the business acuity and power of a theatrical agent. Like all clerks his success depended on his master's, as did his income, a shilling in every guinea Marshall earned. He had not been with Marshall for very long but it was already beginning to prove lucrative. This was not the sort of talk he liked to hear, although he was not too worried. It was part of a clerk's duty to understand his barristers; and although Bowker loved Marshall with something close to hero worship, he was nonetheless a shrewd psychologist and he knew he had only to wait. He had marked Marshall down as a born fighter who would not be able to resist the next sensational murder, however great the strain. But he recognised that for now Marshall was burnt out.

No one who watched his ebullient progress around the Temple would have suspected it. He strode up Middle Temple Lane in the early mornings, always, it seemed, in a tremendous hurry, bellowing his greetings with an indiscriminate warmth and charm to everyone, distinguished judges, colleagues from his chambers, opponents who once met were never forgotten, the Temple crossing sweeper, a passing dog (he adored all dogs). He swept into Inner Temple Hall for lunch surrounded by the youngest members of his chambers, each somehow feeling individually singled out for his attention and encouragement. He would go back to Hall or to the Garrick in the evening, dining with close friends, the best Cuban cigar in hand, the flow of reminiscence unquenchable. But that was the public face.

During Marshall's fallow periods no one else in 3 Temple Gardens got any work done. Highly strung, temperamental, meticulous, he was at his worst when he did not have an all-consuming case into which to throw himself. His restlessness became intolerable for the other occupants of 3 Temple Gardens, and if deprived of attention he was not above throwing what his clerk described as tantrums. Thwarted of DIY in the confines of the new London flat, he indulged his passion in chambers, repairing windows, unjamming doors, his enthusiastic hammering music to his ears if not to anyone else's. Welcome peace only came when he bounded off on a shopping trip, tearing down the stairs still dictating letters at the top of his voice to a flustered clerk following in his wake with a notebook and hurling himself into his motor car. And then he would return in noisy triumph and a better humour, having found a bargain diamond at Tessier in Burlington Arcade or an eighteenth-century snuff box at Rundell and Bridge on Ludgate Hill or pieces of an old clock bought in a junk shop with unrealistically optimistic plans for its reassembly. Once he came back with a whole basket full of Pekingese puppies for Elna. All of it was spilled out on any available desk to be played with, flourished, exclaimed over, quite regardless of the workload of the desk's owner. The truth was that when he was in a good mood no one could resist Marshall.

He had by now joined the club of the famous, as well established, if less clearly defined, then as now. And with membership he became sought after by other members of that exclusive club. Although always acknowledging his lack of legal erudition, Marshall substituted for it a smattering of basic legal knowledge, a lot of common sense, supreme self-confidence and above all his intuitive understanding of psychology. Distinguished lawyers, their names unknown to the public, watched with irony his growing reputation as informal legal adviser to the rich, aristocratic and powerful of his day.

In this unexpected role he had already advised the Sackville-West family when Henry, the product of the second Lord Sackville's indiscretion with a Spanish dancer, had claimed to be the heir to Knole, one of the greatest stately homes of England.[1] Marshall, being Marshall, thought nothing of giving off-the-cuff advice on the highly technical laws of inheritance, nor of giving it to both Henry and the Sackville-Wests despite the painfully obvious conflict of interest. 'My friendship for you', he wrote to the eighth Earl De La Warr, head of the Sackville-West clan, 'is sufficient guarantee that I should not rashly advise [Henry] to do anything to compromise the family honour.' Henry, more interested in Knole than the family honour, eventually got wise to this and instructed solicitors expert in Chancery law. Elsewhere Marshall, unabashed, proceeded to advise the eccentric Alfred de Rothschild in relation to all manner of matters to do with family and estate, the fifth Earl of Carnarvon in relation to defamation proceedings,[2] and Carnarvon's heir, Lord Porchester, with regard to an unfortunate liaison with a woman.[3] Only on the last matter might he have claimed he was becoming an expert and that was on a personal rather than professional basis.

The influential friendships grew and grew and with them came invitations everywhere: to join clubs specialising in his myriad interests (the Cigar Club, the Silver Spoon Club, the Playgoers Club, the Crimes Club, the Stage Guild, the Shakespeare Society); to dinners in London at the livery companies and with the great press barons, financiers, politicians and aristocrats who dominated Edwardian society; and to weekend parties in the grandest country houses. Earl De La Warr entertained in style amidst the ancient glories of Buckhurst Park, Sussex; and in the nouveau riche grandeur of Halton House, Buckinghamshire, Alfred de Rothschild's parties were over the top to the point of vulgarity. There were many other hosts; but most important of all was the Carnarvon family at Highclere Castle in Berkshire.

On 24 November 1910, fresh from the triumph of the Lawrence trial and sore from failing to get the Crippen brief, Marshall, invited for the first time, swept up the long drive to Highclere Castle and felt instantly at home. The great Elizabethan mansion had been remodelled by Sir Charles Barry, the architect of Temple Gardens,[4] in the same elaborate Renaissance revival style, and the surrounding undulating landscape encompassed, he knew, one of the best shooting estates in England. The house parties held in the glorious interiors of Highclere were legendary, with lavish expenditure on fine wines and French menus. Best of all, his host and hostess and the company they entertained were very much to his taste, the well-bred mixed in with the interesting, with a touch of bohemia, not to mention a certain raciness.

Almina, the Countess of Carnarvon, was commonly thought to be the daughter of Alfred de Rothschild and, like him, she was rolling in personal wealth, generous and extravagant, a strange mixture of utter self-indulgence and genuine philanthropy. Her husband, the fifth Earl, famous as the discoverer with Egyptologist Howard Carter of Tutankhamen's tomb, had a passion for speed with almost as many summonses as Marshall to show for it and an obsession with the occult in all its forms.

That gathering was the first of many; until Lord Carnarvon's death in 1923 Marshall was a regular visitor, usually alone though sometimes with Hetty and Elna. He attended shooting parties on the estate two or three times a year and was a constant presence at the house parties, rubbing shoulders with the aristocracy, politicians and intellectuals, flirting with Almina, and upstairs in a darkened guest bedroom known as the East Anglia room, behind locked doors and tightly closed shutters, conducting séances with Lord Carnarvon. These were attended by an inner circle including Carter and other Egyptologists increasingly fascinated by the investigation of clairvoyance, palmistry, spiritualism and the nuttier connections between these and the ancient religions; bowls of flowers were seen to levitate from tables and on one occasion a society lady in a trance was said to have burst into a language that caused Carter to exclaim: 'My God, it's Coptic!' It was all a curious mixture of serious exploration and party game and it was not until some years later that Marshall made a committed and public declaration of his belief in the after-life, a conviction he had held since Ethel's death.

Rackety house parties, no matter how full of influential people, were not compatible with the serious pursuit of practice at the Bar, and Marshall had added to the demands on his time by standing once again for Parliament in the two 1910 general elections and winning the Liverpool seat of East Toxteth. His campaign had been less theatrical than previously but he nonetheless gained overwhelming popularity with large audiences and enthusiastic receptions everywhere. It could not be said that he adopted this new role with even the industry with which he had tackled Southport and by 1913 he announced he would not stand for re-election.[5] Nonetheless constituency visits occupied a considerable amount of time, as did his duties as a newly elected bencher of the Inner Temple; this latter role enabled him to play a part in the running of the Inn and to dine at top table along with the most eminent in his profession and, most importantly, with the judiciary. Marshall had begun to have his eye on the Bench now.

The sky was the limit for a leading silk at this time; during the preceding few years there had been the biggest exodus from Bar to Bench for two generations. At least seven of the top silks had been made judges,[6] leaving Marshall, F E Smith and Edward Carson as the undisputed first-rankers at the Bar, Marshall the most prominent in crime. But Marshall had always been contrary. Now he kept well away from the capital trials that were his for the taking and revelled in a series of jokey cases conducted in the glare of his own personal spotlight. In them he confirmed his populist image by exhibiting a knowledge of the turf and the boxing ring, using sporting jargon which endeared him to the working man and causing the papers to dub him 'man of the people'[7] and 'sporting counsel of the day'.

He began to believe his own publicity to such a degree that he flouted quite flagrantly the rules of his profession. Barristers do not give evidence, they elicit it from others; but Marshall began to rely on his special status to set himself up as an expert on all manner of subjects. On one occasion, he came into court carrying one of his own silver soup tureens to demonstrate a point when cross-examining a silversmith; in cases involving jewellery he would extract from his bag with a flourish the magnifying glass and scales of the trade and proceed to conduct his own examination of the item in question. Anecdotes about his personal experience with guns began to figure in cases requiring ballistics evidence and there were references in speeches to one or other of his previous triumphs and protestations about his personal belief in the innocence of his clients. It was all quite unacceptable but somehow he got away with it. Bar and Bench greeted each new outrage with a smile and a shrug and the press loved it all. High society High Court libel cases earned him substantial brief fees, and lesser cases in lower courts, covered by the press for no other reason than that he was appearing in them, were lapped up by a swooning public.

On one occasion a young member of the Bar briefed on the other side asked for his case to be adjourned simply on the basis that he had not been expecting quite such a terrifying opponent. On another, a (very pretty) actress in the witness box who asked Marshall during her cross-examination whether she was entitled to describe herself as good looking received from him, amidst gales of laughter from those in court, the flirtatious answer 'You are fishing in very deep waters but I am not so easily to be caught'. Another female litigant chose to conduct her own case in Folkestone County Court without the benefit of counsel, suing in respect of an attack on her dog by a St Bernard represented by Marshall. 'I appear on behalf of myself', she began, 'but the defendants have spent a lot of money in bringing down Mr Marshall Hall KC, the most celebrated defender of murderers in the world, to appear for them.' Like many other defendants whose life was at stake the St Bernard must have felt his money was well spent. Every word of the case was reported and Marshall defeated his opponent (whom his clerk afterwards described as 'a gallant little lady') in a series of interchanges in which he exuded patronising charm. 'What do you know about dogs?' she demanded at last, goaded. 'I know something about ladies,' was the response reported by a delighted press.

So he did. With celebrity had come temptations. Marshall revelled in the admiration, nurtured his image as a ladykiller and succumbed to the temptations when he felt like it.[8] Even at an early stage in their marriage, there are question marks in relation to Marshall's fidelity to Hetty. Those interested in genealogy will discover on the internet a family who believe, with significant circumstantial evidence to back it up, that they may be descended from an illegitimate son of Marshall's born in May 1898, only eighteen months or so after his marriage and fourteen months after Elna's birth. The DNA testing to which they and Marshall's brother's descendants sportingly submitted themselves at my request was unsupportive of a link. Whatever the truth, there is no evidence that Marshall even knew of the boy's existence, let alone that he ever had any involvement in his life. By now, however, after fourteen years of marriage, evidence of Marshall's numerous liaisons was clear. Hetty, in the country, was aware of the rumours and did her best to ignore them.

Then he fell in love again. There is no record of when or how he met Louisa Miéville. We know only that in 1919 when he made his will, eight years before his death, he acknowledged her importance to him in a way that was bound ultimately to cause humiliation to his family and a public sensation. Given what we know of his relationship with Hetty, it seems highly probable that the affair was one of long standing and it was to last the rest of his life.

Secrecy would have been no difficulty for Louisa; she had been born into wealth and secrecy and those two overriding factors ruled her life and were to be her legacy. Louisa was the daughter of a Scotswoman, Elizabeth Cameron Robertson, born into a household consisting of her mother, her brother Louis and her sister Elizabeth. At the birth of each of the three children their mother is recorded as 'spinster'. The household was a highly prosperous one; the family lived in Devonshire Street, Marylebone, and young Louis Robertson was sent to Harrow and then to Oxford before being called to the Bar.

In 1885, when Louis, Elizabeth and Louisa were nineteen, seventeen and eleven, respectively, their mother married an extremely rich Swiss banker, Jean-Louis Miéville, who lived close by in immense style in Connaught Square. He was then seventy-seven and their mother was forty-nine. All the evidence suggests that Jean-Louis was the children's natural father. Their Christian names had been Miéville family names throughout the centuries and they eventually inherited Jean-Louis's vast wealth along with the children of his first marriage, all referred to in his will as his sons and daughters. In the box marked 'occupation' on Louisa's own death certificate is stated 'woman of independent means and daughter of Jean Louis Mieville, Banker'.

Jean-Louis's first marriage had ended in 1842 in a manner in those days open only to the very rich, by private Act of Parliament. He had been only twenty-two when he had married his cousin, eighteen-year-old Mary Ann Miéville. He had worked all hours to establish his fabulously successful banking house, Kraeutler and Miéville. Perhaps the hours were too long; after twelve years of marriage and with two young children Mary Ann had an affair with a family friend, a Mr Poley, who was attaché to the Prussian embassy. It was a painful divorce; Jean-Louis was devastated when Mary Ann confessed to not merely 'liberties' with Mr Poley but 'criminal connections' on what she described with some relish as more than fifty occasions.[9] Ultimately she had left England on the *John Bull* steam boat, bound for Berlin, Mr Poley by her side (and in her cabin); and that had been that for Jean-Louis.

Perhaps it was the pain of this first marriage that made Jean-Louis wait more than forty years before he married again. Or perhaps the set-up of Elizabeth Robertson and three children around the corner suited him until old age made him want to regularise his affairs. Whatever the reason, the marriage legitimised Louisa and made her an heiress.

The newly formed Miéville family moved together to Lancaster Gate and stayed there until 1893, when Jean-Louis died aged eighty-six. His vast collection of priceless antiques and pictures was exhibited at Christie's prior to auction, attracting enormous crowds. Louisa, by now twenty-three, moved with her mother to 110 Sloane Street and when her mother died in 1913 she became mistress of the house as well as at some point of Marshall.

Her life was closely entwined with that of her sister Elizabeth, six years older and now widowed, who lived close by at 17 Walton Place, just behind Harrods. Elizabeth had established herself as a hostess, holding literary gatherings at Walton Place that had become renowned. She too had a lover, the eccentric 'Roberto' Cunninghame Graham, aristocrat, politician, writer and adventurer, and through him Elizabeth and Louisa developed a network of famous friends. Joseph Conrad, Axel Munthe, Compton Mackenzie and Sir John Lavery were amongst the distinguished writers and artists who revolved around Walton Place and Louisa, following in her sister's footsteps, held soirées at Sloane Street. The two sisters, attractive, lively and rich, were much admired.

Louisa no doubt experienced all the ecstatic highs of clandestine passion and the humiliating lows of the beloved's other and public life common to most mistresses, but she was not the type to live entirely through her lover nor to languish during his absences. Spirited and independent, from a rich cultivated European background, she must have been well aware of the glamour that surrounded her and reasonably secure that she could hold Marshall's attention.

All in all it was not a happy time for Hetty. She was suffering from a severe attack of insomnia and constituency visits were suspended. She had been sent abroad it was reported and no letters would be forwarded. A frequent visitor to Germany, the strong probability is that she had gone home to Mother. On her ultimate return the vague complaints of years now manifested themselves in serious illness, and a presumably contrite Marshall cancelled all engagements whilst she underwent major surgery.

A new country house was bought, Felder Lodge in Worth, a little village close to Sandwich and the Royal St George's Golf Club. Marshall always called the new house 'the cottage'; the magazines called it an estate, a description that infuriated Marshall, who learned the downside of celebrity when he was immediately inundated with applications from would-be estate employees. In fact it was somewhere between the two, a moderately large establishment with two acres of beautiful gardens. It housed Hetty, whose love for the country and rejection of smart London was ever increasing, Elna during her school holidays, Marshall's newly revived collections and the family's four beloved dogs, Williams, Poodge, Judy and Bunty. But it housed Marshall himself rather less often.

In theory he was attracted to family life in a country house: 'You had a lovely home … with dogs and flowers and everything you cared for,' he once said reproachfully to an unfaithful husband he was cross-examining in a divorce case. Exactly the same could have been said of Marshall himself. But his home life, increasingly lacking in stimulus, had now become an outwardly prosperous and harmonious façade. The plan was that he would go home for weekends, but five days a week of praise and attention, the glitz and glamour of London society, the striving and competition of work, and presumably the company of Louisa, did not mesh easily with weekends of a quiet domesticity which Marshall increasingly found not soothing but intolerable. The routine quickly became looser: 'Gaggie went up yesterday morning and *perhaps* he will come back Sat or Sun,' wrote Hetty wistfully to Elna. It was lonely, she went on, with only the dogs for company. But eventually she settled into the rhythms of village life, and the upheaval to the household on those Friday nights when Marshall erupted through the front door, imperious, bad tempered,[10] accustomed to absolute command in chambers and uncritical admiration from an adoring public, became increasingly stressful for all concerned. The dogs barked for joy when he came home; but Hetty was miserable and Elna sided with her.

Even Elna was proving a bit of a disappointment to Marshall. The adoring little girl was turning out just like her mother: quiet, shy, a little bit frightened of him, undemanding and ultimately unstimulating. The fond letters to Elna still continued but now the whimsical endearments were interspersed with instructions and admonitions to Hetty, and communications with Hetty herself seem to have been limited to the domestic arrangements necessary to the running of the house. From then on Hetty and Elna were joined in timid alliance. Marshall, glamorous but increasingly distant, was regarded as an unpredictable if sometimes generous ogre. 'Gaggie has had the big bill from Madame,' wrote Hetty breathlessly to Elna, now aged sixteen and at finishing school in Paris, 'and he did not mind and says so long as the child has a good time!'[11]

The addiction to passion and turmoil, so uncomfortable for those closest to him, led Marshall to crave new professional challenges; as his clerk Bowker had predicted, he could not resist the defence in 1913 of a murderess of startling beauty, his interests in crime and women irresistibly combined.

She had tripped into the dock of a London magistrates' court swathed in white furs, wiping away her tears with a little lace handkerchief, accused of murdering her lover. Had she anything to say, asked the magistrate? 'I have so much to tell', she whispered, 'that I could not tell it all just now.' Actually it was going to be rather difficult for her to tell it all. Jeannie Baxter[12] was only twenty-four years old and had already managed to pack rather a lot into her life. The lover, Julian Hall, was the public-school-educated nephew of a serving MP with the then unimaginably glamorous status of being a newly qualified aviator. The case inevitably caused a stir, enhanced by Jeannie's deliciously immoral and sophisticated past. When she met Hall she was already being kept in style in a beautifully furnished flat in Maida Vale with a Swiss maid in attendance, a cottage in the country for weekends and a generous weekly income. Her protector, Mr Unwin, was going to marry her once his mother had died, she said. Be that as it may, he was certainly a generous provider which made it all the more quixotic of her to start an affair with Hall, whom she met by chance in a night club.

Julian Hall did not confine his risk taking to flying. He was a reckless heavy-drinking gambler with a penchant for shooting games. He kept loaded revolvers in his pockets like packs of cards, getting them out to play with, whistling over the tops of the loaded barrels and evolving elaborate games shooting at drawing room photographs and over his shoulder through open doors.

Rich (though not, as she naively pointed out in court, anything like as rich as Mr Unwin), handsome and brutal, to Jeannie he was irresistible; the more violent he was, she said, the more she loved him. There was a sort of ghastly inevitability about the course of the relationship. As her passion grew, his waned. The marriage prospects he had held out to her dwindled, and she had burned her boats with Mr Unwin.

Hall was last seen by a neighbour on the morning of 15 April 1913 lying decadently in his bed in his pyjamas smoking a cigarette. Shortly afterwards a volley of six shots was heard from his flat and Jeannie ran out screaming: 'I have shot him – he dared me to do it!'

Marshall was prevailed upon to see Jeannie in prison with the junior barrister instructed in the case, Jack Valetta.[13] On an unseasonally snowy morning they met a girl of translucent beauty with red-gold hair cascading down her back. There was no lace handkerchief in evidence now, only a cool distant confidence. After the meeting, watching through the window for a last glimpse of her as she was taken back to her cell, Marshall caught his breath. 'My God, Valetta, look at that,' he said. The two men peered out into the prison yard. As she was escorted by the burly warders through the grim area miraculously transformed by its white blanket, Jeannie did a little dance watching her footprints in the snow like a child. Marshall was captivated. Despite his resolutions he now vowed to save that lovely neck from the noose.

Her defence revolved around the victim's games. He had pointed the gun at his own chest and dared her to pull the trigger; she had tried to wrest the gun from his hand and during the struggle two shots had been accidentally fired causing the two bullet wounds from which Hall had died. That left a rather inconvenient four extra shots heard by witnesses. Jeannie said she had fired the extra shots into the air in order to empty the gun before running for help. The prosecution said she had let loose all six in a frenzied attack and two had made their mark. The former explanation showed a remarkable amount of forethought for a distraught girl. The latter meant murder. The defence case was not assisted by a statement from a young man who lived in the flat next door to Hall. He reported an earlier conversation with Jeannie (firmly denied by her) in which she had analysed her situation with a rather unfortunate clarity: 'Either Mr Hall must marry me or he must get Mr Unwin back to me or I will kill him.'

Marshall made his way to the Old Bailey on the first day of the trial, 3 June 1913, amidst flags and traffic jams. It was King George V's birthday and the sun was shining. He was facing for the first time a prosecution team that was going to become very familiar to him. The pathologist Bernard Spilsbury, almost as handsome as Marshall and almost as much of a showman, had now taken over the role of Home Office pathologist from Sir William Willcox. Spilsbury had watched Willcox being cross-examined by Marshall during the Seddon trial and had no illusions as to the formidable defence he was facing. Knowing of Marshall's reputation for doing his own expert research and his interest in ballistics, Spilsbury had enlisted the aid of a young gunsmith, Robert Churchill. Between them they had conducted a series of unprecedentedly sophisticated experiments, firing shots at different distances through fabric similar to that worn by Hall, with pieces of leather held behind it to simulate human skin. By observing the effect of the impact at different ranges Spilsbury calculated that the gun was discharged from a distance of about three feet from the victim and not, therefore, in a close struggle. Furthermore the angle of the bullet holes was such that they could not have been inflicted when the victim was holding the gun.

Any barrister would have immediately detected weaknesses in relation to these experiments. However authoritative Spilsbury and Churchill made them sound, they involved some speculative leaps. The fabric was not identical to that of Hall's pyjama jacket and the properties of the leather cannot have been the same as living skin. But Marshall, it seemed, relied on science only when he thought his client would let him down. The dry scientist of the Seddon trial was now transformed back into the showman who had saved Robert Wood and Edward Lawrence. This time he preferred to rely on the impact of the beautiful girl, now in black silk, a wreath of violets around her black hat and once more sobbing into a dainty handkerchief, and of his own advocacy. It was almost becoming a game now, this mastery over the emotions of his jury. It would take the brush of Hogarth, he told them, or the pen of Zola, to convey to them the tragedy of this case. But in the absence of those artists, he did it himself.

Throughout the trial he built detail by detail not so much a defence as a kind of living picture of the victim, 'this magnificent young man well dowered with this world's goods and possessed with a disregard for death which fitted him for the career of an aviator'. It had been drink and his own reckless personality that had killed him, Marshall told them; and he had brought down with him this beautiful butterfly ensnared by her passion for him. The jury was carried away by the pathos. 'He plays on the feelings of his jury like the wind on the strings of a harp,' observed one newspaper, reporting on a much later trial.[14] But in this case, the judge, with enough remaining forensic instincts to know the wool was being pulled over his eyes, suggested to the jury that a verdict of manslaughter was open to them and Jeannie was ultimately found guilty of that offence and sentenced to three years' imprisonment. As Spilsbury's biographer acknowledges, Marshall's hypnotic advocacy and ability to build a poetic picture of a crime ultimately prevailed over Spilsbury's scientific evidence.[15]

Marshall himself was not best pleased with a result which he probably felt rather detracted from his performance. He appealed to the Court of Criminal Appeal on the basis that the judge should not have suggested a verdict of manslaughter to a jury clearly on the brink of a full acquittal. The three judges in the Court of Appeal made clear their disquiet at Marshall's triumph over the evidence, though as they well knew he had transgressed no rules. 'Mr Marshall Hall', they said snootily, 'might very well have hoped for a verdict that he ought not to have got.'[16]

They were not the only ones who began to feel uncomfortable. The public began to wonder whether the accused's life should really rest on the genius of his advocate.

CHAPTER 13

'Nearer, my God, to Thee'

It was 1914. War was declared on 4 August. The new Lord Chief Justice, Marshall's old friend Rufus Isaacs, returning from his vacation, said: 'I seem to have come into another world.' And it was true that war had changed the Temple forever, its upheavals reflecting in microcosm those of the whole country.

The golden afternoon peace of the Temple gardens, which for centuries had been broken only by the caw of rooks, now resounded to the sound of shouted commands as the Royal Naval Volunteer Reserve were drilled on the lawns. On the river steps to the Embankment anti-aircraft guns were installed to protect the ancient grace of the Temple buildings from German attack. By the autumn of 1914 almost all the young men in chambers were called away from their seamless lives in changeless environments – the ancient squares, the cloisters, the rickety staircases up to the double oak doors of their public school studies, their Oxbridge rooms and their chambers in the Inns of Court – to the hell of the trenches. Young men on leave were permitted to appear in court in uniform; judges seeing the youngest in court would try to obtain for them some small case so they had their brief moment as a real advocate. For many it was to be the only such moment they would have. Many never returned; those who did had lost their innocence.

The clerks all went too. Marshall lost his faithful Edgar Bowker almost at once. On 5 August he telephoned Marshall at Felder Lodge: he was leaving now, he told him, but would be back for Christmas. Everybody believed it would all be over by then. Meanwhile old men and very young boys and sometimes even the clerk's wife took over the clerking. Women began to infiltrate the Temple in all sorts of new roles and vacant chambers were rented to people who had no connection with the law and less respect for the peace and traditions of the Temple. Work in court continued in fits and starts. Judges were called away to preside over the plethora of tribunals created to deal with war emergencies, as were barristers to fulfil unpaid duties as special constables and fire wardens. The clerks unable to fight and employed to ensure the smooth running of the law courts were frequently absent whilst they helped in the manufacture of munitions. The ranks of men eligible for jury service was so diminished that the number on a jury in some instances was reduced to seven, although in capital cases it was invariably still twelve. Although there was less litigation there were still some people who, despite the horrors of war, committed crimes, disputed wills, breached contracts and sued for injuries as they always will. War also brought its own litigation with it, as ordinary lives were caught up in extraordinary events. Marshall found himself representing a young artist studying under Stanhope Forbes in Newlyn, Cornwall charged with signalling to the enemy with a flashlight from his studio; Sir Joseph Jones, a former Lord Mayor of Sheffield, charged under the Official Secrets Act with communicating prohibited information to Germany, the country of his birth; an unwitting girl who had strayed into a prohibited area in search of her lover; and many other offences new to him and to the law.

Amongst the influential contacts that Marshall had made through his connection with the Carnarvons was a clutch of names that in the next few years were going to be some of the most prominent players in the war. Principal amongst them were Lord Kitchener, a close friend of the Carnarvons and now appointed Secretary of State for War; General Sir John Maxwell, who was soon to play a leading role on the western front and then to command British troops in Egypt; and General Sir John Cowans, who was Quartermaster General, responsible for the provisioning of Kitchener's newly enlisted army. Marshall attended a house party at Highclere Castle with Maxwell and Cowans two weeks before war was declared. The main topic of conversation was inevitable and a few days later, on 1 August 1914, Lady Carnarvon's reputed father Alfred de Rothschild wrote his now famous personal letter to the Kaiser begging him to cease hostilities. It was to no avail. The Kaiser, unmoved, responded by invading Belgium and war was declared.

Lord Kitchener needed a million men for the army. Marshall, now fifty-six and to his regret too old to fight, possessed other talents and qualities instantly recognised by the authorities as invaluable to the war effort. People loved him; and more to the point they could not resist him. All over the country he dominated the so-called patriots' demonstrations, staged to drum up recruitment. He spoke on these non-political platforms not, as he told the crowds, in a horsehair wig and silk gown holding a brief for some client, but as a member of a great empire in the gravest hour of its history determined to do his little bit. It was, he believed, a fight on behalf of the defenceless, a cause for which in a legal context he had long pledged his support. Now he fought the fight for the safety of the country he loved. With all the old familiar tricks of his oratory, his inimitable and singular mix of exhortation and appeal and his hypnotic rhythms, he whipped the cheering crowds to a frenzy of patriotism: 'To you young men who have wives and children, mothers and sisters, friends and homes you hold dear ... for the honour of your country you will come forward in your thousands ...'.[1] And come forward they did.

Throughout the first year of war Marshall continued in the same vein all over the country, inciting all those young men who were over five feet six inches tall and with a chest measurement of over thirty-five inches to come forward and fight for freedom and 'the defence of the defenceless in this abominable war, an unprovoked war, a scandalous war but nonetheless a war to the bitter end'. But he was not merely a demagogue. In May 1915 he stood on a platform with Sir Robert Baden-Powell. It was the month after the second battle of Ypres, in which thousands of British troops had lost their lives and the Germans had used gas for the first time. Baden-Powell's message was still resolutely upbeat: 'There is a tremendous pleasurable excitement under fire. You are in a funk the first time or two but after that there is ... a joy about it like laughing gas or champagne.'[2] Marshall's sobriety on this occasion, however, was in marked contrast: ever the psychologist, he lingered now on the inevitability of conscription (which ultimately occurred in January 1916); most men preferred to jump before they were pushed.

Professionally, meanwhile, there was a proliferation of new kinds of work: prosecutions of myriad offences created by the Defence of the Realm Act, applications for exemptions from military service, civil actions arising out of the rights and duties of enemy aliens in time of war. The older generation of barristers left behind took on the work of their younger colleagues at the front and the practice grew of splitting the brief fees with the family of the absent barrister. Some observed this custom more conscientiously than others; Marshall, always a generous benefactor whether he could afford it or not, went a step further and refused to accept any proportion of the fee when he undertook the work on behalf of a serving officer. As the war progressed, in what was described in the press as a fine example, he sold part of his beloved collection, a valuable set of prints of London, and invested the substantial proceeds in war bonds.

On a personal level, the whole issue of war with Germany invoked in Marshall a curious ambivalence, his family connections both a qualification and an embarrassment. Frequent visits to Germany to visit his in-laws had given him considerable insight into the German people and their politics. He had predicted a terrible war publicly as early as 1905. He was not the only one of course who watched with growing unease the tensions in Germany, the openly expressed dislike of the English in German newspapers, the rapidly growing population and consequent covetous eye on British colonies, the massive investment in army and navy and the bellicosity of the Kaiser; but he was one of the earliest warning voices on Unionist platforms in his constituency and in letters to *The Times*. When war broke out, acknowledgement of the percipience of his warnings was overshadowed by the fact of his German wife. As the war progressed there was increasing animosity towards people with German connections and Marshall, paradoxically, was amongst those who expressed their feelings most vociferously. On public platforms and in letters to the newspapers he warned frequently of the threat posed by German spies, calling for all enemy aliens to be required to produce sureties from English householders or face internment or instant deportation.

It must have been very hard for Hetty; as it was, within days of the declaration of war she was required to comply with the requirements of the Aliens Act: to report herself to the police station, relinquish all forms of transport including her bicycle and submit to having her telephone cut off. To Hetty, now more English than the English in her tastes and way of life, it must have seemed a slap in the face. Marshall was a kind man and a sensitive one; it is difficult to explain his conduct on this issue. Either his vehemence was an overcompensation in response to any reflection his marriage might be seen to have on his fervent patriotism, or he had persuaded himself that Hetty's German heritage was, after eighteen years of marriage, expunged. 'My wife happens to be German,' he had said on introducing poor Hetty to his East Toxteth constituents, '[but] I have taken a good deal of the German nature and tried to turn it into English.'[3] The context makes it clear this was a joke, but it is unlikely that it was one Hetty appreciated. Her feeling of rejection by her adopted country was now reflected in the personal alienation she felt in her marriage. And she knew about Louisa Miéville too, if not her identity certainly her existence in Marshall's life. But she was not the sort of wife to make scenes, nor did she wish to upset the status quo. Security and status mattered to Hetty.

At least, however, she was now living in the same place as Marshall; Felder Lodge had lost its peace, shaken to its foundations by a battery of anti-aircraft guns a few fields away, and the family was centred in a new flat in Harley House on Marylebone Road. Elna, now seventeen, was summoned home from her finishing school in Paris, whereupon she defied her father by training as a nurse and tending the wounded officers in the private hospital run by Lady Violet Brassey from her own home in Upper Grosvenor Street.

The casualties were rolling in. Distraught judges with dead sons struggled to perform their professional duties. In the Temple Church it seemed that there were almost constant memorial services and weekday organ recitals were introduced to comfort the bereaved. Marshall to his everlasting grief lost his barrister nephew Max Labouchere, Ada's son, who had been a member of 3 Temple Gardens.

Everywhere, in these grim times, there was a demand for diversion. As president of the Playgoers Club, Marshall deplored a movement to close the theatres for the duration of the war; there was nothing so important as cheering people up, he insisted, and proved it by stage-managing wildly successful tea parties for wounded soldiers in Inner Temple Hall, enlisting the aid of his famous theatrical friends to provide the entertainment.

The professional theatres were also providing to the khaki-clad audiences home on leave the desperately needed distraction from thoughts of what they must return to. *The Bing Boys Are Here* at the Alhambra, *The Maid of the Mountains* at Daly's, and *Chu Chin Chow* at Her Majesty's all played to packed houses. But light entertainment was not confined to the theatre; Marshall was providing it in court in the form of a murder trial so gothic as to be almost farcical with a title which would have looked just as suitable up in lights: 'The Brides in the Bath'.

Enter centre stage George Joseph Smith,[4] with a luxuriant moustache just made for twirling, enough charm of manner to make him a magnificent eight-times bigamist and an avaricious evil which eventually made him a serial murderer. To a public hungry for sensation far removed from the reality of the trenches he was manna from heaven.

The extraordinary story of Smith and his brides Bessie, Alice and Margaret got as much coverage in the newspapers as the first Zeppelin raids on the east coast with which the discovery of his murders happened to coincide. All three women, plain, virtuous and close to being on the shelf, came from loving families. Each could hardly believe her luck when she unexpectedly met an eligible man. After whirlwind courtships Bessie married Henry Williams in Weymouth in August 1910, Alice married George Joseph Smith in Southsea in November 1913, and Margaret married John Lloyd in Bath in December 1914. The only problem was that they had each married the same (already married) man. All were induced to take out life insurance and make wills. All the marriages ended in their identical deaths in identical circumstances in strikingly similar baths. No connection between them would ever have been made had it not been for the vigilance of Alice's grieving brother, who happened to see a newspaper account of Margaret's death in the *News of the World* ('Bride's tragic fate on day after wedding') and thought it was rather a coincidence that two healthy young women had been discovered dead in the bath by their newly acquired husband. He contacted the police; publicity resulted in the discovery of a third such death and so one of the most famous cases of the century got off the ground.

Despite inheritances from his dead brides Smith was penniless. The trial was one of enormous expense; there were an unprecedented 130 witnesses interviewed from forty different towns. There were 264 trial exhibits and furthermore there were highly complex issues of law and medicine to be argued. It is unsurprising that Marshall baulked at the fee, the paltry sum of three pounds, five shillings and sixpence (the equivalent of £300 today), to be divided between counsel and solicitor, as provided by the state for representation in capital cases. Smith's solicitor, a careful man of a very different calibre from the chancer Arthur Newton, devised a meticulously drafted scheme whereby Smith would write his life story for a newspaper and assign the copyright in return for funds for his defence. The business-like arrangement had neither the opportunism nor the ethical dubiety of Newton's Crippen proposal; but just to make sure, the solicitor sought an independent opinion as to its legality and propriety from a barrister, who also drafted the terms.

On the strength of these anticipated funds Marshall and two juniors were instructed for substantial fees. Smith, by now in custody, could only sign the contract with the permission of the Home Secretary. The Home Secretary, Sir John Simon, not only refused his permission but expressed the view that the arrangement was contrary to public interest and morals and that the question was academic since no honourable member of the Bar would agree to accept fees supplementary to those available under the fund provided by Parliament for the purpose.

Marshall was enraged on so many counts he scarcely knew where to begin. No respecter of office, he set out his views in a blistering response, castigating a system in which the Treasury and the public prosecutor arrayed all their resources against a man whose life was at stake and then characterised as immoral his attempt to raise funds to defend himself. The Home Secretary remained unmoved by Marshall's concern and apparently impervious to the impossible professional position into which he had put him. Marshall was already committed to defending Smith in a huge trial due to start in a few days. And so, with the good grace characteristic of him, he put aside his own position, and George Joseph Smith in what might be regarded as the greatest achievement of his manipulative career obtained for a paltry few pounds the services of the most famous KC of his day. Even in the eventual Court of Appeal hearing at which he argued a point of law of great importance, Marshall appeared for just seventeen guineas, ten paid by the Director of Public Prosecutions and seven by Kent County Council. He was then commanding fees in the hundreds.

Smith was charged with one murder, that of Bessie Mundy, the first bride. It is a basic legal principle rooted in the presumption of innocence that a defendant is required to face only that evidence which proves the case against him. The jury is not permitted to hear of previous offences or instances of bad character or reputation which do not add to that evidence and are therefore purely prejudicial. This basic rule, however, was subject to a number of exceptions. One of those exceptions was ultimately responsible for putting a noose round Smith's neck.

The trial was to be heard at the Old Bailey in June 1915 by Mr Justice Scrutton, a most distinguished commercial lawyer and the author of an enormously learned book, *The Contract of Affreightment as Expressed in Charterparties and Bills of Lading*. *Scrutton on Charterparties* was and is extremely famous but no criminal lawyer such as Marshall would ever have had any use for it other than as a wedge under a broken desk leg. Scrutton was very clever, but described as bearded and uncouth with a complete lack of interest in bodily comfort, and a preference for hard chairs and dry biscuits.[5] It was quickly apparent that, unlike Marshall, what Mr Justice Scrutton knew about passion could be written on a postage stamp.

Archibald Bodkin, a friend and contemporary of Marshall and soon to be appointed Director of Public Prosecutions, had been instructed to prosecute. Opening the case, Bodkin told the jury the sad story of Bessie's death. It did not take long. Smith was a married man when he met thirty-three-year-old Bessie, he told them. He had had several long absences from his home, his excuse being that he needed to travel around the country in order to buy and sell the second-hand goods from which he made their living. Bessie was the daughter of a bank manager. Her father had died leaving her a significant inheritance in the form of stocks and shares, and having no one but a married brother she lived, rather pathetically, as a paying guest in a boarding house in Bristol. Unsophisticated with money, she had willingly agreed to settle her inheritance on her brother and an uncle, who arranged to pay her an income. She could not by the terms of the settlement dispose of the capital during her lifetime but could do so by her will.

Smith, calling himself Henry Williams, had met Bessie by chance in August 1910 and in less than three weeks had gone through a ceremony of marriage with her, having first got hold of a copy of her father's will and satisfied himself as to her financial position. Smith calculated that the allowance Bessie received was not as much as the interest from the sureties held by her brother and with Bessie's agreement instructed solicitors to extract the balance, which they duly did and handed it over to him. Then in September Smith and the money disappeared. He left a note for Bessie involving, Bodkin told the jury, the unimaginably grossest insults a man could offer a woman. He was going to leave it at that, but the judge, who perhaps really did find it unimaginable, insisted the letter should be read to the court. In it, Smith accused poor plain respectable Bessie of infecting him with venereal disease, thus he said, blighting all his hopes of a happy future.

Bessie moved to Weston-super-Mare and for the next eighteen months resumed her old lifestyle as a paying guest. In March 1912 she met Smith, now penniless again, apparently by chance in the street. Smith was later said to exude sexual magnetism and he must have had something because Bessie forgave him then and there and went with him to a solicitor's office with a request that her brother be informed of their reconciliation. The couple moved to Herne Bay in Kent, to lodgings without a separate bathroom, but shortly after they moved in, Smith bought a bath from an ironmonger. Within a short space of time the couple had made two significant visits. The first was to a solicitor's office, where Smith and Bessie made mutual wills in each other's favour. The second was to a local doctor, Dr French. Here Smith, the anxious husband, told the doctor that his wife had suffered a fit. Bessie did not remember anything after complaining of a severe headache, but the doctor was convinced by the graphic descriptions provided by her husband and prescribed sedatives of a type used in the treatment of epilepsy.

Two or three days later Dr French was called out to see Bessie again; she had had another fit, Smith said. Again Bessie could recall nothing and the doctor prescribed further medication. That night Bessie wrote to her family, saying she had suffered bad fits and emphasising the kindness of her husband.

The next day, 13 July, at eight o'clock in the morning Dr French received a note: 'Come at once I am afraid my wife is dead.' She was. When the doctor arrived she was lying on her back in her new bath, her face and torso submerged in a few inches of water and her feet resting on the bath edge. In her hand she clutched a piece of soap. There was no sign of a struggle, she had no injuries and no one else in the house had heard a thing. She had had a fit in the bath, the doctor said. He did not regard the circumstances as at all suspicious and he did not perform a post mortem. At the inquest, the coroner's jury concluded that the death was by misadventure.

It was not a pretty story, but Marshall was reasonably confident of an acquittal. The financial background might be unattractive, but he was after all used to unattractive defences and defendants. An experienced doctor had been satisfied there was no foul play, as had a coroner's jury. The body, so long buried, could tell no tales. There was no evidence directly linking Smith by any physical act to the death.

Sitting on prosecution counsel's table, however, were two ticking time bombs: papers containing all the evidence relating to two other wives who died in baths. Archibald Bodkin was arguing that as an exception to the usual rules, this evidence should be put before the jury because it was so similar in nature as to amount to what is known as a 'system', that is a course of conduct which transforms a defence of accident, which might be credible in an isolated incident, to one so unlikely as to be incredible. The law was less developed on the topic a century ago than it is now and its applicability to Smith's case was a highly technical point. The bewildered jury, settling back to hear the first witness at what they thought was the end of the prosecution's opening speech, were instead ordered out of court so that the law could be argued.

Technical it might be, but Smith's life was likely to rest on the decision. Mr Justice Scrutton was now in his academic element, and Marshall, despite his reputation as a poor lawyer, dealt with the point with skill and conviction. The so-called similar fact rule did not apply, he argued, in circumstances such as these when there was not so much as a prima facie case against the defendant in respect of the primary crime with which he was charged. But Mr Justice Scrutton ruled against him (as did the Court of Appeal when this ruling was later the subject of an appeal).

On that blazing hot day, the jury filed back in, many of them clutching straw hats in their hands, to be regaled with the whole amazing tale. They were not to use the evidence relating to the two further deaths as evidence that Smith was a man of bad character and therefore likely to have committed murder, the judge scrupulously directed them, but only to help them to decide whether Bessie's death was accidental. Such a direction was as unintelligible to the jury as it was unassailable in its intellectual purity. As far as the jury was concerned, from that moment on Smith was Bluebeard under another name.

The trial descended into something close to farce, the courtroom filled with baths borne in by burly detectives, and the public gallery with women ('morbid neurotic sensation lovers' according to the *Daily Dispatch*[6]) who came to experience Smith's rumoured sexual magnetism at first hand. Registrars to prove marriages, solicitors and bank managers to prove legal and financial transactions, ironmongers to prove purchases of baths, doctors and undertakers to prove illnesses and deaths, gossipy landladies and grieving relatives were called in their dozens. The deaths of Alice and Margaret were revealed in all their gothic horror, Marshall on his client's instructions maintaining that all three deaths has been accidents.

Alice had been nurse to an invalid in Southsea. She too had money of her own, controlled at her request by her family. She met Smith at Sunday evening service a few months after Bessie's death and he bowled her quite off her feet. They were married within weeks and her money was extracted from her father by her new husband. With his help she made her will. They moved to Blackpool; Smith rejected the first lodgings they looked at because there was no bath. They found more satisfactory rooms with a very nice bath. They visited a doctor. Alice wrote to her family; she was sick with headaches, she said, but she had 'the best husband in the world'. Days later the landlady of the lodgings, having tea in her kitchen, was alarmed to see water trickling through the ceiling and to hear Smith calling her to send for a doctor. Alice was found dead in the bath, her sorrowing husband supporting her head above water. The verdict at the inquest had been accidental death from a fit in the bath. It was now December 1913.

Margaret was the daughter of a clergyman. She worked as a companion but at the outbreak of war returned home to Bristol to live with her mother and sister. Now thirty-seven, her future was depressingly mapped out. No one knows how Smith, now calling himself John Lloyd, picked her up. All her family knew was that she had made a number of visits to a local solicitor to arrange life insurance and then one day went out and failed to return for tea. She had run away to marry a man they had never met. On their wedding night the couple had found lodgings in Highgate with use of a bathroom with a nice bath. The same evening they visited a local doctor; Margaret had a bad headache, 'Mr Lloyd' said, and Margaret concurred. The doctor found she had a slight temperature and diagnosed flu. Unlike those of her predecessors her marriage lasted only until the next day. That day she visited a solicitor and made a will leaving everything to Smith. She wrote a letter to her family telling them of her marriage 'to a thoroughly Christian man' and then she went to have a bath. Downstairs the landlady heard the sound of 'Mr Lloyd' playing the harmonium. She recognised the tune. It was 'Nearer, my God, to Thee'. Margaret was still in the bathroom. The landlady heard Smith calling to his wife and then for help. She went upstairs and found him lifting the dead Margaret from the bath. The doctor was called. He conducted a post mortem and concluded that the effect of flu and a hot bath had caused her to faint and drown. The coroner's jury returned a verdict of accidental death due to drowning.

What intrigued press and public was not whether Smith had committed the crimes but how he had done so given the size of the brides and the size of the baths. The baths were of the usual type of the time: free standing, steeply sloping at one end and tapering at the other and, relative to the modern bath, short and narrow. Two of the brides were far from small: Bessie was five feet eight inches tall and Alice was unchivalrously described as very short but very fat. Only Margaret was of a slighter build. None of them had marks consistent with being knocked out or any kind of struggle. Bernard Spilsbury, called by the Crown, gave evidence of the unremarkable state of the exhumed bodies. In a series of questions and answers, during the course of which it was apparent that Marshall had rather more experience of women's conduct in baths than did the judge, Spilsbury rejected all theories that anyone collapsing or fainting in these baths would have gone under water so that their heads were submerged. With regard to their capacity to struggle, he said significantly, only in cases of very sudden submersion would consciousness immediately be lost.

This dovetailed neatly into the prosecution case. Back at the police station Inspector Neil of Scotland Yard had solemnly conducted his own experiments with a policewoman in a bathing dress, very nearly drowning her in the process and coming to the conclusion that Smith had grabbed his brides' ankles suddenly and pulled their heads under water. The judge invited the jury to get into the exhibited baths (minus the water) and try it for themselves when they retired to consider their verdict.

There were undoubtedly matters inconsistent with the theory and Marshall made the most of them: Bessie's tight grip on the soap for instance would generally be expected to slacken when she lost consciousness and then there was the problematic issue of whether a victim grabbed by the ankles would have time to struggle or get their arms over the side of the bath. All over England people had hypotheses: the brides had been killed first by unspecified and undetectable violence; they had been gassed; they had been poisoned; they had been hypnotised. (Marshall after the trial favoured the last of these.) The new breed of so-called psychologists of sex had a field day with their theories of depraved men who exercised irresistible fascination over demure women; it was said that Smith's brides had died because they found his demands literally irresistible and in increasingly lurid language poor Bessie and Alice and Margaret, who had just wanted nice husbands, preferably one each, were described as middle-class women from quiet houses and country vicarages who had 'worshipped Priapus'.[7]

Marshall's closing speech on Smith's behalf was poetic if, unusually for him, lacking in conviction. The exception was a passage that was quoted everywhere as a fine morale booster at a time when the country needed it, tapping in as always to the zeitgeist and the preoccupations of his jury:

> At a moment like the present when the flower of our youth are laying down their lives for their country, does it not strike you as a great tribute to the national character that with all the panoply of pomp and law we have been assembled day after day to enquire into the facts of this sordid case and to decide whether one man should go to an ignominious death or not? It is a great tribute to our national system of jurisprudence.

Despite this much-quoted sentiment he lost. Of course he lost. Three brides dead in baths was just too much for any jury. An appeal to the Court of Criminal Appeal was inevitably unsuccessful and Smith hanged after refusing the customary glass of brandy[8] and the opportunity to confess to the Bishop of Croydon.

From the point of view of public exposure, sensation, numbers of corpses and scale, Smith's trial was going to be a hard act for Marshall to follow. The exhausting prospect of a relentless diet of capital cases was not an appealing one. The press had been hopefully predicting for years his imminent elevation to the bench and in 1917 when a vacancy arose, he was widely predicted to step into it. But whatever public opinion might be, Marshall was anxious. Deep but unforgotten in his past lay the scandal of Ethel's death; not so deep were the confrontations with judges and the making of powerful enemies. Everyone remembered his fall from grace in the early 1900s and the savage criticism of the Court of Appeal. Lord Justice Mathew was dead now but the legacy of his animosity lived on in some quarters. Always one to grasp the nettle, Marshall wrote to Lord Edmund Talbot, government chief whip,[9] harking back to the Chattell libel case which had been the cause of his downfall in 1901. Mathew's attack had been widely felt to be utterly unjustified, he wrote, and deprived of an action for slander since the attack had been made in court by Mathew in his judicial capacity, he had at the time decided to resign his parliamentary seat and challenge Mathew to prove the allegations of professional impropriety at a by-election. He had been dissuaded from taking this course by the party whips of the time and, significantly, by Robert Finlay, then Attorney General, who feared for the safety of the Southport seat. So Marshall had remained under an unjust stigma from which, with no support, he had ultimately extricated himself.

The message in the letter was clear: at the time, whether expressly or by implication, the reward he had been promised for party loyalty had been judicial appointment at the appropriate moment. That moment had come. He was at the top of his tree and Finlay was now Lord Chancellor. In consultation with the Prime Minister, judicial appointment lay within Finlay's gift.

It seems curious to the modern eye, this bartering of party loyalty for a seat on the Bench. At least since the 1701 Act of Settlement, there has been some concept of the separation of the powers of the executive, the legislature and the judiciary and of the desirability of the independence of the last. In practice, however, there had been varying degrees of politicisation of the judiciary over the centuries and Marshall's early career coincided with the period dominated by Lord Salisbury as Prime Minister and Lord Halsbury as Lord Chancellor, both committed to Salisbury's openly expressed view that 'within certain limits of intelligence, honesty and knowledge of the law, one man would make as good a judge as another and a Tory mentality was ipso facto more trustworthy than a Liberal one'.[10] It was in that climate that Marshall's 'bargain' had been struck. With the Liberal landslide in 1906 came a regime more committed to the depoliticisation of the judiciary. The Lord Chancellors thereafter (Loreburn, Haldane, Buckmaster and Finlay) were committed in theory to appointment on the basis of success at the Bar to the exclusion of party affiliation. But this new-found purity does not seem to have extended to Marshall. If the criterion was success in his profession then Marshall fulfilled it. He was one of the highest-paid and highest-profile members of the Bar. If he was not an intellectual heavyweight the same could be said for many King's Bench judges. He was clever enough when he applied himself and he was a man of kindness and integrity. He had proved his worth in the previous year since his honorary appointment as part-time Recorder of Guildford, dispensing justice with firmness and sensitivity, personally finding employment along the way for the many to whom he gave a 'chance'.

But in 1917, contrary to all expectations and until now unaccountably, Arthur Clavell Salter was appointed to the High Court vacancy. It was the richest of ironies. Salter had been called to the Bar two years after Marshall, unusually in those days without a public school and Oxbridge education.[11] With no professional or social connections he struggled in his early years. Marshall with his characteristic all-inclusive friendliness had befriended him, obtained him his first brief, found him permanent chambers, given him devilling work and proposed him for membership of the Garrick Club. Salter had prospered, taken silk in 1904, six years after Marshall, and become

Conservative MP for Basingstoke in the 1906 election. He proved to be an energetic if not particularly inspired politician, a constant attender in the House of Commons and a dogged debater on wide-ranging topics. He remained in his seat for eleven years until his appointment to the Bench.

The reason for his appointment is to be found in in a casual handwritten personal letter lurking in a huge pile of official documents in the Parliamentary Archives. Lord Edmund Talbot, on holiday in Normandy, wrote to Andrew Bonar Law, at that time Conservative Party leader. Amidst chatty personal details ('I am going on to Switzerland to see my boy') and political gossip is the following passage: 'George Younger [party chairman] … said you were inclined to favour Salter. I presume his name will go forward. I have had a letter from Marshall Hall wanting the judgeship. I have replied that … so far as work inside the House had to be considered I had felt bound to bring Salter's name before you – I had reason to think the Lord Chancellor had been approached on his behalf.'[12] It had been, in the end, Salter's political commitment that had prevailed over Marshall's far greater claims.

It was a terrible slap in the face for Marshall and emphasised the ever-widening gulf between the adulation of the public and the disapproval of the establishment which dogged his career. He took the blow with characteristic generosity: 'Salter is a splendid chap and a great friend of mine of thirty years standing. I think he will tell you he owes much to me in the early days,'[13] he wrote wistfully in response to Talbot.

He never recovered from the disappointment. Five years later in 1922 the post of Recorder of London, the senior judge at the Old Bailey, became vacant. This ancient office, appointed on the recommendation of the City of London Corporation, would have suited Marshall's talents and he duly applied. On hearing that the second most senior judge (the Common Serjeant), Sir Henry Dickens,[14] yearned for the post, with a characteristically chivalrous flourish Marshall stood down; Dickens was seventy-three and it was his last chance. When, unexpectedly, Sir Ernest Wild KC was instead appointed, it confirmed Marshall's increasing contempt for the establishment.

The knighthood conferred on him in 1917 was little consolation; Marshall had never coveted honours for their own sake. But it gave Hetty great pleasure, compensating for the difficulties in her German heritage and validating her position in English society. She did not want to be one of the many Lady Halls and so Marshall at last regularised the position by changing his name by deed poll to Marshall Hall.[15]

In 1919 the Kent house was sold and Overbrook, a huge modern house in the then fashionable Tudor style, was bought. Situated in Brook in Surrey, conveniently close to Guildford where Marshall continued as Recorder, it was a house which stood for success. Still standing, it is now split into two large family homes. In three acres of gardens, with garaging for three cars, a vast music room and a library, it housed a substantial staff, the new Lady Marshall Hall, Elna, brought home from London simmering with resentment to be her mother's companion, and Marshall's now priceless collection of Chinese porcelain miniatures, snuff boxes and silver. Marshall kept his two worlds resolutely apart. His wife and daughter were strongly discouraged from going to hear him in court.

Hetty and Elna led a country life caring for Marshall's beloved dogs, attending race meetings and participating in village activities whilst over the next few years, based primarily in London, Marshall wallowed in the unfathomable motives, terrifying psychology and gory brutality of some of the worst crimes of the century.

CHAPTER 14

'It's a shame!'

C rime has always been a social barometer. Witches, highwaymen, counterfeiters, smugglers and poisoners all committed crimes that were the product of their time in history. The aftermath of the First World War brought the return of men hardened to death by the horrors they had witnessed. There was an increase in women snatching anxiously at their now significantly reduced chances of marriage and later regretting their haste. Men came back from hell to humdrum lives they found hard to comprehend as well as to wives who had almost forgotten them and defiant sons who scarcely knew them. All over the country there was easy access to service revolvers that had not been handed into the authorities when hostilities ceased. Combined with the restless gaiety and relaxed moral standards of the twenties, it was a dangerous cocktail and violent crime inevitably resulted.

The ensuing trials brought with them new problems. Juries faced with delivering verdicts on ex-soldiers who had served their country with loyalty and sometimes distinction were reluctant to convict. When they did, judges in all cases but murder, when the death sentence was mandatory, sentenced with noticeable leniency despite strictures from the Court of Appeal that war service, however brave, was no more a mitigating factor than anything else, and certainly not an excuse. Counsel, Marshall in the forefront, were not above exploiting these sensibilities for all they were worth. Marshall described one defendant as 'this grand old soldier with the sands of time fast running out standing in that dock with his head bowed with all his great services to his country to look back upon'. The speech led to one of his best results.[1]

The public unease with the whole law of homicide and the mandatory death sentence for murder, which permitted no concept of degrees of culpability, was not new; but now the particular characteristics of post-war crime made society respond more sympathetically to those who sought reform. Marshall, jumping on the bandwagon, was prominent in the press in his criticisms. The result of the law as it then stood, he told journalists, was that juries were reluctant to convict of murder in cases where no sane man would think the death penalty should be inflicted. Equally, the rigidity of the law relating to provocation was such that they could not return a verdict of manslaughter either, since matters the man in the street would regard as sufficient provocation to reduce murder to manslaughter were not in law regarded as such.[2]

But above all else Marshall, with his now huge experience of passion and suffering, chafed against the rigidity of the laws governing insanity and crime, and here too the war had had its effect on public opinion. In many homicides there were palpable undercurrents of mental illness of a sort now more readily understood although unrecognised by the law. An ill-defined psychological injury termed 'shell shock' was now acknowledged by doctors but its permitted manifestations were narrow and regarded even by some of them as indistinguishable from cowardice. The more sophisticated had begun to discern something more. A syndrome was now being observed: some of these young men had come home apparently normal and resumed their civilian lives. Guns and uniforms were set aside, pre-war or new occupations taken up and after rest and nourishment they seemed to their families to be much the same. But then they began to oscillate between high excitement and deep gloom, seeking restless stimulation one week and complete solitude the next. When faced with reverses, they lost their emotional balance. Even minor arguments and small disappointments led to a passionate loss of self-control, to violent frightening rage and in some cases, inevitably, to terrible crime.

Deep in Marshall's formative memories was the frantic, repressed figure of Christiana Edmunds, the Brighton chocolate poisoner of his boyhood, whose crimes in all their insanity or evil had divided the nation. He had grappled ever since with depicting before juries the one thing the law had always said did not have to be proved: motive. Were apparently motiveless crimes always suggestive of insanity? Were crimes disproportionate to motive the product of some nameless uncontrollable impulse which the law failed to recognise?

Since the seventeenth century there had existed a basic legal principle that no crime could be committed without intent of wrongdoing and that a person of unsound mind could not be responsible in law and should not be executed; unable to repent, he would be sent to God in an unfit state. Over the centuries the law had developed piecemeal in relation to the practical application of those beliefs. In 1843, forty years before Marshall had been called to the Bar, an attempt had been made to formalise the position with the establishment of the M'Naghten rules.

Daniel M'Naghten, attempting to shoot the then Prime Minister Robert Peel, instead shot dead the Prime Minister's private secretary. In the face of what seemed to the judge to be his obvious insanity the trial was stopped and M'Naghten sent to Bethlem. Subsequently, in view of the uncertainty of the law, a panel of judges at the request of Parliament set a series of hypothetical questions to be answered in future cases to test a defence of insanity.

The rules they formulated had started from the premise that the defendant is sane, the onus then being on the defendant to prove his insanity. He had to prove that at the time of committing the act he was labouring under such a defect of reason from disease of the mind as not to know the nature and quality of the act he was doing or, if he did know it, that he did not know that what he was doing was wrong. The strict interpretation of those rules had prevented the law of insanity keeping pace with the progress of medical knowledge or with the development of the conscience and compassion of a more enlightened age. In Marshall's day disease of the mind was interpreted strictly; transient passion, anguish and depression were not enough. Even if a defendant were able to overcome that hurdle the remainder of the rule was often insuperable. Ignorance of the nature of the act was originally intended to cover the acts of those completely frenzied, reduced by illness to animal instincts; but knowledge of wrongdoing was held by the judges to mean legal and not moral wrongdoing. Thus any man who having committed an atrocity hid or ran away on seeing a policeman or indeed did anything to hide his tracks disqualified himself from an insanity defence.

These rigid rules were rooted in the then current (and long-standing) concept that all mental illness arose from disease of the brain, usually accompanied by distinctive facial and cerebral appearances. Experience of 'madness' in the days when there were no sedative drugs frequently involved exhibitions of the most florid behaviour when the sufferer went berserk, a word in itself coined in 1896.[3] Concepts of madness were confused with those of 'simple-mindedness' and 'mental defects' and all were heavily overlaid with those of morality and religious belief. The result was a soup of theories which when applied by the medical profession resulted in treatments of widely varying degrees of enlightenment and compassion. The legal profession, however, was concerned only with the determination of legal responsibility; certainty of definition was paramount and the M'Naghten rules strictly applied, regardless of the increasing sophistication of medical thinking.

Over the ensuing years the terrible results of this outdated perception of mental illness became increasingly apparent and the more enlightened of the medical profession were loud in their condemnation. By the 1920s the M'Naghten rules embodied the medical knowledge of eighty years previously, it was said, and were in flat opposition to present teaching, which discounted the theory that criminal responsibility entailed knowledge of wrongdoing. A man could be well aware that what he did was wrong and be nonetheless incapable of resisting the impulse to commit and this concept of annihilation of willpower should be embodied in the criminal law. Other jurisdictions were far more enlightened; as early as 1911 a committee of the New York Bar Association had condemned the English test as formulated by judges ignorant of psychology and European criminal codes were laying stress on the free determination of will as the prerequisite for criminal responsibility. For years Marshall had grappled with the hopeless rigidity of the English legal system and now he saw an opportunity for reform.

For no one was the debate more important than for Eric Holt,[4] who had been called up from the Territorial Army at the very outset of the war in 1914, had served in the trenches in France and had taken part in the ghastly battle at Festubert, when the British launched an attack on the German positions and advanced barely half a mile into enemy lines at a cost of 16,000 men. By the time he was invalided out in 1916 with the then popular label of neurasthenia, a psychopathological diagnosis covering fatigue, anxiety, neuralgia and depression, there was not much Lieutenant Holt did not know about death. Returning home to Lancashire he threw himself into a frantic social life, met and fell in love with a young and pretty girl, Kitty Breaks, wrote her poetic and passionate letters, became her lover and shot her dead on Christmas Eve 1919.

Kitty's body was found lying in the sand dunes at St Annes near Blackpool. An attempt at comfort had been made: stones piled to form a pillow behind her head and her muff tucked over her feet as though to warm them. Holt's gloves and service revolver were found nearby and his shoes exactly fitted the footprints leading away from the body. Holt was arrested and charged with murder. The Attorney General, Sir Gordon Hewart, was briefed for the prosecution, his presence indicating the immense public importance of the issues at stake, and Marshall appeared for the defence.

Holt, awaiting trial in Strangeways prison, turned rapidly from a charming if rather excitable young officer into a gibbering wreck of a man exhibiting signs of delusional paranoia, asserting that his cell was infested by police dogs sent to attack him and by flies infected with fever germs infiltrating through the grating. Marshall threw himself into an analysis of all the existing case law on insanity and murder. Nowadays the choice between a diagnosis of insanity and consequent indeterminate incarceration in a hospital such as Broadmoor and a conviction for murder and a specified period in prison may not seem to be clear cut. But in 1920, it was mad or dead. Technically it was the accused's choice. But Holt seemed now incapable of making it.

Marshall had a consultation with Holt the day before the trial was due to start. He found it impossible to take any instructions and was driven, after an evening of agonising, to knock on Sir Gordon Hewart's hotel bedroom door at eleven o'clock at night, to inform him that he proposed to take the most extreme position of all in a criminal trial in which insanity is at issue, namely that his client was unfit to plead to the offence at all. In other words the accused was so mad he could not even be said to have the capacity to say if he was guilty or not. That issue had to be determined before the issue of whether insanity was a defence to the crime even arose. Special provisions applied to these rare cases. A jury was empanelled to consider the question of fitness to plead and if they determined that the defendant was fit, a fresh jury was then empanelled to hear the case and determine the question of guilt or innocence. In the ensuing trial a defendant was perfectly entitled to run a defence of insanity but the predetermination that he had been found fit to plead was plainly an unhelpful starting position for the defence.

In Holt's case two doctors were called by the defence, both experts on psychological illness, who separately interviewed Holt and pronounced him to be suffering from delusional insanity and unfit to plead. The prosecution relied on evidence from the governor of the prison, Major Burrows, and the chief warder, both of whom stoutly insisted that they could not see that there was anything wrong with him. The jury preferred this no-nonsense approach and found Holt fit to plead.

A new jury was empanelled to hear the trial. Holt with his upright bearing and military moustache did not seem very mad and pleaded not guilty clearly and firmly. The prosecution case was that Holt had shot Kitty in order to get his hands on the proceeds of a life insurance policy taken out by her a few weeks before her death. But the theory was inconsistent with all that was known about Holt. He was financially secure as the result of an inheritance and well known for his relaxed generosity. True, Kitty had made a will leaving her estate to him only a day or so before her death; but she was regulating her affairs in hope of marriage and anyway there was no evidence Holt was aware of the will. All the evidence was that they had loved one another. 'Mr Dreamer' Kitty called him in her letters to him and their lyrical correspondence, read to the court in Marshall's beautifully modulated voice, reduced not only many of the jurors but the judge to open tears. The one thing real about this Mr Dreamer, Marshall pointed out to the jury, was his passionate devotion to this woman. Poetic though the letters were, however, those written by Holt were somehow uncomfortable in their passion and possessiveness and it was on this indefinable quality that Marshall now relied.

The evidence relating to insanity was confused by the need to try and fit Holt's mental condition into the requirements of the M'Naghten rules. Holt had made a perfectly sensible statement when he was arrested and furthermore, on being approached by a doctor who had wished to examine him in prison, had expressed an eminently sane wish to consult his legal team before he agreed to it. On the other hand all the experts agreed that his subsequent delusional ramblings and strange unresponsive state were not simulated. Marshall, constrained by the insistence of desperate relatives that Holt had in fact been with them on the night of the murder, was forced to run a close to untenable combination defence of insanity (he did it but he was mad) and of alibi (he was elsewhere on the night and did not commit the crime). During the inevitable disintegration of the trial still the burning question remained, tantalisingly unanswered and undeniably tragic. Why on earth had Holt shot a girl whom he loved? As a result, Marshall said, of an impulse born of an uncontrollable passion of possessive jealousy (a letter from an unknown man was found in Kitty's belongings) acting on a mind enfeebled by shell shock and disease and resulting, after the crime, in true 'madness' within the M'Naghten rules. It was a convoluted position to take, complicated by the judge, who also tried to force the medical evidence and the facts into the confines of the rules. A confused jury convicted and Holt, vacant and silent in the dock, was sentenced to hang.

The case provided Marshall with a platform to argue the injustices arising from the law relating to insanity, his position strengthened by a letter that had arrived on the last day of the trial from a doctor who said he had treated Holt in Malaya for syphilis. An application to the Court of Criminal Appeal to subject Holt to 'surgical examination' to ascertain the extent to which he suffered from the disease, if at all, was refused. A few days later, Marshall opened the appeal against the conviction with a characteristic flourish: 'I am going to ask Your Lordships to consider the whole law of insanity,' he began. The court agreed to his request to adduce fresh evidence from the Malayan doctor as well as from other witnesses attesting to various episodes when Holt had shown odd behaviour, along with more detailed evidence than at the trial in relation to the thread of mental illness running through Holt's family.

Marshall's submissions were an exact reflection of medical understanding of the time and in complete contradiction with the legal definition of insanity. He said:

> Will is different from reason. A man may know the difference between right and wrong and appreciate the nature and quality of his acts and the consequences thereof and yet be deprived of that instructive choice between right and wrong which is characteristic of a sane person ... a man's reason may be clear, even his judgment may be clear, yet his willpower is absent or impaired ... so as to deprive [him] of the power to control his actions.

But the court was unimpressed and in unanimous judgments the M'Naghten rules were confirmed.

A public outcry followed. Marshall wrote to the solicitors representing Holt: 'I do not think the judge or the Court of Appeal could do anything. It is not a case for the lawyer but for the mental scientist and the Home Secretary in his extra-judicial capacity ... [It is] not a case of yielding to public clamour or newspaper outcry. Ministerial officials should say the law of England does not execute madmen.' He gave the solicitors leave to send the letter to the Home Secretary. But Marshall's every word was news and the letter was somehow made public and emblazoned across the papers. It had been a strongly felt view professionally expressed to another professional and Marshall must have been deeply hurt by the, for once wholly unjustified, criticism that he had jumped on the publicity bandwagon.

The Home Secretary refused a reprieve. Huge crowds gathered outside Strangeways in the rain to witness the notice of Holt's death being pinned up on the prison gates immediately after the execution. Into the silence a woman's voice rang out expressing the views of many: 'It's a shame!' she cried.

Pressure grew. Two years later in 1922, Major Ronald True stood trial for the murder of a prostitute.[5] The case, in which Marshall did not appear, had striking parallels to that of Holt. True had also served in the war, as an airman in the Royal Flying Corps, and he too had been discharged for eccentric behaviour, in his case compounded by an addiction to morphine. He was a known pathological liar and had expressed an ambition to kill. In his case too, the prosecution contended that there was a 'sane' financial motive for the crime (the victim was robbed and her belongings pawned) and, like Holt, the accused was thought to be insane by the doctors who examined him. The judge, like the judge in Holt, directed the jury as to the need to satisfy the M'Naghten rules, whilst hinting to them that he thought they were unsatisfactory and that ultimately the Home Secretary had the power to exercise the prerogative of mercy. Like the jury in Holt, True's jury also felt constrained to convict and the Court of Criminal Appeal confirmed the conviction. If the M'Naghten rules were extended, it said, the judiciary would be in a sea where there is no shore. On this occasion, however, the Home Secretary, Edward Shortt, exercised his right of reprieve and True was sent to Broadmoor. A cynical public suggested that the difference between Holt and True lay in the fact that Major True was public school educated with a titled mother. Shortt was required to justify his position to Parliament. Public disapproval was compounded by the hanging of Henry Jacoby the day before True's reprieve. Jacoby was perfectly sane; but he was an eighteen-year-old who on breaking into the hotel room of a Lady White in order to steal, panicked when she awoke and killed her. The jury's recommendation to mercy had been ignored.

Public dissatisfaction could not be ignored so easily, however, and in response to it the Lord Chancellor (by this time Lord Birkenhead) set up a committee under the chairmanship of Lord Atkin to consider what changes were desirable in criminal trials in which the plea of insanity as a defence was raised. Committee members included a stellar array of legal and political talent including the Master of the Rolls, the Solicitor General, the Director of Public Prosecutions, Sir Richard Muir, then senior prosecution counsel at the Old Bailey, and several senior Home Office officials. The inclusion of Marshall in the membership belies his reputation amongst some of being regarded as a second-rater by the legal establishment. Undistinguished as an academic lawyer he certainly was, but when it came to understanding the frailties of his fellow man, he was now universally regarded as second to none.

The Atkin committee, having considered extensive medical evidence, ultimately reported in 1923 with a number of recommendations, including the one most passionately supported by Marshall, namely that it should be recognised that a person charged with a criminal offence was not responsible where mental disease had deprived him of the power to resist; the concept of so-called irresistible impulse.

In 1923 Lord Darling introduced a Bill to implement these recommendations by adding an irresistible-impulse clause to the M'Naghten rules but the Bill failed in the Lords. The law lords objected strongly to any blurring of the standards by which mental state was to be assessed and even more strongly to what they perceived as the supremacy of medical opinion over legal principle. Some went so far as to express the view that the law was there to make people resist their impulses.

The subsequent inertia seems astonishing in the face of what was now overwhelming medical opinion. And yet over the next years Marshall appeared in case after case with mounting anger and increasingly openly expressed frustration. It was all very well for those discussing the academic questions but he felt deeply his own position, representing a series of men who had committed crimes of unimaginable violence, whom he believed to be mentally ill, and whose defences had to be shoe-horned into an artificial test unrecognised as valid by the vast majority of the medical profession.

Other murder trials followed, frequently involving ex-servicemen damaged by war who committed sudden acts of violence against members of their families; the results were becoming a lottery. The uncertainty of many of the judges' directions to juries, and the lack of transparency in relation to the Home Secretary's reprieves, injected an increasingly random quality into the outcome of murder trials in which insanity was the defence.

One of the worst instances was the case of Lock Ah Tam. Tam was born in China and had come to England as a ship's steward, ultimately settling in Birkenhead. There was a well-established Chinatown there, hundreds of Chinese seamen having settled around the docks in order to work for the commercial shipping lines then focussing on the China trade. Tam had established a successful life, over the years achieving an unusual degree of assimilation into English culture whilst retaining the respect and recognition of his own. He had married a Welsh girl, Catherine, and had a son, Lock Ling, and two daughters, Doris and Cecilia. He was employed as superintendent of Chinese sailors for three steamship companies and was an active benefactor, raising funds for the poor in his neighbourhood, founding a social club for the sailors and acting as a sort of informal magistrate, consulted in the neighbourhood disputes that occurred frequently in the rougher quarters of the docks. But in addition to being, as he was known, the father to all Chinese sailors, he had a wide circle of English friends and associates in relation to the private business affairs that made him money. He had joined the local Conservative club, went to shooting parties with friends met there, and lavishly entertained English and Chinese alike in his home.

Interceding one night in 1918 in a brawl between Russian sailors Tam was hit on the head with a billiard cue. The blow was so hard that he took two weeks to recover and when he did he was noticed to have changed. He reacted badly to modest amounts of alcohol, had furious bursts of temper and lost his previously highly developed business acumen and along with it his pride. In 1924 he invested massively and disastrously in a shipping enterprise that collapsed and led to his bankruptcy. He retained, however, the loving support of his wife and two charming and cultured daughters, then aged seventeen and twenty, and in 1925 Lock Ling returned from Canton Christian College to help his father rebuild his fortunes. As was the custom amongst the more prosperous Chinese, he had been sent to China to live with his grandparents and learn the language and culture at first hand. Lock Ling's return was a matter of celebration; his parents held a party to welcome him back and mark his coming of age. It was a happy, decorous occasion. There was singing and traditional toasts, Tam danced with his wife and no one, when the party ended at 12.45, was the worse for drink. But after everyone had gone home, Tam threw a terrible scene and threatened his wife and family. Lock Ling ran next door to the neighbours and returned to the sound of gunshots. Catherine and Cecilia were dead and Doris mortally wounded. Tam stood brandishing a gun, literally foaming at the mouth. Then after a breathless frozen moment, he turned on his heel, went into his study and calmly locked the gun away in his safe.

An incredulous Birkenhead constabulary then received a phone call. They knew Tam well; he acted as peacekeeper and if that failed assisted them in ensuring the departure to sea of the disruptive elements of the docks. 'Send your folks please. I have killed my wife and child,' he said clearly and provided his address.

Appalled and loyal Chinese communities from docklands all over England and Wales raised £1,000 for Tam's defence and Marshall was instructed to defend the impossible: a man who had undoubtedly killed his family and just as undoubtedly recognised his wrongdoing at once. Application of the M'Naghten rules would lead inexorably to a verdict of murder and the scaffold.

Marshall called medical evidence to prove that the blow on the head sustained by Tam had when combined with even a modest level of alcohol triggered an epileptic fit in the course of which the attack had taken place. Unsurprisingly the prosecution was able to find two doctors who said Tam was sane and the theory anyway medically implausible. The reality was that, as the prosecution pointed out, the real defence was the crime itself. Marshall in addressing the jury, attempted to bypass all technicalities and certainly expressed what the man in the street thought: 'I do not suppose that if you were to search the Greek tragedians you would find anything more poignant than this tragedy … he was loved by everyone, a peaceable quiet citizen, devoted to his wife and children … let us put doctors and everything else on one side for a moment. Is not the real difficulty you have to face this? How can any man who is a sane man believe that a sane man could do this thing?'

PRESS CUTTINGS FROM MARSHALL HALL'S COLLECTION

The "Brides in the Bath" Murder

George Smith, the prisoner in the dead brides case, with Bessie Mundy, one of the three women he is accused of murdering. The Black Maria, with Smith inside, is seen arriving at the Old Bailey, where the trial opened yesterday.

Photo, Farringdon Photo Co.

The bath in which Smith murdered Miss Mundy.

Ronald Vivian Light, engineer, teacher, and ex-Army officer, in the dock at Leicester Assizes. His trial for the murder of Bella Wright opened yesterday.

Portions of the famous "green bicycle" which figure in the case.

Sir Marshall Hall, K.C., M.P., who yesterday made such powerful appeal on behalf of Ronald Light.

The garden of the Greenwood's home at Kidwelly. Harold Greenwood (inset) said he used the weed-killer in spraying the garden paths at his late wife's request. Also inset, the late Mrs. Greenwood.

GREENWOOD'S ORDEAL.—Harold Greenwood, the central figure in the Welsh poison drama, shielding his face from observation with a bundle of documents on his arrival at Carmarthen Guildhall for yesterday's hearing. [*Weekly Dispatch.*

Putting down sawdust to silence traffic passing outside the court.

Jurymen making their way to the court under police escort on resumption of proceedings after adjournment.

THE FLYING DARK ROOM.—The Instone air-liner, in which "The Daily Mail" photographers developed and printed the Greenwood trial pictures, nearing the Croydon aerodrome.

Sir Edward examining plans of the scene of the tragedy, prepared for reference at the trial.

The judge's lunch being taken into the court at the interval.

GUILTY! — Jack Alfred Field (left) and William Thomas Gray, sentenced to death at Lewes yesterday for the murder of the London typist' Miss Irene Munro, on the Crumbles, Eastbourne.

TRUTH ABOUT ALI FAHMY'S LIFE REVEALED.

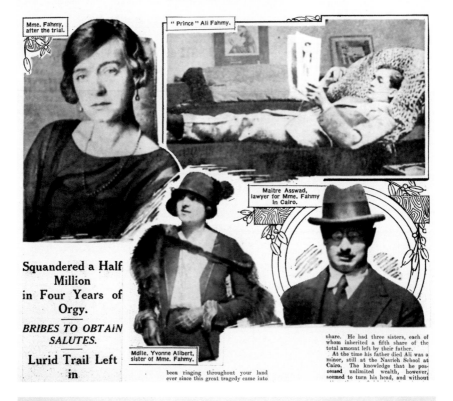

Mme. Fahmy, after the trial.

"Prince" Ali Fahmy.

Maitre Asswad, lawyer for Mme. Fahmy in Cairo.

Mdlle. Yvonne Alibert, sister of Mme. Fahmy.

Squandered a Half Million in Four Years of Orgy.

BRIBES TO OBTAIN SALUTES.

Lurid Trail Left in

been ringing throughout your land ever since this great tragedy came into

share. He had three sisters, each of whom inherited a fifth share of the total amount left by their father.

At the time his father died Ali was a minor, still at the Nasrieh School at Cairo. The knowledge that he possessed unlimited wealth, however, seemed to turn his head, and without

HOW I WAS PURSUED BY FAHMY BEY:
EXCLUSIVE STORY BY MME. FAHMY.

Mad Lover in Dazzling Motor-Cars.

I Am Offered Wealth and Life of Luxury : Trap that Lured Me to Egypt : My Installation "Like a Princess" in Palace of Splendour.

The whole passage and the last rhythmic sentence in particular were pure Marshall. But the directions as to the law were against him. The jury felt constrained to convict. Tam was sentenced to death to the sounds of sobs from those listening and the judge's voice was noticed to break. On the day of execution Catherine Tam's sister handed into the warders a flower to put on his grave and a day of Chinese mourning and fasting took place at all the major docks in England.

Whilst still oppressed by this frustration and failure Marshall took part a year later in an equally tragic trial, that of Edward Flavell, a young man of twenty-four whose mental age was far younger, who had insanity in his family and a history of cruel and disturbed behaviour and who had taken an axe to his sleeping brother. Cross-examining an obdurate doctor Marshall lost his temper: 'Are you one of the class of doctor who thinks no one is mad?' he asked contemptuously.

The Judge was Mr Justice Avory. Marshall was a contemporary of his and an old rival. Avory was famed for his intellectual approach and cold discipline in court and he did not seem to have many soft spots. Despite their diametrically opposed personalities, he was known to have one for Marshall. All the same he was not going to let this pass. 'I hope, doctor,' he said icily, 'that you are not one of the class of doctor who thinks everyone is mad.'

Flavell, too, was convicted though ultimately reprieved in an extraordinary backstage attempt to reconcile law and justice. Immediately after the verdict Marshall wrote an impassioned plea to Sir Ernley Blackwell, chief legal adviser to the Cabinet. It was lucky for Flavell that Blackwell[6] was a friend of Marshall's, a fellow member of the Inner Temple and a keen golfer. The letter was one of Marshall's typical efforts, reading like the spoken word: 'My mind is much exercised over this poor fellow. The man may not be technically within the rule in M'Naghten's case ... he is a sort of village idiot ... a disordered mind not actually insane ... not able to resist a sudden violent impulse. You must not let this man be hanged.'[7]

And he wasn't. In an intellectually dishonest, if merciful, decision the death sentence was substituted by life imprisonment. The Home Secretary advised that there was no question of a reprieve on any grounds connected with his mental condition and the verdict was held to be the right one.[8] The clemency of the Crown was extended having regard to the feelings of the prisoner's mother and local sympathy for her. And so almost on a whim, Flavell's life was saved. It was a very close-run thing. A telegram was sent to the high sheriff of the county at the last minute; the sentence of death was to be respited and the telegram acknowledged at the earliest possible moment.

Eventually Flavell was released after eleven years, improved, it was said, with training and maturity.

The superficial little interchange between judge and counsel in Flavell's trial had in fact exemplified the polarisation of views that now existed. Marshall continued to campaign until the end of his life. And he was eventually vindicated. In 1957, thirty years after Marshall's death, Parliament passed the Homicide Act, recognising another definition of 'insanity', diminished responsibility as a result of abnormality of the mind. The Act also introduced a more enlightened approach to provocation; the standard of the reasonable man was to be used as a test and the question left to the jury. And then, at last, in 2009 a concept of 'loss of control' was introduced into the law of homicide by amendments to the 1957 Act.

But it was all too late for Marshall and for the many unluckier than Edward Flavell who had died on the scaffold despite medical evidence of mental illness.

PART IV

FAME

CHAPTER 15

'A strange magnetic quality'

The year 1920 was an extraordinary one for Marshall. The Holt trial took place in the February and was followed by three of the most celebrated cases of the century. The Green Bicycle murder trial was in June, the trial of the solicitor Harold Greenwood for the murder of his wife took place in November and the Crumbles murder trial, for the ghastly killing of a young girl, was in December. All took place in assize towns distant from London but for their durations the attention of the nation focussed on the ancient courtrooms, Leicester Castle, Carmarthen Guildhall and Lewes Courthouse respectively, in which each was heard.

The periodic exodus of High Court judges from London to the assize towns of England and Wales to hear serious local cases was a centuries-old tradition. In the old days, most of the London Bar went with them, post chaises full of work-hungry barristers swaying in the wake of the judges' carriage, taking over every local inn and lodging house and competing shamelessly for the attention of the country attorneys who held the briefs. As each town was reached, the judges were greeted with pomp and lavish hospitality, before they began their work dispatching hapless defendants to the transportation ships if they were lucky and the gallows if they were not. That was all over by now, but its memory lingered on in numerous arcane traditions.

Judges and barristers were in Marshall's day permitted to travel by train provided the former wore top hats, all travelled first class, and the judges made the short journey from station to court by horse-drawn coach. Although there were still trumpeters and javelin men to meet the judge, dinners given by the high sheriff of the county and a church service to consecrate the administration of justice that was to come, it was all more of a formality and once it had been observed the assize court settled into a disciplined routine that was very different from the drunken roistering of the previous century.

Sensational murder trials outside London were greeted by the Bar with mixed feelings. The ever-present strain of a trial in which one false move or ill-judged question could send a man to the gallows was stress enough without adding the fatigue of travel and the isolation from home comforts. But it was not all bad. A Bar butler ensured the comfort of the visiting Bar. The barristers' robing room and the wine and silver for the lavish mess nights were all under his charge and, like the concierge of a grand hotel, he knew all about local custom and geography. A barrister like Marshall who knew the vital importance of ingratiating himself with local juries did well to engage the Bar butler in conversation and reminiscence. The very isolation intensified the camaraderie between opposing counsel. In a high-profile murder, there would often be six or even eight counsel involved, frequently all staying in the same hotel. Never far from public school culture, there are many accounts of nicknames, private jokes and apple pie beds. There would be at least one invitation to the lodging where the judges were housed for the duration of the assize, and for the county gentry, the assize carried with it the same excuse for entertaining as the local races. London counsel had cachet as a result of the sensational trial in which they were appearing and were something of a catch for country house hostesses. Competing invitations were issued with relentless hospitality.

In the summer of 1920 Marshall arrived at the Bell Hotel in Leicester for the murder trial of Ronald Light[1] to be greeted by a population and press whipped up to fever pitch. The case, known as the Green Bicycle murder, had fascinated everyone and continues to do so to this day. A quick Google search reveals site after site of faithful followers: amateur sleuths ('I have travelled six thousand miles from my home in Oregon to view the murder site,' one claims), bicycling buffs ('It was a quality bicycle with a coaster brake and a broad huge springed leather Brooks saddle,' *Bicycling World* tells us), historians, ballistics experts, ornithologists, canal enthusiasts, you name it. One book in 1930 said Light did not do it;[2] another in 1993 said he did.[3]

The victim was a twenty-one-year-old factory girl called Bella Wright. On 5 July 1919, on a sunny Saturday evening she had cycled to her uncle's house in a nearby village. Three hours later, she was found by a farmer lying dead on a shady green road, her bicycle beside her, her body still warm and bleeding. It was a remote spot, off her direct route home. There was still scant regard for forensics in those days. By the time the police arrived accompanied by the local doctor the body had been moved onto a milk cart. Dr Williams clambered on and had a cursory look. She had died of collapse due to exhaustion, he decided, and they all went home for supper. But the police officer, Police Constable Hall, was uneasy. The next morning, very early, he returned to the site and there, only about seventeen feet from where the body had been lying, he found a bullet. He recalled the doctor, who must have been somewhat embarrassed to discover, on re-examining of Bella's body, the bullet wounds: a small puncture wound in the left cheek, below the eye, and the larger exit wound in the hair over the middle and upper right parietal bone.

Bella had reached her uncle's house that evening as planned. His son-in-law was also visiting. Both men said she had been accompanied by a man on a green bicycle who had waited outside whilst she paid her visit. 'Bella, you have been a long time. I thought you had gone the other way,' he was heard to say when she came out, and the two had cycled off together. From then on, the green bicycle became the symbol of all the violence and mystery of Bella's death; second only to it was a gothic touch that engendered a horrid public thrill. Not far from Bella's body, a dead raven was found. Its bloody claw marks tracked back and forth from the body; it had died gorging on Bella's blood, it was said, and ornithologists have disputed the theory ever since with protestations that there are no ravens in Leicestershire and anyway they do not drink blood. It scarcely matters; the raven, inextricably linked with bullet and bicycle, is now firmly part of the legend.

Advertisements offering rewards were posted everywhere. Suddenly, it seemed, the green bicycle had become the murderer. Thanks to Bella's relatives who knew about bicycles, careful descriptions of the culprit were given: 'Upturned handlebars, level front brake, back pedalling brake worked from crank of unusual pattern ...'. In contrast the description of the rider remained shadowy, almost irrelevant.

The publicity resulted in two young girls aged twelve and fourteen coming forward. On the afternoon of the day Bella had died, they too had been out on their bicycles and had encountered a man who had pestered them. His bicycle had been green. The police interviewed many men with green bicycles, searched fruitlessly for a gun, advertised beseechingly for witnesses, called for assistance from Scotland Yard and six months later gave it up. Bella was buried by her grieving family, the crime receded into the mythology of the villages concerned and the Leicestershire countryside settled back into the remote gold of autumn and then into bleak winter.

On 23 February 1920 a canal man called Waterhouse was taking a load of coal along the river Soar, the light dim, the two horses plodding dutifully along the narrow towpath, the narrow boat low in the water, a quiet timeless scene. It was a journey Mr Waterhouse had done a thousand times, leading ultimately to the factory where Bella had once worked. When his tow rope tightened suddenly it was nothing unusual in that overgrown stretch of the water. But it was very unusual when he pulled it up to discover the frame of a green bicycle on the other end. The borough dredgers found other parts of it, the wheels, the crank, the pedals – enough to assemble most of a bicycle. Dragging further down the river opposite the factory wharf, a revolver holster still holding some cartridges was found.

It was easy after that. It was a deluxe bicycle, and a 'special order' with an identification number on it. Although the number on the exterior of the frame had been filed off, another concealed in the inner frame was still there. It had been sold in 1910 by a Birmingham shop to a Mr Ronald Light. Mr Light had looked after it very well and had it repaired and serviced locally, the last occasion being on the very day of Bella's death.

Ronald Light, the only son of doting middle-class parents, was a qualified engineer. He lived with his now widowed mother in Leicester. He was a pleasant unthreatening-looking man, thirty-four years old, not long discharged from the army, and had recently gained employment as a schoolmaster teaching mathematics in a private school in Cheltenham.[4] He had only been there for a few weeks when two police officers turned up to question him. At first he denied ever having had a green bicycle but at last he agreed that he had owned one and said that he had sold it; he also accepted he had had a service revolver, like all other men who had fought in the war, but insisted that it had been long relinquished.

Light was identified by two witnesses as the man seen with Bella and by a local bicycle repairer who had fixed the bike at Light's request and returned it to Light on the day of the death. A distinguished team of barristers was instructed to prosecute the case. 'It is most gratifying to hear of the splendid array of counsel you have secured,' the chief constable in the case wrote to the Director of Public Prosecutions. 'Undoubtedly the most complete justice will be done to our case.' He meant they were bound to secure a conviction. That was what everyone thought. All in all Light stood in need of a miracle if he was not to hang for Bella's murder.

He got one in Marshall, who, suppressing his own inclination for drama, delivered a defence which was a masterpiece of restraint accompanied by nail-biting suspense.

Leicester Castle is highly picturesque with Norman arches and ancient beams but as far as the Bar was concerned it was notorious for being far too small and extremely uncomfortable.[5] The trial was conducted in what Edgar Bowker, Marshall's clerk, described as a terrible intimacy, judge, barristers and accused so close they could touch one another. Counsel's table was so narrow that nothing would stay on it and the seats were little more than a ledge to lean against. For Marshall, suffering increasingly from varicose veins, it was torture. By this time in his career he had begun to make a point of arriving late for court in order to make an entrance. On this occasion he arrived with his usual flourish and clutching a large cushion. It was to become a trademark like the cigar and the immaculately furled umbrella. As closely clutched to his chest as his cushion was his defence. Not even his juniors knew the line he was going to take until they arrived in Leicester.

Certainly the Attorney General and his team were completely in the dark as to the nature of the defence. They were a formidable bunch; Sir Gordon Hewart KC led another silk, Henry Maddocks KC, as well as a rising star at the junior Bar in Birmingham, Norman Birkett.[6] It was Birkett's first murder trial and he later wrote:

> I shall always remember the moment when Marshall Hall came into court at Leicester Castle. He brought with him a strange magnetic quality that made itself felt in every part of the court. The spectators stirred with excitement at the sight of the man whose name was at that time a household word and a faint murmur ran from floor to gallery. Marshall came of course with the prestige of the greatest criminal defender of the day and every eye was fixed upon him. When he addressed the judge it was seen that to his great good looks there had been added perhaps the greatest gift of all in the armoury of an advocate – a most beautiful speaking voice. He had in this case a terrible task before him.[7]

The prosecution team had been exhaustively thorough in its attempts to cover all evidence linking Light, the green bicycle and Bella. Hewart's opening speech was long and detailed and then the witnesses were called: the county architect to prove the plans of roads on which Bella had cycled; the farmer who had found the body; Police Constable Hall, proud that his vigilance had led to the discovery of the cause of Bella's death; four locals who had seen a girl like Bella with a man like Light cycling along together. Bella's uncle and his son in law identified both Light and the bicycle. Bicycle shop employees gave evidence of the sale of the bicycle to Light and the subsequent repairs it had had. Light's mother's maid, crucially, told of Light's use of the bike on that day in July 1919 on which Bella had died, of Light's late return, tired and dusty, and of the subsequent disappearance of the bicycle. The canal boat man who ultimately found it was called to identify it.

And then there were the police officers who interviewed Light and now recounted to the jury the lies he had told them.

On and on the evidence mounted. With each witness the court waited with breathless anticipation for the legendary cross-examinations and displays of temperament which they had been led to expect from Marshall. No more than the most desultory interest was roused in the sleeping lion; there was a mild question here and there and then the witness was stumbling from the box, released from the long-anticipated ordeal so easily he was dazed. In only four witnesses did Marshall show any interest. There were the two young girls called to regale the court with their lucky escape from the pestering man on the green bicycle. Young Muriel and Valeria, faced with six feet three inches of Marshall fully robed, stern if kindly, readily admitted that their statements had been taken eight months after the event, that by then they had seen and heard a lot about the Green Bicycle case including many photographs of the bicycle in question, that they had eagerly talked the matter over and agreed that their green bicycle incident had been the same day that Bella had been shot and that a kind policeman had helped them remember the date. A satisfied Marshall sat down quickly and purring.

Then there was Dr Williams, the embarrassed and somewhat defensive examining doctor who had managed to miss the bullet wounds. His view was that the bullet had been fired at a close range of a few feet. How did he explain the fact that the bullet landed such a short distance away, demanded Marshall? If there had been no resistance but the girl's head it was absurd to suppose that it would only have travelled a further few feet. The doctor, crucially, agreed. He had already given evidence at the coroner's inquest that he could not give an opinion on Bella's position when she was shot but since then he had thought about it a lot, he said. The girl must have been on the ground when she was shot in the head and the bullet, having passed through her head, must have bounced off the stony road and landed a few feet away. It was contrived enough to satisfy Marshall, who asked no more questions.

That left the ballistics expert, Henry Clarke, a gunsmith who carried on business, appropriately enough, from Gallow Tree Gate, Leicester. He was the type of witness to whom Marshall was particularly partial. He settled down into one of his inimitable cross-examinations somewhere between a chat, expert to expert, and a lecture to both expert and jury. Clarke had identified the type of bullet found at the scene and stated that those found in the cartridges in the canal were of the same sort, issued for use with a service revolver, made to be fired with black powder and adapted for use with cordite. That was the purpose for which he had been called by the prosecution to give evidence but Marshall had a whole lot more he wanted to elicit.

He started with the easy stuff; Clarke agreed he could not say how many thousand millions of these bullets had been produced since the Boer War when they were first issued. Marshall asked him to inspect the bullet. It was correct, Clarke agreed, that the bullet that had killed Bella had marks on it showing its passage through a rifled barrel which could equally have been that of a rifle or of a revolver. Whichever it was, a rifled barrel enormously increased the range of the weapon and the velocity of the bullet. Neither the position of the bullet nor the wounds in the girl's head were consistent with a shot at a close range from a service revolver, Marshall suggested; in such a case, the girl's head would have been half blown off and the bullet would not have been found close by. Either the bullet found nearby was not the bullet that had killed her, or it had been shot from a very long way away, reaching the end of its trajectory when it hit her. 'Have you ever seen a human being who has been shot at a distance of within five yards with a service revolver?' Marshall asked Mr Clarke. 'No, sir,' he replied. And Marshall, who certainly had not done so either, sat down with a histrionically meaningful look at the jury. A few more witnesses and the case for the prosecution was over.

In the hushed courtroom, in his very quietest voice, with no preliminaries of any kind Marshall called his only witness, the accused Ronald Light. And he and Marshall embarked together on one of those perfect question and answer sessions between counsel and witness which hit the right note at every query and every response, as satisfying to the listeners as a rally in tennis, a musical duet or *a pas de deux*. In a court rapt with attention, heads turning from one to the other of the two speakers, against all the odds, together they rowed Light out of trouble. By the end, there was not one unanswered question in the juries' minds nor one false move made.

Light had fought twice in France, in 1916 and 1917, and had been discharged with shell shock and deafness. He had had a service revolver of course; it had been with him at the casualty clearing station where he had been sent after his discharge and he had left it there with the rest of his kit when he came home. The holster had been left at home when he returned to France for the second time. It was indeed the one found in the canal, as was the ammunition found in it. When he had gone to France he had left behind his bicycle, his green bicycle. That was the bicycle found in the canal.

The Attorney General and his team, who had spent so many hours and called so many witnesses to prove Light's ownership of bicycle and holster, began to look incredulous, the jury bewildered. Only Marshall and Light remained supremely confident.

During his convalescence he had begun to take the bicycle for runs in the country. On the day in question, he went out after tea. He had not met either of the two girls, Muriel and Valeria, on that or any other day. But he had come across a young lady standing by a bicycle who had asked him if he had a spanner. He didn't but he had had a look at the bicycle and it had then seemed natural to ride on together, until they came to her uncle's village. She was an attractive girl. She said she would only be ten minutes. He had taken that to mean as a 'sort of suggestion' he should wait. She was a long time and in the end he rode on, taking the higher of the two roads which ultimately led back to Leicester. On the way he had a flat tyre. By then it was just before eight. He thought he would just see where the girl had got to, so he rode back to the house at which he had left her. She was just emerging. He said 'Hello' not 'Bella'. He had not known her name. 'You have been a long time. I thought you had gone the other way.' He had had a chat with the two men at the house about his bicycle. He and the girl had ridden off together. He had stopped again to pump up his tyre and she had gone slowly on. He caught her up again. They chatted some more. When they had reached the intersecting roads, she had said goodbye, and taken the lower road towards Leicester. He had taken the more direct high road. He never saw her again.

Of course a day or two later he had read of the murder and identified the girl; he saw that she had been killed, apparently by a bullet from a service revolver, and that the green bicycle was sought. He had filed the number off his bicycle and thrown it and the holster into the canal. He did it because everyone had jumped to the conclusion that the man with the green bicycle was the murderer.

Light had admitted so much that the rug had been jerked from under prosecuting counsel's feet. They were left with a detailed cross-examination of Light's movements which somehow resulted in lending credence to his story. Why had he not gone to the police with his story as soon as he knew of the girl's fate? 'I did not make up my mind, deliberately, not to go forward. I was astounded and frightened at this unexpected thing. I kept on hesitating and in the end, I drifted into doing nothing at all.' Why had he not confided in his much-loved mother, or the faithful family servant? His mother had a bad heart, she worried about him, and telling the servant would have meant telling everyone. Fear had made him lie to the police; attempts at concealment had been to avert suspicion. He came over as a lonely man in a difficult position, of whom the worst that could be said was that he lacked judgement.

In vain the prosecution dwelled on Light's undoubted and persistent interest in Bella and pointed at the overwhelming coincidences; if his story was true, Bella had been shot within one mile and fifteen minutes of leaving Light and no other possible candidate for the murder had been found. How much more likely was it that he had made advances to her, been rejected by her, threatened her to try and gain her compliance and shot her so that she could not tell her story?

The speculative nature of this supposed motive, the pathos of Light's isolation and his desire to protect his mother lost nothing in Marshall's speech. What was so unnatural about his interest in a pretty girl? If he had shown moral cowardice, wasn't that consistent with the shell shock sustained in the defence of his country? He had drifted into a policy of concealment and he had lied when confronted by the police; was that so hard to understand? Then came his scales-of-justice peroration.

Light was acquitted. Generally speaking the judiciary were rather grudging of Marshall's remarkable results since they disapproved of the theatricality that achieved them. But Mr Justice Horridge sent Marshall a note after this trial: 'Your defence of Light', he wrote, 'seemed to me to be without fault.' It was a rare unqualified accolade. It had been one of his greatest achievements, Marshall said. But then he always said that after each fresh triumph.

By now Marshall was suffering frequent bouts of illness: phlebitis from varicose veins, worsened after he fell through a cucumber frame he was repairing at his country house,[8] lungs subjected to frequent bouts of pneumonia not to mention daily assaults from Havana cigars, but most of all the sickening stage fright which had never left him since his earliest days at the Bar and the constant stress were beginning to tell. Although his ill health suggested at least some psychological component Marshall's careful cultivation of his image in his early years made him reluctant to admit to the strain under which he worked. With fame came candour. 'If you are irritable and over-sensitive – if your work worries you unduly and you are sleeping badly … you are probably suffering from nerves … you need a tonic,' said a 1921 advert for the tonic wine Sanatogen, after that homily continuing: 'Sir Edward Marshall Hall writes "I believe I was one of the first to recognise Sanatogen's value as a nerve food … not only did I take it myself with great benefit but I recommended it to my friends".'[9]

By the time of his third capital case in 1920 he was certainly exhibiting the symptoms referred to in the advert. The stakes were even higher than in the previous two in the case of Harold Greenwood,[10] solicitor, pillar of the community, personification of the stiflingly respectable provincial professional class. Greenwood lived in some style in Kidwelly, Carmarthenshire in one of the largest houses in the little town with a beautifully kept garden that required the generous use of weed killer (he favoured Coopers Weedicide) in the upkeep of its immaculate gravel paths.

Kidwelly was a remote place in those days, twelve miles or so beyond Carmarthen, its nearest assize town. The whole picturesque area is steeped in history, reaching its climax in Kidwelly with its crooked high street, its bridge across the river and its castle. Time moved slowly there in the 1920s; motor cars were few, excitements mild and crime of the more sensational variety almost unheard of. News did not travel fast but all the same the name of Sir Edward Marshall Hall KC and his Green Bicycle triumph had reached the town via the London papers and the revelation that he was to come down and defend Harold Greenwood on, of all incredible things, a murder charge, was greeted with the same degree of excitement as a visit by a famous film star would cause now. He was to stay at the Ivy Bush, the old coaching inn in the centre of Carmarthen, and his room was to be supplied with a special desk so that the great man could prepare his legendary speeches in comfort.

The national press took up many of the other rooms as well as all the local lodgings and the newspapermen in their dark city coats and unsuitable shoes, carrying exotic equipment stood out like sore thumbs in the streets. One or two of them, to the fascination of the locals, even had American accents; it was not just Harold Greenwood's own country that took a fascinated interest in his fate. The dissemination of news from such a remote place posed a problem. Photographers were growing bolder and bolder as the public demand for pictures increased. Marshall's speech during Ronald Light's trial had actually been interrupted when the judge had spotted one taking a photograph of the legendary advocate in action. An ugly scene had ensued; it was a contempt of court to photograph inside a courtroom. Now the *Daily Mail* was determined to scoop the best photographs. Just to add to the town's excitement, a biplane arrived, fitted up as a darkroom.[11] Photographs of the gathering circus taken outside court in the morning left Carmarthen at 11.25 and arrived at the *Daily Mail*'s Fleet Street headquarters in time to go to press for the evening edition. The public could not get enough of it.

Some newspapers were critical of the mounting hysteria. And this criticism was not just aimed at the yellow press; even *The Times* did not escape censure: 'In back corners you could read of the death of the King of Greece, or of men and women being shot like dogs by the Government's forces in Ireland or the destruction of Armenia or the perishing of thousands of children in Austria from disease … all these were neglected in the interests of the discussion of what happened one hot Summer's day in the garden and dining room of one respectable house.'[12]

What had happened? Harold Greenwood lived in Kidwelly with his wife Mabel, the daughter of a well-known county family. They had four children. Irene, the oldest, was twenty-two and living at home, as was her youngest brother, Kenneth, who was being educated by a tutor. The other two were at private boarding schools. Greenwood practised as a solicitor in the nearby town of Llanelli and Mabel was a pillar of St Mary's Church, Kidwelly where the family worshipped regularly. 'There was no more united family at Kidwelly than my wife and I,' Greenwood stated in his police interview. Social life revolved gently around the local gentry, the doctor, the clergyman and the few professional men and their wives. If there was a shadow for Mabel in this idyll, it was caused by Harold's reputation for 'carrying on' with other women. This phrase, it was observed later in a commentary to the transcript of the trial, was 'a convenient term conveying anything from affability to adultery'.[13] Greenwood was a pompous man, dapper and moustached, and his facetious little efforts were more probably attempts at the former than the latter but even so they had been noted with disapproval. Miss Mary Griffiths, the local doctor's sister, told the police that Mabel had been distressed by what she described as 'Harold's weakness'. Miss Griffiths herself had been the subject of some of Harold's attentions though she indignantly rejected the town gossip that she had encouraged him by sitting on his knee in a railway carriage.

Mabel was known to be delicate. She often looked tired and was said to have a weak heart to which she believed she might succumb at any time. It was subsequently regarded as sinister that her husband, far from discouraging this belief, seemed to foster it. Nonetheless, she did her duty with tireless good works and church attendances.

On Sunday 15 June 1919, the Greenwoods uncharacteristically missed church. Mabel said she felt unwell and sat and read in the leafy garden whilst Harold worked on his car. The morning passed quietly and in the spacious kitchen the cook prepared the Sunday luncheon, a joint with vegetables and a gooseberry tart. Laying the table was delayed; the maid, Hannah, later told the police that the master had gone into the china pantry and remained there for half an hour and she had not liked to disturb him. Eventually, however, she performed her duties with china from the pantry and cutlery from the silver basket. Luncheon was served at one o'clock to the four members of the Greenwood family, and the servants ate the remains afterwards in the kitchen. The master had drunk whisky with his meal, Hannah recalled, the children water and the mistress her customary burgundy wine.

At half past three Mabel began to suffer from profuse diarrhoea and at about six she took to her bed with violent sickness and chest pains. Harold

Greenwood called Dr Griffiths, who lived opposite. He prescribed sips of water and brandy and then strolled into the garden to play clock golf with Harold. They played several games and when the doctor popped in to see his patient afterwards she seemed better. He sent across some bismuth medicine later. Mabel then suffered a relapse, and Irene called the district nurse to help care for her. Dr Griffiths made a series of visits and prescribed some pills, the contents of which were the subject of much discussion later. She seemed to get worse after taking them. At 3 am she died. The doctor certified death due to valvular disease of the heart and she was buried the following Thursday in the graveyard of the church to which she had given so much of her energy.

The whispering in Kidwelly started almost immediately. The Reverend Ambrose Jones, the vicar, who had spent the day before Mabel's death engaged in parish duties with her, could not believe the speed with which death had overtaken her and the district nurse was uneasy about the symptoms of that last day. As for Harold, a scandalous four months later he announced his engagement to a Llanelli spinster, Miss Gladys Jones, and if that were not enough, it transpired that during his lightning courtship of Miss Jones, he had been carrying on a violent flirtation with Miss Griffiths, the doctor's sister. It had been anyone's guess which one he was going to marry but ultimately it was Miss Jones, on 1 October 1919. Miss Griffiths retired to her room that day, in tears.

The effect of his behaviour on an already suspicious neighbourhood was incendiary. He came back from his honeymoon to a police interview and an application for an exhumation of Mabel's body. Harold should be relieved of this terrible suspicion, said the chief constable; and on 16 April 1920 the peace of Kidwelly churchyard was shattered when Mabel's body was removed from her grave. Analysis revealed small amounts of arsenic in all the organs examined. It was now concluded that the violent vomiting caused by the ingestion of arsenic had acted on Mabel's weak heart and killed her.

An inquest belatedly held concluded that Mabel had died at her husband's hand and amidst demonstrations of public hatred Harold was conveyed to the county gaol to await the arrival of Sir Edward Marshall Hall KC, briefed for the defence at a dramatic 300 guineas with a daily 'refresher' of 50 guineas for the duration of the trial.[14] The Director of Public Prosecutions had had no illusions about the difficulties of proof: '[There is] undoubtedly evidence of opportunity means and motive. The content in the case will arise in connection with whether there is sufficient evidence to show that the prisoner in fact utilised the opportunity and the means,' began the prosecution brief sent to Sir Marlay Samson KC, counsel for the prosecution.

The theory was that the arsenic, in the form of weed killer, had been secreted in the only thing consumed by Mabel alone, the burgundy wine. Marshall, connoisseur of the Garrick Club and Inner Temple wines, must have been amused by the label on the bottle, 'Pure Foreign Red Wine of Burgundy Character', and unsurprised by the Home Office pathologist's view that 'the addition of a possibly fatal dose of arsenic ... in a wineglass of [this] wine has no appreciable effect on the flavour of the wine', but he too was well aware of the wine's crucial importance to his client's case.

Marshall, already ill with a combination of nerves and phlebitis, booked into the Ivy Bush Hotel the weekend before the trial was due to start. When he drove to see his client, by now incarcerated for nearly four months in the county gaol awaiting trial, the entire route from his hotel was lined with eager crowds thronging to catch a glimpse of him. For them, it was like some great royal procession; but it was not so festive for Marshall, this grim visit to a cell stinking of damp and fear where a respectable man was waiting to be saved from hanging in three weeks' time.

By the first day of the trial, the town was so packed that Sir Marlay Samson KC had to lodge with a local dignitary; the Ivy Bush was full. The little courtroom was overflowing with ticket holders and the rest of the crowd had to make do with standing room in the square outside to watch the trumpeters announcing the judge's arrival, the horse-drawn carriage bearing the prisoner from the gaol, the procession of the twelve chosen jurors and, always last for maximum impact, Marshall, his pain overtaken by adrenalin, striding across from the Ivy Bush, a head higher than the rest of the crowd.

This time, unlike in the Light trial, the defence team insisted that everything had to be proved; nothing was admitted. It was one of Marshall's best diversionary efforts, and its focus was Dr Griffiths, now retired, who had treated Mabel during her last twenty-four hours. This tactic the doctor himself assisted in, his bungling confusions in the witness box creating an impression of incompetence. He had given Mabel an excessive dose of morphine, Marshall suggested, and poor Dr Griffiths ended up so confused that he was unclear as to whether the tablets he had prescribed had been opium tablets (containing a fortieth of a gramme of morphine) or morphia tablets (containing half a gramme of morphine), let alone the dose he had given. To make matters worse, he had mislaid his prescription book.

Perhaps, suggested Marshall, emboldened by this success, he had confused the arsenic and bismuth bottles in his surgery and given Mabel the former instead of the latter? The doctor floundered and the judge objected to this last attack. It was the first of a series of clashes of the old kind:

Marshall oppressed by pain and responsibility was irritable with witnesses, outrageous in his completely unfounded allegations such as this one and audacious in producing with a flourish items that were not exhibits in the trial. A surreptitious visit to the Kidwelly chemist's shop had enabled him to buy two bottles, one of arsenic and one of bismuth, in order to emphasise his point. It was infuriating for the prosecution but press and public, and more particularly the jury, loved it. And such was Marshall's public image that the judge, Mr Justice Shearman, appeared surprisingly anxious to keep the peace. 'I can trust you, Sir Edward,' he said pathetically at one point when Marshall was being particularly obstreperous, 'and you can trust me.' The plea had little effect and throughout the remainder of the witnesses called, the judge interposed frequent and equally ineffective injunctions to Marshall not to 'get excited'.

But getting excited was Marshall's tactic in this trial and he was now in one of what his clerk Edgar Bowker described as his naughty moods. By the end of the prosecution case, red herrings galore had been introduced to the dazed jury, and the Home Office scientists and doctors had been subjected to bewilderingly technical cross-examinations. 'I don't know much about the law but I know a lot about figures,' Marshall observed cheerfully to the jury, before embarking on a series of mind boggling and ultimately irrelevant calculations with the Home Office analyst and Sir William Willcox, the pathologist. When he had exhausted those, he turned like a man at a cocktail party seeking topics in common with a fellow guest, to a chatty analysis of the domestic products that contained arsenic. Wasn't it true it was an ingredient in Epsom salt? In magnesia? In boric acid? In borax? The list seemed never-ending. Then he explored all kinds of fascinating and obscure facts about poisoning. It was true, was it not, that the symptoms were indistinguishable from food poisoning? And with regard to food poisoning it was a fascinating fact that several persons could eat the same food with only one affected? Gooseberry skins were a known irritant? It was possible, was it not, to inhale arsenic through the air? Might Mabel have absorbed it as she walked the garden paths? Might she have ingested it through gooseberries in her portion of tart? Was it right that there was arsenic in very minute quantities in every human body? Was it correct that strict control over substances containing arsenic had been lost during the war? It was present in tonics and beauty products? On and on went the questions to which the scientists were forced to agree, their attempts at qualifications lost in the onslaught. But crucially, in the welter of facts, they made admissions: if the death had been due to morphia, it was possible it would not have been detectable by the time the body was exhumed; the amount of arsenic had been ascertained by the method also used in the Seddon trial and was, when calculated up to the amount that must have been administered, the very minimum dose that could be fatal; none of Mabel's symptoms were inconsistent with food poisoning; and her heart had anyway been weak.

Marshall was satisfied. He had got what he wanted despite a reproachful judge and an infuriated prosecutor. In defence, he told the jury, he was going to call expert witnesses 'from your own neighbourhood' to back up these many possibilities as to the cause of Mabel's death. Nice trustworthy Welsh witnesses were of course what this Carmarthen jury wanted. And he was going to call the daughter of the house, Irene, who would say she had drunk wine that day from the same bottle. And he would call Harold Greenwood. The jury must forget the gossip; 'trifles light as air are confirmation strong as Holy Writ to jealous people,'[15] he reminded them, in his beautiful voice.

When he called Greenwood to the witness box, the court settled down to witness the great forensic duet that Ronald Light's trial had led them to expect. Marshall, with a casual contempt for the entire prosecution case, asked Greenwood if he had been happy with his wife? If he had had anything to do with her death? If he had benefited financially either by her death or by his remarriage? And then: 'Are you ready to answer any questions my learned friend may ask you relative to this case?' 'Yes,' said Greenwood. And Marshall sat down. It had taken all of three minutes.

After the fireworks during the prosecution case, the contrast was extraordinary, as Marshall intended it to be. Sir Marlay Samson, taken by surprise, embarked on a lengthy cross-examination which got him nowhere. Greenwood was followed into the witness box by Irene, whose frequent references to 'Daddy' and touching devotion to her mother lent credence to her insistence that she too had drunk from the red wine bottle.

'Members of the jury ... I am suffering from an illness. It is probable that after making my speech I will have to leave the court,' Marshall began on Monday 8 November. He was by then feeling so ill that he had requested the attendance of Sir William Willcox, who was staying at the Ivy Bush Hotel and who, ironically, after a day of being cross-examined relentlessly as to his competence, had prescribed for Marshall in order to keep him going for the rest of the trial. But for the admission, the jury would never have known of Marshall's illness as they listened to a wonderful speech. He was a complete master of the court. Early on, the judge interrupted him to point out that he made an undoubted error of fact. Marshall did not like having mistakes pointed out; nor was he going to be interrupted. 'I don't know whether my Lord has ever had the responsibility of conducting the defence in a case like this,' he observed sweetly to the jury. 'At any rate he probably has not done so under the physical discomfort I am experiencing at the present moment.' It was probably the sheer temerity of it that caused Mr Justice Shearman to lapse into silence. For the next three and a quarter hours, at extraordinary speed yet with impeccably close reasoning, Marshall addressed the jury, his gaze never wavering from their faces, his entire energy transfixing them, intimidating them with the constant reminders that one life and four children's futures were at stake. And then at last, after his demonstration of the scales of justice falling in his client's favour, he ended as he had begun, with *Othello*, recalling the moment when Othello snuffs out the burning light before strangling the life out of Desdemona:

> 'If I quench thee, thou flaming minister,
> I can again thy former light restore,
> Should I repent me; but once put out thy light,
> Thou cunning'st pattern of excelling nature,
> I know not where is that Promethean heat
> That can thy light relume.'

> Are you by your verdict going to put out that light? Gentlemen
> of the jury, I demand at your hands the life and liberty of Harold
> Greenwood.

Marshall left Carmarthen immediately afterwards, leaving his junior to listen to the speech of prosecuting counsel[16] and the judge's summing up. Awaiting the London train at Cardiff, a porter told him of the acquittal, anticipating by a few hours the massive headlines dominating the world's newspapers.

Less than four weeks later, Marshall was standing graven faced in trilby and muffler, the collar of his long dark overcoat turned up against the cold on a remote stretch of shingle, gazing into the shallow grave that shortly before had contained the body of a young girl with her head smashed to pieces by a rock.

CHAPTER 16

'Unsuitable for the eyes and ears of pure women'

S ir Archibald Bodkin, Director of Public Prosecutions, was a worried man. The body buried in the shingle had been identified as that of Irene Munroe, a pretty seventeen-year-old, and two men, Jack Field and William Gray, had been charged with her murder. The police were convinced that they had got their men, but the evidence against them was all identification evidence, never the most reliable.[1] The defence was being funded by *John Bull*, the weekly news magazine owned by the trenchant and eccentric newspaper proprietor Horatio Bottomley. Jingoistic, reactionary, and a self-appointed mouthpiece for the common man, *John Bull* had become dangerously influential. The funding of Gray's defence provided it with a story to illustrate one of its periodic pushes for a Poor Prisoners' Defence Fund. Its special crime investigator was already sniffing around the witnesses, and it did not take a genius to guess who *John Bull*'s chosen counsel would be. Bottomley was one of Marshall's greatest fans. Once Marshall was appointed, the magazine's eulogies of his invincibility as defence counsel were such that serious consideration was given by the Home Office as to whether the articles, published in the context of a particular anticipated trial, could be said to amount to a contempt of court.[2]

There was by now a real concern amongst the establishment that the cult of personality surrounding Marshall's cases might distort the proper administration of justice and there was in this case a strong desire for a pair of safe hands to steer the prosecution home. The safest hands of all were those of Charles Gill KC and furthermore Marshall's deep affection for him was well known. He would not take liberties with Gill. Gill found the stress of capital cases intolerable. He had refused to prosecute Harold

Greenwood and now he refused the Field and Gray brief. Bodkin persisted, however, and in the end he accepted on the understanding that he would share the 'responsibility and load' with another KC as well as an experienced junior.[3]

The extraordinary assize circus began once more. The Honourable Stella Gwynne, wife of the Member of Parliament for Eastbourne, wrote from her home, Wootton Manor, renowned for its country house weekends:

> Dear Mr Gill
> I wonder if you would care to make use of our house while the Crumbles case is on at Lewes … Sir Edward Marshall Hall is coming so do come and complete the pleasure …[4]

It was for all the world as though the terrible murder had marked the start of the season.

This sort of invitation was exactly to Marshall's taste but Gill firmly booked himself into the Metropole Hotel, Brighton and concentrated on his obsessive colour-coded trial preparation, every piece of evidence analysed in columns labelled 'untrue', 'the truth', 'Gray says', 'Gray omits' and so on. Unusual by any standards, it was a style as far as could be imagined from Marshall's instinctive but haphazard approach. It was no use preparing elaborate scripts for Marshall, his juniors had learned; he received them with enthusiastic praise, then jettisoned them within moments of beginning his case as he followed a scent like a truffle hound, straight to the prize he sought.

There was no cosy Agatha Christie aspect to the Crumbles murder.[5] It was sordid, brutal and somehow very contemporary. Irene Munroe had had her head pitilessly smashed in with a rock and then, alive or not, who knew, had been superficially buried in the loose shingle of an area bordering the sea just outside Eastbourne and known as the Crumbles. The strange topography and reputation of the Crumbles became central to the investigation. Remote and isolated, it was rich in vegetation and populated mainly by seagulls. A few desolate bungalows fringed it and a sinister narrow tramline ran across it. It was a very secret place in those days, and the few people who went there had reasons for wanting secrecy. In a time when all sex was illicit save that within marriage between a man and a woman, it was a place to go, away from prying eyes or interruption. Its reputation had led to the activities of an unsavoury group of men known as the Eastbourne Foxes who roamed the Crumbles looking for victims to blackmail. It had long had a reputation for being haunted and the spookiness of the area was much enhanced after Irene's death; the police set bloodhounds loose across the sands looking for clues, and a local medium held a séance there in an attempt to elicit from Irene herself the identity of her killers.

Irene, on holiday from London, had known nothing of the reputation of the Crumbles when she went on an afternoon walk with two men; and the reasons she did so are unknown. Theft or sex were the conventional motives put forward by Gill at the trial; but Irene had possessed nothing worth stealing and she had not been sexually assaulted.[6]

Field and Gray, the two men soon arrested for the crime, were an odd couple. Field was nineteen years old, living with his mother and grandmother, unemployed since his discharge from the navy. Gray, aged twenty-eight and also unemployed, was married, living with his wife on a small army disability pension. The two men had met a couple of months before the crime and had become inseparable, loafing around the Eastbourne pubs and amusement arcades, chatting up young women holidaymakers and visiting afternoon cinema shows. Photographs of the two belie the descriptions at the trial of their seedy down-at-heel appearance; both could be described as attractive to a young woman, as it appears one or other or both were to Irene.

The evidence against them was very strong. Several witnesses came forward who had seen the three of them walking on the Crumbles; the men had tried to create for themselves a false alibi; and Gray had had highly incriminating conversations with fellow inmates in Maidstone prison whilst awaiting his trial.

It was anticipated that the two would seek to blame each other and they were therefore separately represented, Field by two junior barristers and Gray, with *John Bull*'s substantial backing, by Marshall and a junior. But in fact the two men remained loyal to each other, sticking resolutely to the same story of an innocent afternoon in each other's company. Watching reporters noted that they huddled together in the dock as though for comfort. The defence was exceptionally difficult, every point amounting to a two-edged sword. The glorious clarity of a sunny August afternoon, for instance, was the most unlikely light in which to choose to kill someone on an open beach; but on the other hand, the same clarity aided visibility and therefore identification. Equally, the generally seedy undesirability of both men made them unlikely magnets to pretty young Irene, but heavy emphasis on such a characteristic made them far more likely to have committed the crime.

Gill's performance was anxiously thorough, and any point he missed was picked up by the judge, Mr Justice Avory. ('What a pity', Marshall said acidly afterwards, 'he can't do a summing up rather than a speech for the prosecution.') Marshall's own performance, to the disappointment of the assembled press, was restrained in the extreme for reasons he explained afterwards in a letter to Gill:

> How little the outside public understand these cases. – They talk about Greenwood and the Green Bicycle, those cases were child's play compared to this and it is only the expert like yourself who can realise the real difficulty in a case like the Crumbles murder is to put any sort of defence that does not turn round and hit you in the face. Never have I been at such a loss for something to say and never was I more pleased to come to the end of a case.[7]

The verdict was a curious one: both men were found guilty of murder but with an almost incomprehensible rider that there should be a recommendation for mercy on the basis that the crime had not been premeditated. Commentators since have interpreted it as a tribute to Marshall's closing speech, compelling despite the evidence.

The two men, sentenced to hang, as was mandatory once convicted of murder, at last turned on each other. Each subsequently made a statement saying his defence had been lies to protect the other.

The whole muddle went to the Court of Criminal Appeal, which heard appeals by Field and Gray as well as a referral by the Home Secretary in relation to the oddities of the verdict. It was an extremely rare case in which the court not only considered the evidence given at the trial but permitted Field and Gray to give their new accounts and heard fresh evidence from the warders who had had the two men in their custody at Lewes railway station after conviction. The court ruled on 18 January 1921 that the convictions had been right and just, and Field and Gray were kept in separate cells at Wandsworth prison until 4 February, when they met again as they approached the scaffold upon which their double execution took place.

Marshall was back in London, his company sought everywhere, his views sought on everything. His portrait[8] had been the star attraction at the Royal Academy and dozens of publishers and newspaper editors were importuning for his memoirs. His personal and private life, his every word, was the subject of constant press comment. When he told a joke, or had a holiday abroad, or contracted influenza or said anything on any subject, however far removed from his own expertise, it was reported in the popular press. The newspaper coverage of his cases of 1920 was such that man and legend were inextricably entwined; it became increasingly difficult for anyone, including Marshall himself, to distinguish between the two. His supposed enormous wealth, however, was one subject on which he at least was clear and increasingly touchy. He sought to suppress what was the growing mythology around his fabled riches.

It had probably begun when he sent to auction an item which attracted international interest and was associated with a name that really was a byword for immense wealth, Rothschild. Alfred de Rothschild, his old friend from Highclere house parties, had died in 1918, leaving the then almost unimaginable sum of £1.5 million and appointing Marshall as one of his executors. Marshall remained heavily involved in the administration of the estate for the rest of his life.[9]

The demands seemed never-ending. Alfred left two vast properties, 1 Seamore Place, Mayfair and Halton House in Buckinghamshire. Each was fully staffed and stuffed with priceless and grossly underinsured works of art. Seamore Place was inherited by Almina, Lady Carnarvon, rumoured to be Rothschild's illegitimate daughter, who instantly sought approval from Marshall to sell a Gainsborough and a van Dyck. Despite his friendship with Almina, Marshall withheld permission, refusing to pay duties on the sale in deference to Alfred's wishes that the contents remain intact and therefore tax free. Being Almina, she did it anyway. The reasons for her desire for funds were to have future implications for Marshall.[10] Meanwhile the vast expenses of the Halton estate prior to sale were administered by Marshall and his co-trustees, who also had discretionary powers over the large charitable donations to be made from the residuary estate, and responsibility for those claiming to be destitute as a result of Alfred's death. Alfred had been open handed but un-business-like and many had come to rely on an ill-defined largesse which had now ceased. For the onerous duties as an executor, Marshall received a handsome £5,000 fee. But in addition he had been left a personal bequest, an eighteenth-century bonbonnière composed of plaques of Sèvres porcelain exquisitely painted by Dodin. He sold it at Sotheby's in 1922 along with a selection of his renowned snuff box collection. The Rothschild bonbonnière caused a considerable stir; Queen Mary herself went to Sotheby's to view it and it sold for £4,000. The entire sale realised £9,025, the equivalent today of more than £400,000.

But it was the whispering surrounding his professional fees that really infuriated him; it eroded his carefully guarded image as a man of the people and it insulted potential jurors who, misunderstanding the 'specials' system, thought that he demanded higher fees to persuade him to come to their far-flung home towns. 'Can you keep your men off the fee question in their effusions about criminal trials?' he wrote to Ralph Blumenfeld, the editor of the *Daily Express*, after an article had triggered a dawn 'raid' on his chambers by the Inland Revenue.[11] But the truth was of course that like many others in the public eye he criticised and suffered from the publicity he assiduously courted and fed, jostling for his position in the centre of everything newsworthy that ever happened in the law and shamelessly exploiting whatever element might assist the client he was representing.

A significant change in the legal system[12] had passed almost unnoticed when on 28 July 1920 women jurors sat for the first time, in a criminal case at Bristol Quarter Sessions. One anxious article in *The Times* had preceded the event, speculating on the impact such a duty might have on the role of women in the home, but other than that there had been little public attention. Inevitably it took the added ingredient of Marshall to catapult the issue into the public's notice a few months later in January 1921 when women were for the first time called for jury service in a divorce case in the Royal Courts of Justice in London.

A private room had been especially prepared for their use with a plentiful supply of hairpins and a mirror but no other special provisions had been made. Had it not been for the fact that Marshall was representing the wife, the six women on the jury – all, we are told, women of refinement in 'neat workmanlike costumes and trim toques' – would have fulfilled their new roles with the same lack of fuss as had those at Bristol Quarter Sessions. Equally Major Allen of the Royal Garrison Artillery would have obtained a divorce from his wife with the minimal publicity he no doubt wanted.

On the first day of the trial the jury were waiting in eager anticipation. Marshall, representing Ethel Mary Allen, got to his feet; he was neither a prude nor a puritan, he said, but the evidence in the case included pornographic photographs and obscene letters and was utterly unsuitable for the eyes and ears of pure women, particularly those who were unmarried. He could not bring himself to put before them material from which he would do anything to protect his own womenfolk.

He caused a furore. The judge was Mr Justice Horridge, who the year before had praised Marshal unreservedly for his defence of Ronald Light. Now encountering for the first time Marshall's manipulative games, he was furious at an intervention calculated to cause a sensation. The six new jurors, though keen to show their professionalism, were not immune to an appeal to their purity by the man described as the handsomest in England.

The newspapers went to town on the issue of sex equality and letters poured in from correspondents ranging from those who thought Sir Edward Marshall Hall had been patronising to those who thought he was a hero. George Bernard Shaw wrote tongue in cheek to the *Daily Mail*,[13] enquiring as to why Sir Edward thought that men were familiar with obscene letters and pictures. He, a sixty-five-year-old married man, would be just as shocked as any pure women.

Major Allen's ground for divorce had been adultery and Ethel Mary was undoubtedly in trouble on the evidence; she had spent the night at the Waldorf Hotel with a man and the family governess was to testify that Mrs Allen had bought a new nightgown for the occasion. But whatever the rights and wrongs, Mrs Allen did not want a divorce. The women jurors, faced with Marshall's outrage, had said they did not wish to see the evidence; they were content that only the men should do so. The trial proceeded on that basis and the jury were unable to come to a verdict. Marshall had got his publicity; but he had got what his client wanted as well.

Divorce work was highly lucrative and Marshall's views on the desirability of dissolving an unhappy marriage were ahead of his time and no doubt fuelled by personal experience. Just as the law relating to murder and insanity had evolved through a complex patchwork of moral, religious and legal principles, so too had the law relating to divorce, with the added components of profound sexual inequality and pragmatism regarding the importance of certainty in the laws of succession thrown into the mix. The whole issue had become highly controversial by the early 1920s.

For the preceding sixty years, since its creation in 1857, the divorce court, taking over from a previously ecclesiastical jurisdiction, had administered the law established at the same time.[14] The divorce jurisdiction was exclusively exercised in London and geographical and economic restraints meant that only the most prosperous could benefit from it. A husband could obtain a divorce on the grounds of adultery, as could a wife but only if coupled with some aggravating factor such as incest, bigamy, rape, sodomy, bestiality, extreme cruelty or desertion. The subtext was clear: women could not have affairs but men could, provided they did not compound them with socially unacceptable behaviour.[15]

In 1909, shortly before his death, Edward VII, better qualified than most in the vicissitudes of married life, had appointed a Royal Commission on the whole subject of divorce. The final report, after three years of deliberation, was delivered in 1912. The Royal Commission suggested radical reforms: an extension of the divorce jurisdiction countrywide, financial assistance for the poor, equality between the sexes and extension of the grounds upon which divorce could be sought to include those such as incurable insanity, habitual drunkenness and long terms of imprisonment. Allowing divorce on the grounds of what was rather charmingly called 'unconquerable aversion' was regarded as a step too far, however, as was the concept of divorce by mutual consent. In other words where one party loathed the other or both agreed to loathe each other, they had to put up with it; divorce was not recommended by the Royal Commission as an option for them.

Controversy as to the recommendations raged for years. There were still those who thought the law even as it then stood went too far. Devout Catholics such as Lord Braye and eminent lawyers such as Lord Phillimore were united in an unshakable conviction that marriage should be dissolved only by death. Reformers argued for a more enlightened approach than existed at that time whilst still rooting their arguments and prejudices in the Christian concept of the sanctity of marriage. Marshall, however, in a plea for reform delivered in a speech at a then smart social venue, the Aldwych Club, argued that marriage was a moral contract and should be dissolvable at the instance of the contracting parties subject only to certain minimal safeguards. 'Marriage is often the most immoral relationship in the world,' he said, frequently founded on considerations of financial expediency, social pragmatism and slavish compliance with the laws of legitimacy. Like many of Marshall's speeches it was highly contemporary, its courage touching a public nerve. His widely reported pleas for divorce reform now fuelled the growing discontent.

The welter of attitudes to divorce from the puritanical to the prurient found fertile ground between 1921 and 1923, when Christabel, the Honourable Mrs John Hugo Russell insisted she was a virgin despite evidence to the contrary in the form of little Geoffrey, her son.[16] This case had it all: sex, scandal and the aristocracy. Little Geoffrey, if legitimate, was heir to the Ampthill barony, the title attaching to a branch of one of the oldest aristocratic dynasties in England, the Russells, who had bred Prime Ministers, ambassadors and noble landowners since the time of Henry VIII.

Christabel had married John Hugo Russell, a year younger than her, when she was twenty-two. By then she had trained as a fashion designer at an art school in Paris, won many admirers and, she insisted, developed an aversion to sex. When John Hugo proposed to her, she accepted on condition that she did not want a baby and there was to be no sex for the foreseeable future, and it was John Hugo's case that he had complied with her stipulation.

Two-and-a-half years into their marriage she found she was pregnant. John Hugo insisted the baby could not be his; Christabel insisted it must be. 'We must do something … for the sake of the baby,' Christabel wrote. 'He is an awfully nice one.' But her husband did not care if the baby was awfully nice or not. He was adamant that no sexual activity that could have resulted in the creation of little Geoffrey had taken place between them. Christabel was equally adamant that although the marriage had never been fully consummated, John Hugo's attempts must have led to her pregnancy since nothing else could have done so. Backed by a family who had been unhappy with his marriage to a girl they regarded as irredeemably middle class, John Hugo sued for divorce on the grounds of Christabel's adultery with two named co-respondents, Gilbert Bradley and Lionel Cross, as well as an unknown man alleged to be the father of the child. He instructed a stellar team to prove it.

Sir John Simon KC, Douglas Hogg KC, Robert Bayford KC and the Honourable Victor Russell as junior were instructed by the Russell family. It must have cost a fortune. By the time Christabel and the co-respondents had all instructed counsel to defend the case, there were no fewer than eight barristers involved, five of them KCs. The president of the Divorce Court, Sir Henry Duke, presided. The gallery filled with fashionable society and the press. A jury of ten men and two women was arraigned. One of the women did not survive through the opening speech. As Simon spoke of Christabel's aversion to consummation and her husband's attempts to persuade her otherwise, she sent a note to the judge. She was unmarried and it was all too much for her. She asked to be discharged. The case proceeded with the remaining eleven jurors, now including only one woman. They sat transfixed through the ensuing romp around the aristocracy, the Mayfair house, the Parisian weekends, the titled protagonists, and the most intimate details of their lives. And against that backdrop they heard also of the 'incomplete relations' between husband and wife. Doctors gave evidence that though pregnant Christabel had 'showed signs of virginity'. Christabel's rackety life, sharing a *wagon-lit* with one co-respondent and the bachelor room of the other, was closely examined.

It was better than any keyhole. Beautiful, racy, independent, Christabel was more than a match for Simon. He was a brilliant man, a fellow of All Souls with a first in jurisprudence, but his chilly delivery interspersed with attempts at contemporary slang looked pompous and out of touch when countered by Christabel's too, too Noël Coward insouciance:

'Some people might call [a co-respondent] a "divine dancer"?'

'I did.'

'Sometimes when you danced with him, would you put your head against his cheek?'

'That was the fashion at the time. It has gone out now.'

'You followed the fashion?'

'Implicitly, in dancing.'

And in the end, having inspected the baby in their private rooms, the jury found Christabel had not committed adultery with either of the two named co-respondents, despite the *wagon-lit* and the bachelor flat, and could not agree as to the unknown man. A triumphant Christabel got her costs, as did the two co-respondents, who were dismissed from the suit. A retrial was ordered in respect of the unknown man. But before the hearing came on, John Hugo came up with another potential lover, Edgar Mayer, a smooth good-looking divorcee living in a flat in Mayfair who wore white flannel trousers and, appropriately enough, brown and white 'co-respondent' shoes. The divorce petition was amended to add Mayer as the new co-respondent and a new trial date set.

Sir John Simon found himself 'unable' to appear for the Russell family in the new trial. He may have had another fixture; but the rumour in the Temple was that he could not face Christabel again. Douglas Hogg, the second KC representing John Hugo, had just been appointed Attorney General. It was he who advised the Russell family as to a suitable substitute. 'There's only one man at the Bar who might pull it off for you. He might win you a brilliant victory or he might make a terrible mess of it. But I really believe he is the only man who can do it – Marshall Hall.'

Marshall hated briefs that had first been offered to other people; it offended his pride not to be the first and anyway he could not bear to inherit another barrister's already formulated tactics. But in December 1922, he received a visit in chambers from a distressed Lady Ampthill, John Hugo's mother. The family line was imperilled, her son's name besmirched; she begged for help. And Marshall, sympathetic and susceptible, it must be acknowledged, to the company of the aristocracy, agreed to take the case on.

Hogg's assessment had been a fair one; Marshall might just pull it off, with his charm and lightness of touch, his understanding of society and of women, his sophistication and well-known liberal views. He must not, on the other hand, lose his temper, treat Christabel like a murderer or most fatal of all, make her cry; nothing gained the jury's support like a beautiful sobbing woman.

And so the second Russell v Russell trial began, in front of Mr Justice Hill, and Marshall proceeded briskly through John Hugo's now well-rehearsed evidence of the 'incomplete relations'. But what everyone was waiting for was the duel between Christabel and Marshall. Newspapermen recorded the drama of that first moment when the protagonists faced each other. Christabel, young, slim, dressed in the height of fashion with her blond hair in immaculately corrugated waves and her eyebrows plucked pencil thin above her heavily made-up eyes, personified the brittle sophistication of the flapper age. Emboldened by the success of the first trial, she exuded a flippant indifference to the coming ordeal. Marshall stood facing her, grey haired beneath his wig, austerely handsome, a huge imposing man, half-moon spectacles on the end of his nose, his eyes fixed on her, his demeanour stern. He was a past master at drawing room conversation but he had no intention of playing Christabel at her own game. No one would have guessed, as he cross-examined her about her free and easy life as a fashion student living in the Latin Quarter in Paris, that he was drawing on personal experience. He was all stuffy disapproval.

The duel lasted for four hours and was afterwards said to be one of the most transfixing cross-examinations ever heard in the divorce courts. Edgar Bowker summed it up: Marshall was at his fighting best, he said, but so was the Honourable Mrs John Hugo Russell.

No holds were barred. Now it suited him, Marshall had lost the reticence he had shown when facing his first women jurors in the Allen case only a year before. No euphemisms were permitted; fondlings, erections, emissions, positions of both John Hugo and Christabel, not to mention that of their silk pyjama trousers, were minutely investigated by him with an almost crude insistence on pragmatism and anatomy. Christabel's responses had sounded like slick repartee when Sir John Simon was cross-examining her; now they sounded vapid and incredible:

> 'Have you never had the smallest curiosity to know what that portion of the man's body was intended by nature for?'
>
> 'I had not the smallest curiosity.'
>
> 'Do you know now that in moments of passion that portion of a man's body gets large?'
>
> 'I did not know … until you have just told me.'
>
> 'What!' exclaimed Marshall involuntarily. But he was not going to stop. 'I am afraid we must go into a little detail. Was he on top of you or beside you?'
>
> 'Beside me.'
>
> 'Did you know the purpose for which he wanted to put his person inside yours?'
>
> 'It seemed to me objectless.'[17]

It sounded pretty unconvincing in a sophisticated married woman who had lived in the high society of Paris and London.

The case culminated in one of Marshall's impassioned speeches in which, to those in the know, personal resonances were clear: 'Free this husband from the life which he once hoped would be a life of love but which is now a rusty chain that burns into his soul.' The jury found for John Hugo; they concluded that Christabel had not committed adultery with Edgar Mayer but they were satisfied that she had done so with an unknown man. A decree nisi was granted by the judge. The first step towards breaking John Hugo's rusty chain had been taken.

Christabel, now a vilified and convicted adulteress, promptly went to the Court of Appeal, who dismissed her appeal. Marginalised by the society so important to her, her name referred to in whispers and little Geoffrey now a bastard, Christabel fought back with an appeal to the House of Lords.[18] Only a point of law of public importance would get her a hearing there; running through all the court proceedings had been references to an old principle of law that a spouse could not give admissible evidence that he or she did not have sexual intercourse if that evidence would tend to bastardise a child prima facie born in wedlock. On this basis, the evidence the jury had heard from John Hugo would be inadmissible.

Marshall had always known his limitations and he recognised them disarmingly now. Had he been more arrogant, or perhaps less conscious of his public image he would have argued John Hugo Russell's case in the Lords. But he turned to Douglas Hogg, now back in private practice, to lead him; the pure intellectual legal arguments in the Lords with no jury to appeal to and no human emotions to invoke was not for him and he knew it. In fact, Christabel triumphed. The rule was upheld: John Hugo's evidence had been inadmissible, and Geoffrey would succeed to the title. But as far as the public was concerned, the Lords were was shutting the stable door after the horse had bolted. The salacious evidence had not only been given in court, it had been plastered (with omissions of the most explicit bits) over every newspaper in the land.

Ever since the inauguration of the divorce jurisdiction in 1857, disquiet had been expressed about the public nature of the hearings. Within two years, in 1859 Queen Victoria wrote to the then Lord Chancellor, Lord Campbell, condemning the scandalous publicity of proceedings in the new court: 'It makes it almost impossible for a paper to be trusted in the hands of a young lady or boy … none of the worst French novels from which careful parents would try to protect their children can be as bad.'[19] But it was all too new, too sensational and too lucrative to the newspaper business to be easily suppressed. The divorce courts were becoming known as a place of legitimised pornographic entertainment and those too far away to scramble for entry got it second hand over the breakfast table.

The Russell case evidence of partial penetration and erections and emissions was certainly the most explicit yet and George V now stepped into the fray. This desecrating of holy intimate relations must stop. But despite attempts to introduce a Bill to regulate reporting, vested interests ensured its failure.

Then in 1925 Marshall did it again, in the case of Dennistoun v Dennistoun.[20] In the Russell case, he had fulfilled the first half of Douglas Hogg's prediction and achieved a brilliant victory. In the Dennistoun case it could be said he achieved the second half, a terrible mess. Not only that, he damaged his reputation yet again, exceeded the bad taste even of the Russell case and besmirched the name of a national hero.

It was all because he could not resist the blandishments of Almina Carnarvon. Lord Carnarvon, the fifth Earl, had died in April 1923 in Cairo, the victim of an infected mosquito bite or of Tutankhamen's curse, depending on point of view. The sixth Earl inherited the family seat, Highclere Castle, and Almina, eight months after her husband's death, married Lieutenant Colonel Ian Dennistoun of the Grenadier Guards.

Ian Dennistoun had been married before, to Dorothy, a close friend of Almina's. She divorced him eleven years later. After Ian's subsequent marriage to Almina and all her Rothschild millions, Dorothy took proceedings against him in relation to small loans she claimed were owing to her and to an agreement she said had been made on divorce whereby she did not claim alimony on the understanding that when Ian was in a financial position to do so, he would voluntarily provide for her.

Almina, now Mrs Dennistoun, was used to getting her own way and she resented Dorothy's claims, which she interpreted as an attempt at blackmail. Her own adventurous love life and the fact that she had kept Ian Dennistoun in a Paris flat (albeit, she insisted, out of the purest of motives) during the last year of Lord Carnarvon's life was only too well known to Dorothy. Almina insisted that Ian contest the action and turned to her old friend Marshall to represent him. The friendship between Marshall and Almina had been a close one. When, as Alfred de Rothschild's executor, Marshall had refused Almina's request for permission to sell the Gainsborough and the van Dyck he may or may not have known that she wanted the money in order to buy Ian Dennistoun the flat in Paris. But he certainly knew Dorothy Dennistoun well, and was well aware that during her own marriage to Ian she had been having an affair with General Sir John Cowans, Quartermaster General during the First World War and also a friend of Marshall's.

When Cowans died, Marshall had given legal advice to Dorothy and the Spanish lover she then had in tow in relation to her wish to take proceedings against Cowans's estate. He had advised her against advertising her adulterous relationship to the world. But now it was likely to come out in another context.

That much Marshall certainly knew of what was to develop into a seedy parading of dirty linen. He very probably knew a lot more of the extraordinary network of love affairs, not just illicit but sordid as well, that was to be revealed in Dennistoun v Dennistoun. It showed a crashing lack of judgement to agree to represent Colonel Dennistoun and would have led to disaster for him personally had it not been for Norman Birkett, now also a KC, who was briefed to appear with him and ultimately saved the day.

The trial opened in March 1925 and the nature of Ian and Dorothy's transactions was revealed for all to hear. Dorothy, according to Ian, had had affairs with a Hungarian nobleman and a Polish major as well as the Spaniard, who had been a bullfighter. But despite the European flavour it had been her affair with a very English general that really attracted the attention. The relationship with Cowans (referred to initially as Colonel X until the judge, Mr Justice McCardie, ordered his name to be revealed) could not have reflected more dishonour on all parties. Dorothy had embarked on it when she and Ian had run out of money. Cowans for his part obtained Ian's advancement in the army to the rank of lieutenant colonel in return for Dorothy's sexual favours and Ian connived in his wife's relationship and latterly advised her on tactics to keep Cowans interested. General Sir John Cowans was a national figure as a result of his service as Quartermaster General, and two years previously had been given a state funeral on his death. The nation was appalled to discover this now tumbled hero's feet of clay and horrified to hear the allegations and counter-allegations of myriad adulterous affairs on all sides. Marshall's cross-examination of Dorothy did him no credit: he was aggressive, bullying and contemptuous, and his personal support for Almina was painfully obvious. It all culminated in this disastrous exchange when he asked her about the action she had begun in relation to Cowans's estate:

'You must remember', she said, 'as you did it all for me.'

'If you wish me to tell the court what you told me, I am prepared to do so.'

'You persuaded me not to go on with the case.'

'You said you did not want a certain name brought into it and I withdrew the case at your wish. At that time you were living at Lady Carnarvon's house?'

'Yes, I had just gone there.'

'Do you know it was at the special request of Lady Carnarvon?'

'Yes, she paid you.'

'You know', Marshall shouted, 'I was never paid a penny. I did not receive one farthing but as Lady Carnarvon's friend I consented to advise you.'

It was all grossly improper on a number of fronts. Counsel should not appear on the other side to a party he has previously represented in a closely related action; he should not disclose information supplied in confidence; he certainly should not give evidence as to his personal role in that other case. His friendship with Almina had 'warped his independence and I think his judgment', Sir Ellis Hume Williams, who appeared for Dorothy Dennistoun, later said.[21] It was a generous exoneration for what was inexcusable for a barrister of Marshall's experience and many in the Temple were far less forgiving.

The day was saved by Edgar Bowker, who, seeing Marshall was suffering from a flare-up of his phlebitis, persuaded him to let Norman Birkett take over the next day. Marshall agreed to take a secondary role, wisely relinquishing the closing speech to Birkett. The jury's findings on the complex claims and counter-claims were such that by the time costs had been allocated neither party gained a penny. And Mr Justice McCardie sought to reassure a public whose admiration of their supposed superiors might have suffered a blow. 'Cases like the present do not in any way represent the general way of life of well-to-do people in England. They give a wholly false impression of English social and family life.'

Punch called it 'The Dustbin Case'. George V, still reeling from Russell v Russell, expressed himself in even stronger terms: sex was one thing and bad enough, but the Dennistoun case undermined the very structure of England. 'The King deplores the disastrous and far reaching effects throughout all classes and on all ranks of the Army [of] the wholesale press advertisements of this disgraceful story,' wrote his private secretary to the Lord Chancellor.[22]

This time his view prevailed. The Judicial Proceedings (Regulation of Reports) Act became law in 1926. From then on, reporting of divorce cases must contain no indecent material. Dennistoun v Dennistoun was far from being Marshall's finest hour; but it was another example of his extraordinary ability to be associated with the case of the moment; whether brilliant victory or terrible mess, it scarcely seemed to matter.

CHAPTER 17

'God's great Western sun'

Being a country solicitor's wife in Wales, until then an innocuous occupation, now seemed to be getting rather risky. In April 1922, eighteen months after the trial of Harold Greenwood, Herbert Armstrong, another solicitor who practised in Hay on Wye, decided to adopt precisely the same means, arsenic extracted from weed killer, to dispatch Mrs Armstrong. An increasingly jumpy Archibald Bodkin, as Director of Public Prosecutions heavily criticised for the defence triumph in Greenwood's trial, was probably heartily relieved when Marshall, obvious first choice, refused the defence brief for Armstrong, giving pressure of work as the reason. Armstrong achieved the distinction of being the first (and only) solicitor to hang for murder. In December of the same year, Marshall also resisted an offer to defend in the famous Thompson and Bywaters case. Twenty-six-year-old Edith Thompson and her eighteen-year-old lover Frederick Bywaters were charged with the murder of Thompson's husband. They too hanged.

Both cases were defended by Henry Curtis Bennett KC. He was outstandingly able. Convictions and acquittals are not reliable indicators of quality of advocacy, as Marshall would be the first to say. All the same, he would not have been averse to the effect of these results on his own reputation, increasingly regarded by the public as mystical. Although basking in the acclaim, Marshall was determined not to be typecast. A financier facing a huge fraud trial had indignantly refused to have Marshall as his counsel on the basis that everyone would think he was a murderer. It was a warning Marshall took to heart. The bouts of bronchitis were becoming more frequent; 'I have quite made up my mind', he wrote to Charles Gill, 'if I don't get alright after this bout I shall do something else than spend my life fighting desperate cases for inadequate remuneration.'[1] He began to concentrate on fashionable divorce and libel, non-criminal cases of a heavily fact-based kind in which his reputation as the consummate psychologist would get him work. The press greeted this new departure with enthusiasm. Now that Sir Edward Marshall Hall was appearing in high-profile divorces, public interest intensified: 'Kisses and Champagne on the Riviera'; 'Millionaire's Romance'; 'Bride in Name Only'. The headlines grew ever larger and more salacious.

In 1923, whilst Marshall's attentions were focussed on preparation for the Russell v Russell divorce, the world was fascinated by one of the greatest discoveries of the century. Marshall's friend Lord Carnarvon with the archaeologist Howard Carter after six seasons of Egyptian excavations had discovered their holy grail, the tomb of Tutankhamen.[2] As its treasures were slowly revealed, fashionable society flocked to Egypt.

Shepherds Hotel in Cairo was booked out by royalty, aristocracy and newspaper moguls and amongst the many smart tourists gathering at Luxor were 'Prince' and 'Princess' Fahmy, a newly married couple of immense wealth who sailed up the Nile in their private yacht to see the marvels they had read about. Serious trouble was already brewing between them. There had been bitter and often public rows and recriminations in palaces in Cairo, in yachts on the Nile and at balls in Paris. Marguerite Fahmy, though she may not then have known it, was going to need Marshall's services; but it would not be for a divorce. It would be because she was on a murder charge.[3]

On Sunday 1 July, the Fahmys' limousine swept up to the Savoy Hotel and disgorged the Louis Vuitton luggage stuffed with couture clothes and fabulous jewels; the obligatory little lapdog; the secretary, Said Enani; the twenty-two-year-old Egyptian millionaire, Ali Fahmy Bey; and his French wife of a few months, Marguerite. Marguerite, ten years Ali's senior, was beautiful and sultry with hooded eyes and a sulky mouth, wafting veils and furs and one of the dozens of heady perfumes for which she had paid hundreds of pounds in a Cairo perfumery. They were fresh from Deauville, Biarritz and Luxor and underneath the superficial glamour lay deep layers of scandal and intrigue.

Ali Fahmy was described so universally at the time as an 'Egyptian playboy' that it becomes impossible to think of any other term to characterise him. Born into an upper-middle-class Egyptian family, he had inherited an enormous fortune in his teens and proceeded to buy a clutch of luxury sports cars and speedboats and to party and show off in the grand hotels of Europe. When at home he lived in a lavishly furnished palace in Cairo and owned a flashy seaside villa in Alexandria. Photographs of the time show him, the epitome of decadence, reclining on leopard skin cushions. Had *Hello!* magazine existed then he would have featured in it. The claim to royal blood with the adoption of 'Prince' as his title followed soon and it became accepted as appropriate to his lifestyle if not to his birth.

His closest adviser and friend was his secretary, Said Enani. Enani was six years older. He administered Ali's business interests and his lavish charitable donations and such was the size of both that he even employed a secretary of his own. The three men were inseparable and in Cairo there were rumours, so scurrilous that they could only be hinted at in public and whispered about in private, that the relationship between them was also a sexual one. If so, Fahmy was bisexual. More open were his relationships with many mistresses and amongst them had been Marguerite, whom he had met and courted in 1922.

Marguerite had been well known by another name, Maggie Mellor. The daughter of a Parisian cab driver, she had become pregnant at fifteen, gone on the streets and worked her way up to become the sought-after courtesan of the rich and titled. On her way she had acquired and abandoned one husband and many rich lovers.

During their short marriage, neither Ali nor Marguerite appeared to have any illusions about the other. In their frequent screaming rows he flung 'prostitute' at her and she retaliated with 'pimp'. Their arrival at the Savoy in July 1923 happened to be a day of relative harmony. They booked into one of the most lavish service suites, replete with the requisite gilt ormolu and marble of the grandest hotels. In the opulent luggage unpacked on their arrival was the .32 Browning semi-automatic pistol with which Marguerite always travelled in case her conspicuous jewels attracted attention of a less welcome kind than the sort in which she revelled.

Ignoring the broiling heat of the next day, the Fahmys booked theatre seats and in the evening, despite the discomfort it must have entailed in the tropical temperatures, the three of them put on full evening dress and awaited the chauffeur in the hotel foyer, the two men in tailcoats and starched white shirt fronts and Marguerite in white pearl-embroidered satin. They were going to Daly's Theatre to see a popular operetta, *The Merry Widow*. They did not know then the irony of the title. Late in the evening, ominous thunder now rolling overhead, they returned to supper at the Savoy. Over the white linen, crystal and silver Marguerite and Ali rowed again. It was not the first argument that day, but it was the most public.

Contrary to her husband's wishes, Marguerite was insisting on returning to Paris. She needed an operation, the reasons for and nature of which were to prove significant at her subsequent trial. The row escalated into a yelling match; but eventually it subsided and the trio went downstairs to the ballroom, where they sat, a morose little island, whilst around them the band played out and their fellow guests danced.

At one in the morning Marguerite went to bed, as did Said Enani. But Ali went out again, still in his evening dress, borne away by a taxi to the

West End, in search of boy or girl more accommodating than his wife was likely to be.

By now London was in the grip of one of the worst electrical storms ever witnessed in England. Fireballs of lightning burst overhead and thunder rolled. Ali returned an hour later in the deluging rain, to another row with his wife. A night porter, John Beattie, on duty on the floor on which the Fahmys' suite was situated, was startled when the door was flung open and Ali, now in a silk dressing gown, ran out followed by Marguerite, still in evening dress. Each tried to show Beattie injuries they claimed the other had inflicted but Beattie, in the best traditions of the Savoy, was concerned only with preserving the hushed carpeted calm of the public parts of the hotel and ushered them back into their own room. He continued with his duties, and a little later, passing by the end of the corridor, he saw that Marguerite's little dog was now in the corridor and that Ali was standing just outside the door apparently whistling to him. Beattie continued on his way but in seconds, above the roar of the thunder and rain, he heard gunshot. Turning back, an operatic scene met his eyes: Ali was slumped on the floor in the corridor with a ghastly wound in his head from which brain and bone protruded; and there was Marguerite, gun in hand, a pool of blood and the crushed pearls from her dress at her feet, screaming incoherently in French. She flung the gun to the floor and ran towards Beattie, who, with remarkable presence of mind, grabbed the gun, threw it into a nearby lift, and restraining Marguerite by both arms led her to the nearest service telephone. Soon the dark corridor had filled with the bright lights and normality of the aftermath: doctor, ambulance, night porters, general manager and finally police, called from nearby Bow Street. It was whilst Marguerite was being interviewed at the police station that the news arrived that Ali had died.

There could be no doubt as to the culprit. Throughout the night a weeping Marguerite had signed her own indictment in a series of heartbroken confessions: '*J'ai tiré à Ali*' (I shot Ali) and '*Je perds la tête*' (I'm losing my head).

Money was no object; Mr Freke Palmer, a highly regarded and experienced solicitor, was retained to represent Marguerite and he wanted Marshall Hall. And Marshall had vowed to do no more criminal cases. But this was the Savoy, the home of his youth, the scene of all those convivial evenings since. And it was a shooting; for Marshall, always regarding himself as a ballistics expert with few rivals, they held an irresistible fascination. And the murderess was beautiful and from his beloved Paris. And the victim, if not an actual prince, was certainly the Eurotrash equivalent. And there had been blood and pearls and chaos on the night of the worst storm in living memory, and sex too aberrant to be mentioned in polite society. And to cap it all there was limitless wealth. He could not let any other barrister hog the limelight or the brief fee in this one. With Marshall's fluent French, sense of drama, understanding of society, this case had his name on it. And so ultimately of course did the brief: 'For the Defence: Sir Edward Marshall Hall KC and with you, Sir Henry Curtis Bennett KC and Mr Roland Oliver'. And Marshall was back in court number one at the Old Bailey, defending the sultry Marguerite.

The only flaw was that there seemed to be no defence.

But Marguerite had a story to tell and furthermore she had (almost too convenient) evidence to back the more salacious bits up. After the romantic courtship, the marriage, according to Marguerite, had turned into a reign of terror and the palaces and yachts into prisons. From the very beginning, immediately after the wedding ceremony that had required her conversion to Islam, things had changed, she said. She discovered that she was expected to pay for the furs and jewels in all kinds of unspeakably dreadful ways. And one of them was particularly well documented. On her arrival at the Savoy, Marguerite had had a consultation with the hotel's doctor. She showed him the bruises that she said Ali had inflicted on her; but her major complaint was the agony she was suffering from haemorrhoids and an anal tear, caused, she told the doctor, by her husband's predilection for 'unnatural intercourse'. On being told she needed surgical advice, she decided to seek it in Paris and it was this decision, she now told her advisers, that had triggered the rows between the couple on that last day.

Here, then, was Marshall's defence: an attack on the dead Ali, addicted to horrible sexual deviance, a wife beater, above all a foreigner and an exotic one at that. It all slotted beautifully into the stereotyping of the time, but it needed handling with extraordinary care. Attacks on the prosecution witnesses would entitle the prosecution to argue that Marguerite's own character and background, otherwise inadmissible as evidence, could be put before the jury. Marshall was prepared to have his client described as 'a woman of the world' but he did not want the jury to know she was a tart, even a high-class one.

There had been a fevered interest in all things Eastern since the turn of the century. Anybody who did not originate in the western hemisphere was an 'oriental' and anyone not determinedly pink was 'black'. By the early 1920s this fascination had intensified, fuelled with authenticity by Lord Carnarvon's recent discoveries.

Women in particular were gripped in a fascination for the exotic: dresses based on ancient Egyptian styles in colours such as Nile green were the height of fashion, sphinxes and camels featured on handbags and cigarette holders, scarabs appeared on fingers and lapels, and kohl outlined eyes. But it was not just appearances that fascinated them; it was men too, as love affairs between 'Western' women and 'Eastern' men became the subject of ever-increasingly lurid 'desert romances'. This unhealthy genre was personified in the ludicrously overwritten *The Sheikh*, written in 1919 and turned into the 1921 film that made Rudolph Valentino a star. A young aristocratic English girl is kidnapped, raped, beaten and humiliated into love for her 'Arab' captor. In that story, all turns out well in the end when it transpires that the 'sheikh' is really the son of an English nobleman and not an Arab at all, that his swarthiness is attributable to his Spanish mother and that he was educated in Paris. His bestial behaviour is thereby transformed into titillating masterfulness and they live happily ever after in a beautiful tent with oriental hangings and all the mod cons the heroine requires. It was the first of many such books in which heroines revelled in the perfumes and splendour of the so-called 'orient' and learned to their cost, or delight, as the case might be, that with all the alluring exoticism went a cataclysmic clash of cultures as a result of which they end up enslaved in more ways than one.

It was a fertile time for a trial in which a sophisticated Western woman told of her overwhelming seduction and the price she had paid for it; no excesses of stereotyping, as Marshall well knew, would be too great for his jury to swallow. And so he set himself to create one of his living pictures, as he had done for Jeannie Baxter. With a magnificent contempt for the fact that in English law no concept of *crime passionel* exists, Marshall ran a defence which was in reality just that. It was also racist, homophobic and jingoistic. Marshall was none of those things. But like a tabloid journalist he gave his public what they wanted, even if it meant selling himself in the process.

The trial at the Old Bailey opened with the familiar fever pitch of excitement and to a packed court. Counsel's row attracted particular attention. There sat the prosecution team, a monument to the hereditary traditions of the Bar: Percival Clarke, son of Marshall's great hero Sir Edward Clarke KC; and Eustace Fulton, son of Forrest Fulton, Marshall's early mentor. Beside them sat Marshall himself, Henry Curtis Bennett KC and their junior, Roland Oliver. Another KC and junior represented Ali Fahmy's sister, now head of the powerful dynasty; but most striking of all, as Marjoribanks tells us with unmistakable superiority, 'cheek by jowl with these members of the English Bar sat swarthy Egyptian lawyers' also retained by the Fahmy family. What they were to hear shocked the entire Egyptian nation.

The prosecution did not anticipate a very hard task. There was no doubt, after all, that Marguerite Fahmy had shot her husband dead and not even

Marshall could argue otherwise. The law at the time presumed every homicide to be a murder. It was for the defendant to prove the circumstances that either exonerated him altogether or reduced the killing to manslaughter.

The first significant witness was the Fahmy's secretary Said Enani. Marshall started as he meant to go on with a noisy objection to Enani, a Muslim, being sworn on the New Testament. There was no Koran available; neither the judge nor prosecuting counsel nor Enani himself raised any objection to the course taken, but now Marshall suggested that Enani was not bound to tell the truth on an oath taken in these circumstances. The jury got the message: here was an exotic foreigner whose word could not be trusted, whose religion was alien. Through the medium of cross-examination Marshall began to build his picture.

In the first months of her marriage, he suggested, every bit of life had been crushed out of this beautiful woman, his client. Ali was a man of strong sexual appetite, he had had many girlfriends, he had treated them all brutally, he had lured Marguerite to Egypt and married her under a system that entitled him to have four wives and divorce them at will. Six black servants had watched her constantly and Ali had abused her until she was wretched with misery. Marshall's extraordinary skill turned his cross-examination, an exercise designed to elicit evidence, into the evidence itself and a picture was emerging. Enani's protestations and qualified responses scarcely mattered at all.

Amongst all the allegations, the most sensational was the least explicit. In 1922 a cartoon had appeared in a Cairo satirical magazine showing Ali Fahmy, Enani and Enani's secretary under the caption 'The light, the shadow of the light and the shadow of the shadow of the light'. Undoubtedly suggesting inseparability between the three men, it had in some quarters been interpreted as an allegation of homosexuality. Now, Marshall produced the cartoon and asked whether in Egypt the relationship between Fahmy and Enani had been 'notorious'. Enani denied it; but again, the seed had been sown, and sown so insidiously that the judge rejected the prosecution's suggestion that Enani's character had been traduced.

With his usual habit of skating over the bits he did not like, Marshall scarcely questioned the night porter at all. The domestic picture of a prince in pyjamas whistling for his wife's little dog was not one he wanted implanted on the jury's mind. He concentrated his attention instead on the gunsmith Robert Churchill, who, as a prosecution expert, had become an old protagonist. With his own expert knowledge of firearms Marshall had recognised that in the technical characteristics of a semi-automatic weapon, so damaging to the defence, lay what, if carefully handled, might equally provide a plausible explanation for an accidental firing of the gun.

A semi-automatic has a far more sophisticated mechanism than the revolvers used in the Edward Lawrence and Jeannie Baxter trials, in which Marshall had had such success. Once loaded, the breech cover has to be manually pulled back and released to bring the cartridge into its firing position in the breech. The shot is fired by pulling the trigger, and once that first shot is fired the remaining seven rounds (eight being the full capacity of the gun) will automatically be brought into firing position one by one after each successive shot. This characteristic was at first glance an embarrassment to the defence: experience, or at least knowledge, was required in order to fire the first shot.

Marshall had spent anxious hours at Whistler's, gun dealers in the Strand, consulting with Mr Stopp, the manager. Stopp was used to giving him informal advice. An old friend, he supplied Marshall with his sporting guns and shared his expert knowledge. In this trial with money no object he could of course have been called as an expert for the defence. But Marshall made it his practice to keep his experts backstage. It suited his vanity to provide the 'expert' knowledge as his own; but it also suited his tactics. Experts owe a duty to the court to give factually correct evidence, however inconvenient to the party they are representing; what Marshall unashamedly delivered was 'expertise' with a spin. In the unusual mechanism of the weapon he detected the beginning of a defence; someone ignorant of it might plausibly believe that in discharging the gun they were emptying it when in fact they were automatically reloading it. Flourishing a gun provided for the purpose by Whistler's, Marshall demonstrated the theory to Churchill and crucially Churchill accepted its credibility.

Enough ground was laid for what Marshall was really relying on, a vivid picture of Marguerite's marriage which he was to paint with the assistance of his client. Marguerite, unlike Ronald Light in the Green Bicycle murder, was not quite pitch perfect; early in her evidence he asked her why she had come to London. 'I had to come to London for family reasons,' she replied. That was not the answer Marshall wanted. He wanted the jury to swell with protective insularity. 'Did you think you would be *safe* in London?' he asked her in a shamelessly leading question. Even then she did not respond as he wanted: 'I passed from despair to hope and hope to despair,' she said.

But eventually she got the message and the story emerged. She knew nothing of guns, she insisted; and under Marshall's gentle tutelage she made a timid and fruitless attempt to pull open the breech cover. The brutal violence she had suffered at Ali's hands transfixed the court and culminated in her description of the final scene. She had begged for the money that would enable her to return to Paris for the vital operation; he had grabbed her and told her she had to earn it. Though unreportable it was implicit that he was demanding anal intercourse despite her injuries. She had struggled and fought and at last freed herself and run into the corridor; this was the occasion of the first encounter with Beattie, the night porter, who had ushered her and Ali back into their suite. As Ali approached her again she grabbed the pistol lying on top of her suitcase. Loaded for her some time previously by Ali, she believed it now to be harmless, because, she said, she had earlier attempted to draw back the breech cover and to shake the cartridge out of the barrel as she had often seen him do. She had been afraid of the presence of the loaded gun in the climate of threats and violence. In her attempt to empty it, however, it had discharged harmlessly out of a window. Now she had seized what she believed was an empty weapon to hold him at bay. Somehow they had ended up again in the corridor. He threatened to kill her and leaped at her, grabbing her by the throat. She pushed him away and as he crouched to spring again 'I lifted my arm in front of me ... and pulled the trigger ... I do not know how many times the pistol went off'.

It could not be described as a watertight defence. There were very obvious gaps in Marguerite's account, not to mention the inherent unlikeliness of Ali's murderous pounce in such a public place as a hotel corridor; but the difficulties were obscured by the general pathos and the tears and collapses that punctuated her evidence. Midway through a cross-examination that Marguerite was finding hard to cope with, Marshall told the judge that she could not follow the court interpreter, whereupon a young Frenchwoman, Odette Simon, herself a barrister, who had been listening from the public gallery, offered her services. It may have been a tactic to direct the jury's attention away from the cross-examination; it may, as Marjoribanks suggests, have been a romantic notion of Marshall's that two young Frenchwomen supporting each other in a strange land would appeal to the jury; or it may simply have been that Marshall had an undoubted predilection for Frenchwomen; but from then on Odette Simon took over from the court-appointed interpreter.

There has been a recent theory as to why, given Marshall's attack on Said Enani's reputation, the judge would not allow Marguerite's background and character to be put before the jury and in relation to the supposed lack-lustre nature of the prosecution's cross-examination of her. In 2013 it was revealed that Marguerite had been a mistress of the Prince of Wales, the future Edward VIII, during her early career. The theory is that in exchange for her silence on this and the return of damaging letters to the prince, the trial was rigged to secure her release.[4] Whether true or not there is no evidence to suggest that either Marshall or his instructing solicitor was included in the plan and nothing detracts from the theatre that was his closing speech, commonly held at the time to be the reason for her acquittal. Certainly it was in the tradition of all the other miraculous acquittals with which his name was associated around this time.

Delivered to a mesmerised jury, it was pure Marshall. No juror's eye wandered away from his tall figure during the hours of the impassioned lyrical diatribe and the whole court was gripped in a motionless silence. As he appealed for Marguerite's life, he seemed, the newspapers reported, to cast a spell as compelling as that of a hypnotist. His gestures were those of an actor, his modulation of tone that of the greatest orator, changing by the minute 'from irony to passion, from passion to grave and serious sonorousness'.[5] 'Strip off the external civilisation of the oriental,' he now begged the jury (and a delicious collective shiver went through the public gallery crammed with fashionable women), 'and you have the real oriental underneath'. The oriental, he reminded them, to whom women were chattels and who changed after marriage, from plausible lovers to ferocious brutes. This Eastern man, with his pride in the possession of a Western woman, had treated her cruelly, subjected her to unnatural demands and deprived her of her freedom from the day of her marriage until a bullet sent him to eternity.

She was, said Marshall, warming to his theme, at the mercy of this brutal man and his six black servants. He asked the jury to imagine the horror for this white woman of a black servant watching her, even when she was in her bedroom. 'It makes one shudder to think of it.' By now the jury were shuddering too. And so, at last, to the night of the killing. 'When the accused saw the pistol on her chair in her suite at the Savoy something came into her brain. She remembers the threats, she remembers the brutality. She knows it is charged and ready to fire.' And Marshall imitated Ali's last ghastly threatening crouch, 'like an animal, like an oriental' ready to spring, and he gripped the pistol as Marguerite had done. The jury were on the edge of their seats. And the weapon fell from Marshal's hand onto the wooden desk in front of him, its clatter resounding ear-shatteringly through the silent courtroom, like gunshot.

Anything else might have come as an anticlimax. But Marshall had a last trick up his sleeve. He reminded the jury of *Bella Donna* by Robert Hichens, one of the most famous of the desert romances. At the end of the novel, the garden gate of the safe colonial home of the heroine opens and she goes out into the dark, into the desert to God knows what. 'Members of the jury,' he said, 'I want you to open the gates where this Western woman can go out, not into the dark night of the desert but back to her friends ... back to her child ...'. The courtroom, dull for most of the morning, was suddenly illuminated with a beam of late September sun catching the gold of the sword of justice suspended above the judge's chair. Marshall pointed to it. 'Let this Western woman go back into the light of God's great Western sun.'

The imagery lingered as though relayed on a vast screen which formed an imaginary backdrop to the judge's summing up. At the end of it all, Marguerite reeled into the arms of her wardresses and was carried below to await her fate. When the jury returned with their verdict of 'not guilty' to murder, the hysterical crowds tightly wedged in the public gallery rose in a yelling cheering mass so out of control that it was several minutes before sufficient order was restored to hear the foreman announce that the jury had also found Marguerite not guilty of manslaughter. She was free.

The day after the trial finished was Marshall's birthday. He was sixty-five. Amongst the vast amount of post arriving over the next few days was a telegram from Marguerite Fahmy: '*De tout mon coeur je vous suis, profondément reconnaissante*' ('With all my heart, I am deeply grateful to you'). Letters from her followed, passionate in her relief. It is interesting that of all his clients, it was Marguerite, the French tart, with whom he kept in touch; not only did the pistol join the display on his wall, but so did a portrait of Marguerite at her most sultry, bearing another personal message of thanks, and Marguerite herself came to tea at 3 Temple Gardens on a subsequent visit to London.

Congratulations from all over the world poured in. Amongst them, promptly delivered to the correct address, was one addressed simply to 'Marshall Hall the greatest lawyer on earth'. The newspapers, deprived of the daily sensation of Marshall's oratory during the trial, now relived every word of it all over again. The re-enactment by Marshall of Ali's oriental crouch, the electrifying clatter of gun on floor and the shafts of sunlight infusing the courtroom lost nothing in the retelling. Sir Edward Marshall Hall, said *John Bull*, 'overlays with the skill of an accomplished actor, the deadly and dangerous dexterity of a great forensic artist'. The legend grew and grew.

The admiration was not universal. The worldwide exposure the trial had received whipped up what nowadays would be termed racial hatred as self-congratulatory headlines such as 'Beautiful English justice' appeared in all the press. One paper with the headline 'Sheikh glamour' spoke of 'sinister Egyptian enchanters who lead white women astray' and another under the heading 'The twain that will never meet'[6] warned against the horrors that lay in store for white brides in the East.

The Reuters correspondent in Cairo was officially requested to forward a statement to the English newspapers deploring the rash generalisations made about the Egyptian people. Outraged by the headlines, the Batonnier (leader) of the Egyptian Bar wrote to the Attorney General, leader of the English Bar, complaining of Marshall Hall's indiscriminate 'lashing' of not only Egypt but the whole East: 'The Egyptian Bar protests with all its force against the principle followed by Sir Marshall Hall in his defence as unjust and deplorable.' In loyal defence Sir Douglas Hogg replied: 'I am quite confident that Sir Edward Marshall Hall would not willingly hurt the feelings of any foreign people and he is far too distinguished and experienced an advocate to transgress the limits properly restraining the conduct of his client's case.' Privately he then hauled Marshall over the coals. Marshall wrote a disingenuous, albeit slightly sheepish, letter: 'If by any chance, in the heat of the advocacy I was betrayed into saying anything that can be construed as an attack on the Egyptians as a nation, I shall be the first to disclaim any such intention and express regret if I was so represented.'[7]

Marshall had lived now for years with life and death. On more occasions than any other living barrister he had seen men and women facing the possibility of the cold planned ritual of their own deaths. He knew better than most how facile was the public understanding of hanging, hedged around as it was by false comfort deliberately created by officialdom. The victims all went bravely, or at least quietly, to their deaths, the public were told. They were usually said to have confessed on the scaffold; there was no question of an unjust verdict. Their last utterance usually contained a reference to God. An inquest immediately held on the scaffold reassured everyone that it was all over in a second.

A few journalists who had witnessed the actuality spoke out against the barbarity. 'I have never seen a man afraid before … and I prayed I might never see that shameful sight again,'[8] wrote one after a contemptuous rejection of the anodyne reports on a particular hanging. Marshall had seen that unimaginable fear on many occasions now, and as he sat in condemned cells advising on appeals, he had been seen by desperate men as their only saviour. No sensitive man could fail to seek answers to the unanswerable questions around death. Of all the condemned he had seen, he was ultimately most affected by the fatalism of the patriarchal Lock Ah Tam, plainly mentally ill. Asked, as was customary, if he had anything to say on why the sentence of death should not be passed upon him, Tam merely shook his head slowly from side to side. 'Life cannot be such an important thing if all the million and millions of Easterners treat it with such unconcern,'[9] said Marshall in a letter to a friend.

Impressed though he was, fatalism was not an answer for Marshall, with his optimism and hunger for life. Spiritualism appealed far more. He wanted to believe not only in a life after death but in one with the recognisable pleasures of the life he knew. If Marshall had had his way, spirits would have smoked cigars and frequented the theatre and the Garrick Club. From an early age he had hovered around in the vague hinterland where Christianity met spiritualism, inspired by listening to William Boyd Carpenter, who, when Canon of Windsor and chaplain to Queen Victoria, used to preach in the Temple Church. Boyd Carpenter ultimately became president of the Society for Psychical Research. At home as well, Marshall had been early exposed to the influences of spiritualism. His sister and brother in law Ada and Arthur Labouchere had a close friend, Miss Kate Wingfield, a trance medium who received and communicated messages through automatic writing. An irreverent young Marshall when first watching the writing appearing on the page had infuriated his sister by asking Miss Wingfield if she could predict the winner of the Derby, but later, in 1894, an uncanny prediction by Miss Wingfield relating to the death of his brother in South Africa at last convinced him.

Marshall's older brother James had, by the standards of the day, gone to the bad. A highly successful businessman, his work entailed frequent trips to Paris, and when it came to his wife's attention that he had taken a woman with him, she not only left him, but ensured that his business partner and the woman, a long-term mistress, also did so. James, ostracised by society, fled to Kimberley in South Africa and took to drink. Marshall had always been the admiring little brother, fifteen years younger. Now he refused ever to speak to his sister-in-law again and became James's lifeline, sending regular remittances for his support. These were entrusted to an English cleric, Archdeacon Gaul, the rector of the church in Kimberley, with instructions to make sure they were not spent on drink. James, resenting the arrangement, wrote vituperatively to Marshall, and Marshall, visiting his sister Ada in March 1894, had the letter in his pocket. Miss Wingfield was also visiting and Ada begged Marshall to test once more Miss Wingfield's psychic powers. Marshall handed over the letter in an unmarked envelope and asked Miss Wingfield to identify where the writer of the letter lived. A message came through via Miss Wingfield's automatic writing: 'The writer of the letter is dead. He died yesterday in South Africa.' The statement turned out to be true; Marshall subsequently received a letter from the archdeacon telling him that James had been found dead in his lodgings. The incident, apparently inexplicable by any rational analysis, had a dramatic impact on Marshall.[10]

Marshall had been highly vulnerable at that time when still grappling with the tragedy of Ethel's death. The experience had been the beginning of a strong belief in the after-life from which he derived enormous comfort. For the next thirty years he neither advertised nor hid his beliefs and discovered many other fellow travellers. Most prominent amongst them was Sir Arthur Conan Doyle, an old friend from the Crimes Club. Also an ardent believer was Arthur Balfour, briefly Prime Minister during Marshall's time in Parliament, and a member (and one-time president) of the Society of Psychical Research. Like Marshall's, Balfour's interest had stemmed from the traumatic loss of his first love and after the carnage of the First World War many others sought comfort from the same source. As a consequence, the spiritualist movement became more mainstream. Miss Wingfield had sunk into obscurity by then. The daughter of a Guards officer, she had caused some embarrassment to her family in relation to her spirit communications with an ancient Egyptian doctor called Semirus and in deference to their wishes had abandoned her sittings. The new climate now encouraged her to publish a book, *Guidance from Beyond*,[11] and Marshall agreed as an old friend to write the foreword endorsing her powers. As a result, *Guidance from Beyond* got more publicity than Miss Wingfield could ever have dreamed of, with banner headlines announcing Marshall's conversion.

After that there was little point in reticence; Marshall addressed his first spiritualist meeting in October 1923 in Bournemouth. Three years previously he had chaired a public debate on spiritualism but this was the first time he had spoken publicly of an allegiance. The spiritualist movement welcomed him with joy; not only was he popular and high profile, but his profession was one that enabled them to make much of the significance of his belief. Here was a man, Conan Doyle pointed out in welcoming him, whose skill in the evaluation of evidence was second to none and who in applying his forensic genius to the question of life after death was convinced by what he had learned.[12] Marshall was rather more cautious in answer to all the questions posed to him; we should not reject evidence merely because it was improbable, he pointed out. It was an interesting observation from a lawyer, who is trained to do just that.[13] Perhaps he had been influenced by the adage Conan Doyle put into the mouth of Sherlock Holmes: '… when you have eliminated the impossible, whatever remains, however improbable, must be the truth.' As knowledge advances, Marshall insisted, the seemingly impossible is explained; our grandfathers, after all, would have found the concept of wireless lunatic. He later summed it all up in one of the poetic phrases typical of him: 'my knowledge is nil, my belief strong, my hope infinite'.

CHAPTER 18

'You damned swine, you have seduced my wife'

London in the 1920s was not all about sipping cocktails in Mayfair drawing rooms and its crimes did not principally consist of society murders in the Savoy Hotel. Nor was Marshall the man to confine his interests to those of the upper classes. The racetrack, the boxing ring, the music hall and the so-called transpontine melodramas, which took place south of the river Thames, at the Elephant and Castle and Lambeth theatres, all held an irresistible appeal and an early career in the London police courts had left him with a lifelong attraction to plausible rogues, forgers and fraudsters.

All the same, in November 1924 Marshall must have been taken aback when he answered an evening knock at the door of his London flat to be confronted by Charles 'Darby' Sabini, head of London's most vicious and famous underworld gang. What the Kray brothers and Esmeralda's Barn in Knightsbridge were to the 1960s, the Sabini family and the Eden Club in Hampstead were to the 1920s.

It had all begun on the racecourses of the south east of England where the Sabinis offered bookmakers 'protection' and the elimination of rivals in exchange for a share in their rich pickings.[1] They ruled their empire with the casual emotionless violence of professional gangsters but inevitably other gangs moved in, sparking off the 'racecourse wars' as they fought for supremacy. By the mid-twenties the pitched battles had spread from the racecourses to the streets of London and of Birmingham, home to the principal rival gang, in an orgy of violence recently depicted in the BBC2 television series *Peaky Blinders*. Slashings and shootings were commonplace in 1921 and 1922, reported by the press in all their gore with dire warnings of anarchy on the streets. There were prosecutions of course but as is usually the case, it was the expendable small fry who ended up in court, never Mr Big. Then came a short lull; most of the small fry were in prison and Mr Big, Darby Sabini, was preoccupied with a libel case, all righteous indignation at a newspaper which had had the temerity to suggest he was the mastermind.

The peace did not last long. In September 1924 there was another ghastly fight which left a gangster, Barnett 'Barney' Blitz, dying in a river of blood in the road. Barney Blitz could not be said to be white as snow as victims go. He had notched up nine convictions for wounding by the time he met his end on the night of 23 September. The Eden Club in Eden Street, Hampstead was hopping that night, the gambling stakes high and the drinking heavy. Alfred Solomon and his friend Edward Emmanuel, both Sabini confidants (at the time, anyway; Emmanuel was not known for gang loyalty and regularly crossed sides), had arrived at the club at midnight. There they encountered Blitz, a bookmaker who had a score to settle. Emmanuel, he believed, had grassed on him in relation to an affray at Epsom Races the year before. He threatened Emmanuel with a broken glass and Solomon leaped to his friend's defence. A fight broke out and all three men, thrown out of the club, continued it on the pavement outside. There, a crowd of some forty people watched Solomon knife Blitz. Only a brave few could be persuaded to assist the police with their enquiries, still fewer to give evidence when Solomon was duly charged with murder.

And so Darby Sabini knocked on Marshall's door with wads of cash in his pocket and a request for representation for one of his boys by the man recognised by the underworld as the 'Mr Big' of criminal defenders. It could have been either arrogance or ignorance that led him straight to the horse's mouth with his request, but in either case it was an unheard-of solecism. Barristers could not be instructed directly; the client had to consult a solicitor and the solicitor then had to negotiate with the barrister's clerk. Marshall, with considerable presence of mind, told him so and Sabini, redirected to Edgar Bowker, obtained Marshall's services in the orthodox way. Bowker probably did not ask too many questions about the source of the brief fee, respectably presented as having been raised by 'the Jewish community' on Solomon's behalf. And Marshall, as his client had done, went into battle.

From the basic position that the attack had been self-defence, Marshall's representation of the level of violence offered by Blitz culminated in a demonstration less famous but just as dramatic as the dropping of the revolver in the Fahmy trial. Arming himself with a glass, he smashed it on the table in front of him and conducted his speech waving it in the jurors' faces, its glittering shards bringing home to them the ghastly injuries that such a weapon could inflict.

Only Marshall could have countered Solomon's reputation for violence by emphasising it; he had been a ferocious fighter for his country, he pointed out, and had medals to show for it. In Marshall's expert hands the image of the brave soldier prevailed over the thug Solomon had become and that image combined with the mesmerising effect of the shattered glass led ultimately to a verdict of manslaughter. Solomon was sentenced to three years' imprisonment. Given that the threatened glassing had been not of Solomon but of another man and that the time lapse between that event and the stabbing had been significant, it was a remarkable result. Sabini's ill-gotten gains had been well spent, at least so far as Solomon was concerned, although the citizens of London may have felt differently.

Only a few weeks later a very different life was saved with an exquisitely sensitive speech as far removed as could be imagined from the bravura of Marshall's performance in the Solomon trial. Young James Doyle was a miner recently engaged to his sweetheart, Doris. 'Courting' (as it was euphemistically described in court) one evening in a field near Doncaster, the couple were surprised by two local men. Albert Needham and William Thrussle were peeping toms; attired in rubber knee caps they would creep noiselessly close to couples, watch them and then turn on a flashlight to expose them literally and metaphorically. On this occasion, caught in the act, aflame with embarrassment, the purity of his love sullied, Doyle sprang up and stabbed Needham to death with his pocket knife. Only some dirty marks on his shirt supported his story of self-defence, but an emotional jury, enjoined by Marshall to show mercy and send young Doyle home to his Doris, acquitted after a short deliberation.

It is difficult to overemphasise the emotional toll of these cases, in which Marshall won his results by the sheer imposition of will. He was ageing noticeably. The umbrella held jauntily throughout his life upside down under his arm was now specially reinforced to serve as a walking stick and he leaned heavily on it. There was no longer any golf; he satisfied his passion for sport by refereeing boxing matches at the National Sporting Club. He was handsomer than ever; the blurring of his features caused by too many good dinners had now fallen away, revealing once more the god-like bone structure of his youth, and his tall frame, which in middle age the unkind might have described as portly, was now spare again. In court, he frequently had to ask to conduct his cases sitting down and his striking authority was less compelling as a result. The perpetual cigars had taken their toll; the beautiful voice, legendarily husky, was now a little less commanding and the glass of Worcestershire sauce, his remedy for years, was not so effective in restoring its strength. Hetty, receiving treatment for her own fragile health at Dr Carl von Dapper's sanatorium in the German spa town of Bad Kissingen, wrote acidly to Elna: 'I am sure it would do Gaggie good to come here – but suppose it did not, I should be blamed.'[2]

Back in London, Marshall, in a hurtful declaration of independence and completely unbeknown to Hetty, had sold the family flat in Harley House and bought another in nearby Wimpole Street. Nonetheless, having already arranged to consult a specialist in Paris, he now decided to join Hetty in Bad Kissingen first, for a three-week overhaul in the rarefied environment created by Dr von Dapper at his internationally famous sanatorium. Here the nobility, politicians and military leaders of Europe congregated to walk and drive in the Bavarian countryside and benefit from the spa waters, professional opinions, urbane charm and excellent champagne that made up Dr von Dapper's prescriptions for all ills. Some of the diagnoses were eccentric to the modern eye (Hetty seemed more gratified than distressed to learn that she had 'anaemia of the brain') but Marshall was satisfied with the theory that his throat problems arose from his speaking so fast that he gulped in air at too rapid a rate. It was the beginning of the throat spray that joined the cushion and the exquisite little pill boxes essential to all his last court appearances, carried over by the long-suffering Bowker.

Whilst Marshall was away, the newspapers, deprived of his cases to report and knowing of his ill health, made a stir by announcing his imminent retirement. The peace of his Bavarian retreat was disturbed by the news from England that his chauffeur,[3] believing the reports, thought he would soon be redundant and walked out. Marshall was furious; it was 'all rot', he exploded, this constant harping on about his retirement every time he took a vacation. He was determined to reach his fifty years at the Bar and just to prove it flung himself back into work.

'Times change', Marshall was fond of quoting, 'and we change with them.' He was ever receptive to all that was new and methods of communication in particular fascinated him. Had it existed, social media with all its potential for mass manipulation would have been a joy to him as great as was the newly developing film industry. In 1921 he conducted the first libel case brought against a film company. A silent film, *The Amazing Quest of Mr Ernest Bliss*, featured a theatrical agent called Montague depicted as 'a despicable hound'. A real Mr Montague bore such a striking physical resemblance to the fictional hound that other men at his club remarked upon it. Marshall took up cudgels on his behalf against Hepworth Picture Plays Ltd,[4] one of the very first English film studios, built at Walton on Thames. And then there was a new medium to conquer; in December 1922 the newly formed British Broadcasting Company transmitted its first broadcasts and the first major trial to be reported on in detail had been Marguerite Fahmy's. Three years later, in 1925, Marshall's voice was broadcast for the first and only time in a bravura performance as Serjeant Buzz-Fuzz in the farcical breach-of-promise case in Dickens's novel *The Pickwick Papers*.[5] Joining him in the cast were Henry Dickens KC, the novelist's son, and an old friend of Marshall's, the then famous author William Pett Ridge.[6]

The significance of the part he played would not have been lost on Marshall. Large and eloquent, Serjeant Buzz-Fuzz, who cajoled and flattered his jury in a torrent of unstoppable oratory punctuated with thumps on the table and mesmerising changes in pitch and pace all fuelled with passionately expressed conviction in his client's innocence, had very obvious resonances:

> Serjeant Buzz-Fuzz began by saying that never in the whole course of his professional experience – never, from the very first moment of his applying himself to the study and practice of the law – had he approached a case with feeling of such deep emotion or with such a heavy sense of the responsibility imposed upon him – a responsibility he would say which he could never have supported were he not buoyed up and sustained by a conviction so strong that it amounted to positive certainty that the cause of truth and justice, or in other words that the cause of his much injured and most oppressed client must prevail with the high minded and intelligent dozen of men whom he now saw in that box before him.[7]

Marshall's performance on the wireless was a great success; the next morning in court he took the ribbing from his opponent, in front of broadly smiling judge and jurors, in good part. 'Having listened to Sir Edward Marshall Hall's powerful appeal to the jury,' said his opponent, Sir Ellis Hume Williams KC, who had missed the performance, 'I can only say that I am more than ever convinced that he must have filled admirably and to the very nature the part which he took in last night's broadcast entertainment.'[8]

Marshall had become a National Treasure; but even National Treasures are vulnerable to the jealous jibes of their professional colleagues and it did not escape unnoticed that in 1924 he was taking a backseat role in a prosecution team fronted by Sir Patrick Hastings KC, then Attorney General and twenty years Marshall's junior.[9] Then in 1925 came the Dennistoun v Dennistoun divorce, in which he was generally thought to have shown a disastrous lack of judgement from which he had been 'rescued' by Norman Birkett; and then in 1926 the trials of Edward Flavell and Lock Ah Tam.

Though the latter was generally regarded as one of his most moving performances, Marshall himself regarded Tam's execution as his most bitter failure and, being Marshall, made no secret of it.

It was beginning to be felt in some quarters that the great star that had been Sir Edward Marshall Hall KC was on the wane, his legendary career in its last chapter. Everywhere there was a clamour for his memoirs. Marshall had been tantalising press and publishers with the prospect for some years, holding off from committing himself whilst he still hoped for a judicial appointment. If it came, it would rule out the sensational revelations about his past triumphs that he had in mind. But it had not come; and now it would not. It was too late. Now it was all about money and Marshall, his love of dealing to the fore, embarked with relish on a campaign to push his price up. Two newspapers and three magazines approaching him for articles were refused on the basis that he did not want to anticipate the contents of the planned sensational book. Negotiations continued meanwhile with John Lane, an old friend, co-founder of the Bodley Head and known for his controversial publications,[10] and with an offer from the *Sunday Express* for the serialisation rights to follow.[11] But then came a far more attractive offer: £25,000, the equivalent in today's money of £1.4 million, then the highest known brief fee ever offered in the Temple. With all expenses paid, Marshall was to go by luxury liner, accompanied of course by Bowker to look after him, to represent the Maharajah of Indore in a commission of inquiry in India.

The maharajah had kept in his colourful collection of concubines a twelve-year-old dancer, Mumtaz Begum. After some years in her gilded purdah she had made a break for freedom taking with her, according to the maharajah, jewels from his treasury. She quickly put herself under the protection of a new lover, a rich Bombay businessman called Abdul Bawla. A little while later Mumtaz and her lover were driving in the prosperous Malabar Hill area of Bombay when their car was forced off the road by another containing a group of men, subsequently found to be members of the maharajah's household. They were apparently hell bent on kidnapping Mumtaz. In the fight, Bawla was shot dead and Mumtaz received knife wounds to her face and head. She was saved by the serendipitous arrival on the scene of three English army officers. In the ultimate cliché of colonial life, the three young men were travelling from an afternoon round of golf at the Willingdon Club to evening drinks at the Taj Mahal Hotel. With reckless public school heroism and chivalry they went into battle against the guns and knives armed only with their golf clubs, captured the assailants and rescued Mumtaz. Bawla's murderers stood their trial in the Criminal Sessions of the

Bombay High Court in 1925, the proceedings conducted in English and according to British Indian law. The main assailants were found guilty and sentenced to death.

During the trial, the maharajah and his household were heavily implicated in the vengeance inflicted on Mumtaz and her lover. As a sovereign prince, the maharajah was not under the jurisdiction of British Indian law, but by virtue of a resolution passed in 1907, the Viceroy of India had the power to appoint a commission of inquiry. The then viceroy, the Marquess of Reading, Marshall's old friend Rufus Isaacs, proposed to take this course. The maharajah had already raised British eyebrows in relation to his exotic personal life and significantly he had been amongst those Indian rulers who were most fiercely protective of their autonomy. An inquiry that could legitimately lead to his downfall was in line with a newly formulated policy of the British rulers in India to assert the paramountcy of their powers.

The maharajah now offered Marshall the brief fee beyond dreams for representation at this inquiry. The inquiry was to be heard during the English legal vacation in order that the long weeks away would not interfere with normal work in the Temple; Marshall eagerly anticipated the lavish colonial hospitality and gentlemanly hearing in a specially constituted courtroom in the Murree Hills, an enchantingly beautiful hill station in the Punjab province.[12]

Faced with the realities of the imminent inquiry, however, the maharajah was plainly anxious as to his chances; even Marshall Hall, he concluded, in all his fame and with a fortune in his pocket, was unlikely to triumph over the might of British India. Forty-eight hours after Marshall had accepted the brief, on 26 February 1926 the Maharajah of Indore abdicated. A ruler in his position, he said, would sacrifice his sovereignty before he submitted to a committee of inquiry whose jurisdiction over him he could not recognise or accept.[13]

Marshall was thwarted of his dream case and his dream fee; but the fact that his reputation as the greatest defender had reached an Indian maharajah and that he had been offered the highest brief fee to date in the Temple confounded those who had prophesied his decline. Nonetheless his increasing exhaustion was only too apparent. The strain and distress of his battle against the laws of insanity in the trial of Loch Ah Tam, also in February 1926, and of Edward Flavell in the June was too much for him. In November, he collapsed in court. He could not go on, it was whispered.

Three weeks after his collapse he rallied like an old war horse responding to the sound of battle in his last great capital case, the Stella Maris murder. It was the story of the destruction of domestic hopes and dreams, a great passion and a tragic death all played out in the tasteful drawing room of a seaside villa in Whitstable, Kent, named Stella Maris. In this trial Marshall achieved the last miraculous result with all his now famous trademarks, enactments of the crime, a spectacular stand-off with the judge and the creation of dramatic tension, in this case so intense that his peroration on the nature of human passion induced what was little short of mass hysteria.

He insisted on driving himself down to Maidstone Assizes in appalling weather; it had become his custom to arrive in court seconds before the trial began but this time it was fog and not showmanship that caused his last-minute arrival to represent Alfonso Francis ('Frank') Austin Smith.[14] Smith was public school, Cambridge University and Sandhurst educated, an ex-Dragoon Guard and heir to a railway fortune. He was charged with the murder of his friend John Adam Tytler ('JT') Derham. Derham had been the Old Etonian grandson of a brigadier general and VC, and had also been a graduate of Cambridge University as well as an internationally renowned ice hockey player. The motive for the shooting was clear enough: Derham had been having an affair with Smith's wife Katherine, who, just to provide the last touch for the fascination of the public, was so strikingly beautiful that it is apparent even in the unflattering cloche hats and grainy press photographs of the day.

Only Smith, his wife and the victim were present in the drawing room where Derham sustained the gunshot wounds from which he later died. The prosecution could not call Katherine as a witness; the law did not allow the wife of an accused to be called as a witness for the prosecution in a murder charge. And judging by the story that emerged, the defence dared not call her. The terrible two-edged defence that Marshall was to run was based on the emotional cruelty inflicted on Smith by Katherine's inability to decide between the two men. The jury might be moved to sympathy for her husband; but on the other hand the worse the cruelty the more it could be said to make the motive for murder compelling.

Central to Smith's case were his letters; when his marriage broke down he bombarded his wife and her lover with emotional threats and appeals. His vocabulary was conventional and limited ('you damned swine, you have seduced my wife' and 'you dirty white-livered fool' were the best he could manage to her lover) and his grammar sometimes rendered his meaning ambivalent ('You have made me happier than I ever hoped to be … I could never love anyone like you,' he wrote to his wife). Even so, no one could doubt in these anguished laments the genuine emotions expressed or the rollercoaster of despair, of rising hope and dashed dreams, that he was experiencing. It was this real desperate emotion that Marshall planned to exploit.

The affair between Katherine and Derham had begun about two months before the dénouement in the Kent drawing room. Smith had moved out of the house, leaving his wife to care for their three small children. Unbeknown to him Katherine had had a deed of separation drawn up and on discovering this, mad with jealousy and grief Smith had smashed up Derham's flat, and threatened both violence to Derham and suicide.

On 9 August 1926 he had visited his wife at Stella Maris and begged her to return to him. She had promised to think it over and with painful hope he had slept that night in the spare room. The next day there was a passionate reconciliation; she had decided to give her lover up and for two nights Smith was reinstated in bliss in the matrimonial bedroom and Katherine blew hot. On the third morning she wavered, and then blew cold. She told him he should go; then that he should stay; then, having received a letter from Derham, she told him to go again. Smith was determined that the three of them should have it out once and for all and sent a telegram in his wife's name (a decoy, said the prosecution) inviting Derham to Stella Maris.

When he duly arrived, the confrontation which Smith believed would clear the air led instead to a united position between the lovers, who now told him Katherine was set on a divorce. Smith with a melodramatic flourish took out a gun concealed in his trouser pocket and threatened to kill himself.

The good manners of upper-middle-class English life seem to have prevailed: the gun was removed from his grasp (though not from his possession; it seems to have been restored at some point to his pocket) and the three went out together to an uneasy but civilised dinner at the nearby Marine Hotel where, sipping champagne, they continued to discuss their future. The waiter thought they all seemed a bit tense. On their return to Stella Maris, Katherine made up a spare room bed for her lover, laughing off her husband's protests at the white-livered seducer remaining under his roof. Maintaining her brittle hostess manner she went into the drawing room and proposed a card game, which she proceeded to lay out.

'I did not want to play cards,' said Smith pathetically when he gave his evidence, 'and I told them I was going to do away with myself. It did not appear to distress them. They did not believe it.'

There was something infinitely poignant about the little picture he painted, his agony ignored by his wife and her lover intent on playing cards in the polite drawing room. It could drive anyone to take desperate measures. But what was the nature of those measures? Smith took out the gun he still had in his pocket. And moments later the civilised façade was stripped away; the drawing room curtains were hanging off their poles, the playing cards and flowers carefully placed in the brass vase were all over the floor, and on the blood-soaked carpet lay the once cheerfully indifferent Derham, shot through the abdomen. He died two days later.

Marshall read to Smith the letter he had written to his wife during those last days of reconciliation:

> You have made me happier than ever I dared hope to be. I have been mad lately and in hell … the mad criminal folly I have been steeped in is a thing of the past from yesterday forever … you asked me to forgive you last night but I could only say I love you and that covered everything … I feel like a man who has been in a terrible fever delirious and … am just waking … do not throw a lifebelt to me and draw it away at my last grasp …

The metaphors were a bit mixed but, as was later reported, it was not the words but the extraordinary delivery in Marshall's beautiful voice that brought the house down. As he read, a sudden scream ripped through the court followed by blood-curdling moans and wails. One of the two women jurors was having hysterics and as attendants and police rushed forward with water and smelling salts other jurors were seen to have tears rolling down their cheeks. In the public gallery women spectators began to sob hysterically in sympathy.

There was an adjournment to restore order. The trial then resumed and Smith told his story. He had taken the gun from his pocket; he did not intend to kill either Derham or himself, he had removed it merely 'for comfort and convenience'; the two lovers, misinterpreting the action, had sprung at him; there was a struggle and then it had 'all happened in a flash'. Crucially he insisted that he had never touched, let alone pulled, the trigger.

Marshall's closing speech was a shameless appeal to the already overcharged emotions of his jury: 'He begged his wife not to withdraw the lifebelt she had thrown to him as he was struggling in the water. That lifebelt had been withdrawn once. Members of the jury, it is now for you to say whether you will throw him that lifebelt once more, given him the chance of grasping it and being pulled ashore to resume his old and happy life with the woman he loves …'

Mr Justice Avory, the presiding judge, had by this time just about had enough. He had long experience of Marshall as a man and as an advocate; Marshall always said that he was the only man at the Bar who dared to call the judge by his Christian name, Horace, after his elevation to the Bench. They were sneakingly rather fond of each other but Avory, a pure technical lawyer, a cold man and a strong supporter of capital punishment,[15] deplored Marshall's tactics. The whipping up of emotion that Marshall indulged in was anathema to him. Now he had had to put up with hysterics in his court and an outpouring of emotion by both Marshall and his client that he regarded as not only unseemly but more importantly of little legal relevance. It was his turn, and in his summing up he sought to redress the balance.

Forget all these references to crimes of passion and unwritten laws, Avory told the jury. The law was clear. If Smith had pulled the trigger intending to kill Derham, it was murder. Since suicide was a criminal act,[16] if he had pulled it intending to shoot himself and shot Derham accidentally it was still murder. If he was provoked by an assault or was grossly negligent in handling a loaded gun, or if he was taking it out of his pocket intending to shoot himself and it had gone off accidentally, in all these cases it was manslaughter. Only on Smith's account, exactly as he had told it, could there be an acquittal. He then pointed out to the jury all the reasons why that account could not be true. What about all the threats Smith had made? What about the telegram sent to lure Derham to Stella Maris? Why should there have been a struggle if Smith had been intending merely to retrieve the gun from his pocket? Why had he not simply given it up? Why wasn't Mrs Smith a witness for the defence? The jury must think that very significant! He ended with the sternest of warnings: 'I have told you the law of this country as it must be applied. If you apply … any notions of your own you are violating the oaths you have taken.'

But Avory lacked Marshall's consummate psychology and his intimidation backfired. Juries can do what they like. And now they did it. Two hours and ten minutes later they delivered verdicts of not guilty to murder or manslaughter. Smith's life was saved amidst screams and sobs from the public gallery.

Instead of discharging Smith from the dock, a by now furious judge instead invited a further forgotten charge to be put: Smith had had in his possession a revolver and six rounds of ammunition with intent to endanger life. After a rapid consultation with Smith, still in the dock, Marshall bowed to the inevitable. Smith had already said that he had originally bought the gun with the intention of killing himself with it; if the statute covered possession with intent to endanger one's own life then Smith was constrained to plead guilty. Avory ruled that it did and Smith duly pleaded guilty. It was a technical offence that cried out for leniency; but Avory, ungracious in defeat, now took his revenge. The jury, he said, had taken the most lenient view possible of the story they had heard; he was now constrained to sentence on the basis that the only life Smith had intended to endanger when he bought the gun was his own, although he could not resist adding: 'I have my own opinion on it.' With that, he sentenced Smith to twelve months' hard labour. In 1926 to a man of Smith's background such a sentence was, as the judge well knew, ruin.

If the judge intended to punish despite the verdict, he certainly did so. Smith never resumed his 'old and happy life'. Katherine did not carry out her expressed intention to 'stand by him'. He died almost destitute and quite alone in 1944 in an Ilfracombe boarding house. By that time the few who knew him at all knew him as 'Mr Smith upstairs'.

At the end of December 1926 Marshall was suffering from one of his periodic bouts of bronchitis. He rejected with fury Edgar Bowker's suggestion that he took a longer Christmas break than his usual few days – inactivity was intolerable to him. Immediately after the festivities at Overbrook with Hetty and Elna, he was on his way to south Wales. It was hardly court number one at the Old Bailey but his brief fee of 500 guineas for the day was one seldom heard of in Bridgend Police Court. The case encapsulated a highly topical little slice of social history and was also one of immense legal importance.

Brynmore John, an eighteen-year-old miner, had been out on strike with his workmates in the stuttering aftermath of the General Strike some months before. In the unaccustomed freedom of a late summer afternoon above ground, John, four of his fellow strikers, a ferret and a number of dogs went on a ratting expedition during which the excited dogs led the no less excited boys into the grounds of a local colliery. The deprivations of the strike had led to thefts of coal and the mine owners had erected an electric fence around their coal bunkers, which they had activated that very afternoon with 110 volts of electricity. Young John tripped and fell on it face first and was killed instantly. All the bitterness left by the General Strike, after which miners were being forced back to work on lower wages for longer hours, seemed encapsulated in the tragic little incident, John a martyr to the cause.

A belligerent South Wales Miners' Federation took up the case and through the dead boy's brother mounted a prosecution against the colliery bosses. It was a highly sensitive time for mine owners, already perceived as having a brutal disregard for the working man; a conviction against the company for 'setting a man trap calculated to destroy human life' and worse, for manslaughter, was the last thing they wanted. A prosecution against a company was now possible under new legislation and so Marshall was instructed to defend not a man but a company against a charge of homicide with a reputation rather than a neck at stake.

It was a dismal case in the bleak January of 1927 and Marshall in an unfamiliar role faced hostility from the local community in his defence of the colliery owners. The case was committed to the local assize court for a hearing in March. Walking back to the railway station Bowker, who now accompanied Marshall everywhere, noticed he was lagging behind. His anxious enquiries elicited nothing more than an impatient wave of the hand.

The newspaper stories relating to this case are the last in his series of press cuttings albums, which now extended to thirty-eight volumes; the final entry is on page 110 of the thirty-eighth volume, the remaining 129 pages poignantly blank. It happens to be a cutting from the *Western Mail* dated 12 January 1927 and Marshall would have liked this last report; 'IN A DRAMATIC OUTBURST Sir Edward Marshall Hall asserted that behind the prosecution was a subtle influence, a scheme of propaganda …'

The day after he finished in Bridgend, he was due in Derby. It was a complex fraud case. The hours were long and Bowker increasingly uneasy. Marshall returned to the London flat for the weekend, leaving wig and gown, brief and bags in Derby. On the Sunday evening, 16 January, Bowker received a telegram: Sir Edward was too ill to return. Whilst his junior, faced with every junior's dream or nightmare depending on his constitution, battled on with the case, Marshall battled for his life.

Pneumonia followed the bronchitis. All visitors were banned. Letters poured in from distinguished well-wishers; prayers were offered at the spiritualist healing service, and at the Society for Psychical Research Sir Arthur Conan Doyle tabled a motion, enthusiastically carried, that a warm message of sympathy should be sent. Messages of love and encouragement came from the august members of the Crimes Club and the Garrick Club. The King himself enquired as to the patient's progress.

In every newspaper, in breathless daily bulletins over the next six weeks, the details of Marshall's last fight were recorded as faithfully and in as much detail as had been his forensic battles. Sir Edward had had a restless night; he was a little more comfortable; he was gravely ill; his wife and daughter were by his side; his favourite dog had been sent up from the country to comfort him; and then he was at death's door.

On 23 February 1927, with his usual consummate timing, he died at midnight exactly. He hovered briefly in those seconds that end the old day or begin the new one; and then he was gone. 'Peace be unto his restless and dramatic soul,' said the *Sunday Times*.

The tributes began arriving. In the Lord Chief Justice's Court in the Strand and in the Old Bailey, Bar and Bench gathered the next morning to mourn the loss of a man who, for all the flaws affectionately acknowledged in every speech, had been at his best one of the greatest advocates ever heard. These barristers, themselves skilled in oratory, struggled to convey in words, as people always did, the extraordinary magnetism of Marshall's performances. Amongst the overwhelming praise Marshall would have been highly amused by that of Mr Justice Avory, fresh from the fireworks of the Stella Maris trial: 'No-one who has known him as a personal friend, as an opponent at the Bar, as an advocate practising before one, as I have, can have failed to recognise … his striking individuality and above all his peculiar talents as an advocate … I am sure the public at large will regret that his services are no longer available.'[17] He would probably have been most pleased by that of Sir Ernest Wild, the Recorder of London: 'Sir Edward was a great and outstanding advocate … he leaves a gap in the forensic world, in the social world, and in the artistic world and we mourn the loss of a many-sided big-hearted highly gifted virile handsome man'; and most touched by that of Sir Archibald Bodkin, Director of Public Prosecutions, ideologically opposite to him and an old friend: 'There was nobody quite like him at the Bar.'

Obituaries appeared in the United States, in Australia and on the continent. George V sent a telegram of condolence to Hetty. Members of the aristocracy and judiciary, famous actors, authors and politicians packed the Marylebone church where the funeral service was held.

Hetty and Elna led the huge procession of mourners. Discreet to the last, Louisa Miéville, supported by her brother Louis and nephew Jean-Louis, was fifty-ninth in the list of mourners. It was only to be expected. She had never had any public recognition of her central role in Marshall's life. She may or may not have known then of the newspaper headlines she was to face when his will was published.

Outside in the Marylebone streets, shops closed and crowds gathered along the funeral route to mark the procession, the hearse followed by extra cars laid on to carry the hundreds of wreaths. The traffic stopped. Pedestrians and passengers on buses, 'persons of every class among them many in working clothes removed their hats and remained reverently uncovered as it passed'. It was an extraordinary funeral fit for a great film star or statesman, unique in the history of the law. No other barrister through all the centuries of distinguished advocates has ever achieved anything like it.

Marshall had lived his life in a blaze of publicity. And he had kept a trick or two up his sleeve to ensure that it did not die with him.

CHAPTER 19

'Some great statue of mourning'

LOCKED IRON BOX: SIR EDWARD MARSHALL HALL'S GIFT TO WOMAN FRIEND.[1]

It had been a long and detailed will but that was the item that made headlines in nearly every newspaper in England, as Marshall must have known that it would. The box was a handsome one, bound with gilt bands and fastened with a Chubb lock, and Marshall had kept it in his safe in his chambers. Now, together with its contents it had been left to Louisa. No one today knows what it contained.[2] And that was not all; all the longest-loved and most personal items in his chambers room and his London flat were also left to her. From 3 Temple Gardens, the original sketch by 'Spy' for his *Vanity Fair* portrait, the bronze statuettes of Rousseau and Voltaire that had stood for decades on the mantelpiece and the portrait of a lady that hung above it; and from Wimpole Street, the two Chinese cabinets hanging in the drawing room containing his most cherished items of Chinese porcelain, a small part of the now vast collection which was mainly stored at Overbrook. Most significantly of all he had left Louisa his beloved gold repeating watch made in the previous century by Thomas Boxall of Brighton, its chain festooned with a silver pencil top, a little matchbox and charms. He had always worn it. It was the thing quite literally closest to his heart.

The message was unmistakable, to Hetty and to the world.

Hetty and Elna were scrupulously provided for. Overbrook and all its contents went to Hetty and after her death to Elna. The London flat and all the valuable collections were to be sold, the proceeds to be used to set up trusts for Hetty and Elna as well as to provide for impecunious members of the Inner Temple.[3] Although she had constantly complained about the size and value of the accumulating collections at Overbrook and had lived in fear of burglars, Hetty sought legal advice as to the proposed dispersal of Marshall's beloved collections. On a strict interpretation of the will, it would seem that right was on her side; since the collections were part of the contents of Overbrook she should have been able to retain what she wished. For some reason the sale went ahead, however, attracting huge attention and publicity. The dealers, mainly old friends of Marshall's, had a field day. Bluetts, Malletts, Tessiers, Welbys, Finks, Ackermans – all the big London names gathered for seven days of sales devoted to Marshall's collections of pictures, porcelain, furniture, silver, snuff boxes and *objets de vertu*.

The Christie's catalogues[4] bring home the sheer scale of the collections. The lyrical descriptions cover page after page. Peonies and magnolias, hunting scenes and cherry trees, ladies and sages, peacocks and petals, waltzing across the vases, ewers, fluted cups, salt cellars, jardinières and candlesticks of the Nanking porcelain collection. A riot of colours, aubergine and white on green and yellow grounds, *familles verte* and *rose*, stippled green and coral in the Chinese enamelled porcelain collection. Décolleté ladies, gentlemen in pink coats, in wigs, in armour and in braided uniforms romping against gold backgrounds with jewelled borders in the miniature collection. There were pearls and pendants, cufflinks and earrings in the jewellery collection. The *objets de vertu* went on seemingly forever: scent bottles and pencil cases, pocket watches, needle cases, badges and scarf rings, cases of shagreen, leather and silver and countless snuff boxes. No item seemed too obscure for Marshall's acquisitive eye; amongst the enormous collection of silver were no fewer than twelve eighteenth-century marrow scoops.

Neither Hetty nor Elna attended the sale but the handwritten notes of the auctioneer, interspersed through the catalogues, tell their own story. Lady Marshall Hall wished to buy back five pictures including the Zoffany; she put in a bid for the lady in the décolleté dress (she failed to get it); she bought back several small items of jewellery; the executors had telephoned; Lady Marshall Hall could have the original drawing of Serjeant Buzz-Fuzz and a Frank Lockwood[5] cartoon given to Marshall by the artist depicting 'An honest citizen before and after cross-examination', provided she paid the executors two pounds for them. The humiliation for Hetty must have felt complete.

In one way or another, Marshall lived on for all those he loved through his belongings. The faithful friend R E Moore, corrector of his grammar and researcher of his legal arguments, was left the legal reference books for which Marshall had had so little time. His beloved niece Violet, Ada's daughter, was remembered with jewellery. Lady Carnarvon, now the ill-fated Mrs Dennistoun, her children Henry, Lord Porchester, and Lady Evelyn, the

Garrick Club, clerks and servants were all left mementos. Even his remaining cigars had been allocated.

Louisa maintained a dignified silence about her inheritance throughout the hype surrounding the sale. During the years until her own death she maintained a friendship with Marshall's niece Violet and she travelled extensively with her sister Elizabeth and Elizabeth's lover. She was bereft when Elizabeth died. She herself died in 1948 aged seventy-four, by which time she was living in a flat in Kensington, still surrounded by Marshall's belongings. In her own will she left Marshall's portrait by 'Spy' to the Garrick Club and directed that the watch, chain and attachments be sold and the proceeds donated to the Prisoners Aid Society, a charity whose work Marshall had particularly admired. The treasured little collection of porcelain remained in her family until in 2010 they sent it to auction. Its provenance had not been forgotten: 'The secret collection of Sir Edward Marshall Hall KC,' said the catalogue. The family connection with Louisa has through the passage of time become a remote one but despite that they remain protective of her memory. If they know anything of the detail of the relationship beyond the bare fact of its existence, they were not willing to divulge it to me.

Marshall's executors, so scrupulous in carrying out his wishes despite Hetty's protests, were less so when it came to his vast archive of correspondence and papers. They had all been bundled together by him personally into large packets on which he had written 'To be destroyed'. He gave the same instruction in his will.[6] But the pressure for a biography was now mounting. The executors must have known they were sitting on a fortune for someone. Marshall had never thrown anything away. He had left records of his Brighton youth and schooldays, the intimate six-year diary of his first marriage and a lifetime's correspondence. He had been a prolific letter writer who valued entertainment over discretion and had written to most of the great names of his day. Hetty was consulted as to a suitable biographer and she in turn sought advice from one of the few of his London friends with whom she was familiar. J C Squires, editor of the *London Mercury*, an influential literary journal, and hard-drinking networker, was an old friend of Marshall's and lived near to them when in the country. It was Squires who suggested Edward Marjoribanks for the job. Marjoribanks had literary ambitions, had been liked by Marshall, had influential legal contacts despite his youth and seemed the ideal choice. Everything was now handed over to this very young member of the Bar with very big aspirations.

Marjoribanks was a twenty-seven-year-old golden boy. He had been a scholar at Eton, a member of 'Pop'[7] and captain of school. He was a scholar at Christ Church, Oxford and became a fine oarsman and president of the

Oxford Union, leaving with a double first in Mods and Greats.[8] As though all that were not enough, he was a member of a famous legal and political dynasty. His father, a Scottish baron, had died when he was a few months old and his mother, an American heiress, had then married Sir Douglas Hogg, later first Viscount Hailsham. By the time Marjoribanks came to the Bar in 1923, his stepfather was Attorney General and was shortly to become Lord Chancellor. It did not seem as though anything could dislodge the silver spoon.

In 1923, the young Marjoribanks had been instructed in a minor junior role in a case in which his stepfather was leading counsel. It was a libel case; Vera, Lady Terrington was standing as Liberal candidate for Wycombe in Buckinghamshire and had given an interview to the *Daily Express* in which she was quoted as saying: 'If I am elected to Westminster I intend to wear my best clothes. I shall put on my ospreys and my fur coat and my pearls. Everyone knows I live in a large house and keep men servants and can afford a motor car and a fur coat. Every woman would do the same if she could. It is sheer hypocrisy to pretend in public life that you have no nice things.' Published under the headline 'Aim if elected – furs and pearls' the article made her look vain and superficial, Lady Terrington complained, and she sued the newspaper for libel. Sir Douglas Hogg was instructed to represent the proprietor, Lord Beaverbrook. Hogg was cautiously optimistic about the outcome but the case was taken over at the last minute by Marshall to whom the word 'cautious' was in a foreign language and who expressed supreme confidence in the result.

At trial it became quickly apparent that Marshall had underestimated Lady Terrington. She was a charming witness and a vulnerable one. Marshall's cross-examination reduced her to floods of tears and the jury began to assume the ominously protective attitude which it adopts when a sympathetic witness receives what it perceives as a mauling. At the end of the first day the general consensus in court was that the tide of opinion was in Lady Terrington's favour. It is hard to row back against such a tide; Marshall was struggling as he began his speech the next day. It happened to be Armistice Day; as the clock struck eleven he saw his opportunity and grabbed it unhesitatingly, stopping dead mid-sentence, as though he had been shot.

The two-minute silence is always impressive in court, the ritual held in sudden suspension, the participants frozen, the combat stilled in memory of the far greater one. On this occasion the scene was dominated by Marshall's compelling presence, his head bowed in grief 'like some great statue of mourning'. Everyone in court looked only at him. It was only five years after the worst carnage the modern world had known. Marshall knew there would be men on the jury who had seen it first hand.

When he resumed, he abandoned the argument he had previously been pursuing and spoke as though illuminated by some great truth.

Members of the jury, we have been celebrating the anniversary of the greatest national sacrifice which the world has ever seen. We have all suffered loss in the war; you have suffered; I have suffered; and every year comes this two-minute silence for remembrance' sake. And now turning from this great national ceremony we find ourselves in this court and have to address ourselves to the trifling grievances of this lady ...

It was masterly, it was outrageous and it worked because it was Marshall. Lady Terrington no longer seemed sweet and frivolous and Marshall was no longer perceived by the jury as her attacker; he was a man like them who had suffered, who had, like them, far finer things to think about than a petty claim for damages by a rich society woman. After that Marshall had it all his own way, and he went from strength to strength in the most mesmerising eloquence young Edward Marjoribanks had ever heard.[9] The shameless piece of posturing was a revelation to Marjoribanks; he was deeply impressed not only by the style of advocacy but by Marshall's enviable aura of glamour. Prior to this his impression of the Bar had not been favourable: everyone was too industrious; no one was sparkling or witty or smart enough to meet his exacting standards. But Marshall, with his dominating personality, his fame and his society friends, was more like it.

Alongside all his achievements Marjoribanks had many very unattractive characteristics.[10] He was self-absorbed in the extreme and pathologically ambitious. 'I would rather die', he wrote to a friend on his twenty-sixth birthday, 'than not be a great person in the world's eye.'[11] And he worked very hard to achieve that. He was both an intellectual and a social snob. To dowagers needing a walker, society hostesses looking for a spare man and distinguished old men who basked in flattery he provided the perfect answer. Entertaining and personable, extravagantly elegant in dress, his closest companion his dog Bryden, he assiduously and successfully courted the contacts that would lead to the position in society he sought.[12]

Marshall became one of his targets. He cannot, given his background, have needed Marshall's advice as to his career; but he sought it and Marshall, who had been fond of Marjoribanks' father, loved the company of young members of the Bar and was highly susceptible to admiration, responded. Lunches and first nights followed. For the last two or three years of Marshall's life they became friends.

The commission to write Marshall Hall's biography was to satisfy Marjoribanks' literary ambitions, his desire for recognition at the Bar and his self-confessed 'inordinate longing for fame'.[13] He eagerly grabbed the opportunity with scant regard, it seems, for the wishes of the man whom he had claimed to be a friend. A contract was drawn up with the executors; the papers were to be handed over to him in their entirety, the only proviso being that the book was to be written 'as expeditiously as possible' with 7.5 per cent of the profits ploughed back into the estate.[14] Marjoribanks took out an insurance policy to cover potential libel actions arising from the then recent cases the book would cover[15] and plunged in.

The book was published two-and-a-half years after Marshall's death by Victor Gollancz, with a preface by Lord Birkenhead which in its praise of Marshall's extraordinary advocacy and consummate psychology contributed as much as the book itself did to the growing legend. Birkenhead wrote:

> Courage was [Marshall's] outstanding characteristic. He was utterly fearless in what he conceived to be his duty, both as a lawyer and in other, less vicarious parts of life ... the elan with which he swept down upon a doubtful jury, brushing aside their prejudices, and persuading them against their will, sometimes possibly against their better judgment into accepting his own sanguine view of his client's innocence won many a day which a more timorous, if not less skilful advocate must have given up for lost ... To watch him in court was an educational process in the study of human nature.

The Life of Sir Edward Marshall Hall caused a sensation and captivated a public already disposed to hero worship. The rave reviews, including a glowing recommendation from Lloyd George in the House of Commons, ensured it became a best-seller. Within the first three years it had gone into eleven reprints and sold a then exceptional 30,000 copies in Britain and the United States.

Marshall did not need Marjoribanks to make him a household name, but the success of the book crystallised his image in the public mind, the biography and its subject soon indistinguishably famous. Marjoribanks' portrait of Marshall depicted his achievements on a heroic scale, with glorious battles, black despair and histrionic oratory worthy of Sir Henry Irving. The lens through which Marjoribanks looked at his private life was kept firmly in soft focus with all the reticences of the period in which it was written. Errors of judgement were excused, mistresses expunged and displays of bad temper portrayed as lovable childishness. All that said, it is a wonderful biography, embodying in one man's life all that is most romantic about the Bar.

Hetty hated the book. This seems to have been primarily because of the account of Marshall's despair at the breakdown of his first marriage and Ethel's death, but she would not have been human had she not also resented the absence of any mention of her role in Marshall's life (she figures in two sentences in the whole book) and its depiction of a Marshall so far removed from the complex, difficult man she had known. Marjoribanks wrote anxiously to her. By this time his own world seems to have been unravelling; he was ill and overworked, he told her amidst fulsome apologies for any offence caused and protestations that he had done his best. 'I do ask you not to make things more difficult for me than they already are' he concluded.[16]

It had seemed at first that after publication of the book he was going from strength to strength; its huge success had resulted in a commission to write the life of Sir Edward Carson; in the same year he was elected Tory member of Parliament for Eastbourne, the first step in his ambition to be Prime Minister by the time he was sixty. Those following his political progress, however, began to feel some unease. He was seen to align himself too eagerly to the grand and elderly mandarins of the Tory Party and there were jokey reports of his near-hysterical oratory. He was nicknamed 'Clarence' and in one speech in the House of Commons was said to have foamed at the mouth and waved his arms around so wildly that he nearly knocked out Lord Salisbury, who was standing close by. It is tempting to speculate that he was modelling himself on Marshall's dramatic perorations without Marshall's inimitable magnetism.

Socially, however, he had attained his ambition to move in the grandest of society. On 31 March 1932, he attended a reception at the Egyptian legation where a glittering crowd had gathered to celebrate the birthday of King Fuad of Egypt. After it, he went down to his stepfather's home in Sussex for the weekend. On 2 April he was found, elegantly dressed as ever in his country tweed suit, dead in a chair in the billiard room. He had shot himself with his stepbrother Quintin's[17] double-barrelled twenty-bore shotgun.

Theories have abounded ever since as to the reason; overwork, two broken engagements and a realisation that he was homosexual but unable to acknowledge or live with it have all been mooted. They are not of course mutually exclusive but his troubled past makes the last theory at least the most probable deciding factor. At Eton he had been famous as a passionate beater of small boys,[18] often under a charge he had invented known as 'generalities' rather than any specific misdemeanour. At Oxford, one of the uneasy generation who had experienced the effects of the First World War bloodbath whilst being too young to have taken part in it, he became one of a group of self-consciously nihilistic aspiring poets. Michael Llewelyn Davies (the adopted son of J M Barrie and the inspiration for Peter Pan) had been at Eton with him, as had Roger Senhouse and Robert Boothby. Rupert Buxton, the last of the group, was odd man out as an old Harrovian. Llewelyn Davies and Buxton died in their third year at Oxford in a mysterious drowning incident interpreted by many as a lovers' suicide pact when their bodies were found clasped together after an afternoon swim in Sandford Pool near Oxford. Marjoribanks, who gave evidence at their inquest, never got over Llewelyn Davies's death. The nearest he came to a clarification of the nature of their relationship was a poignant love poem[19] and a line in a letter to a friend: 'I have really touched the bottom of my grief. Five years almost exactly Michael Davies died and it was not merely that I lost what will be the only great and perfect friendship I have ever had but there was something else. I have often referred to it but never told you …'[20] The sentence peters off.

Of the remainder of these young men, Roger Senhouse survived what seems to have been a group philosophy and went on to have a sado-masochistic affair with Lytton Strachey, while Robert Boothby became a portly Conservative politician and lived until he was eighty-six, thereby losing all the romance of the slim youths who had died young.[21] Boothby was so sexually enthusiastic with his male contemporaries at Oxford that he was known by them as the Palladium because he performed 'twice nightly'. He did not embark on heterosexual relationships until he was twenty-five, though he made up for lost time then, becoming openly bisexual in a far more enlightened age. For Marjoribanks, who died in 1932, the year in which George V remarked in relation to an aristocratic scandal, 'I thought chaps like that shot themselves',[22] it was a different story. With his craving for establishment recognition it seems safe to assume that any scandal that might damage his ambitions would be intolerable to him.

It seems the final irony that Marjoribanks' only lasting claim to the fame he so craved should be through Marshall, as a shadowy Boswell to Marshall's Dr Johnson.

All biographies inevitably reflect the life of the writer. We can only explore the life of someone else through the prism of our own experiences. Our preoccupations dominate our understanding of the subjects. Even this short account of Marjoribanks' own life throws considerable light on his *Life of Sir Edward Marshall Hall* and his portrait of Marshall. Marjoribanks' cynicism and decadence, born of natural inclination and the post-war spirit of his time, led him to interpret Marshall's worthy Victorian values as what he constantly describes as naivety; with his own brilliant intellectual achievements he could only see Marshall's lack of classical scholarship as a sign of a deficient intellect; his own all-consuming desire for political success led him to judge Marshall a failure as a politician. In truth Marshall had, like many others of his time, regarded membership of Parliament on a simplistic level as a representative of local interests and as an adjunct to his real career at the Bar. Equally Marjoribanks' own undoubtedly troubled attitude towards women confused his analysis, such as it was, of Marshall's personal relationships[23] and he reflected in his interpretation of Marshall's behaviour the hysteria of his own reactions to reverses.

For my part I found a quite different man, charismatic and flamboyant as described by Marjoribanks but far cleverer, far more self-aware, more sophisticated and manipulative than Marjoribanks had portrayed him, a pragmatic hard-working professional, an expert self-publicist and builder of his own public image. He may have been a dreadful show-off but the ultimate aims were calculated and subtle. Newspapers paid for defences; Marshall gave them their headlines; but more than that they developed his reputation for being invincible and it became the ultimate self-fulfilling prophecy. He started every trial with a public (and so jury) expectation that he would pull off the impossible. It was consummate public relations.

Marshall's creation of illusion was inimitable, close to that of an actor yet delivered with the objectivity of an observer. 'My profession and that of an actor are somewhat akin', he once said, 'except that I have no scenes to help me and no words are written for me to say. Yet out of the vivid living dream of someone else's life I have to create an atmosphere, for that is advocacy.' And so for over forty years with extraordinary stamina and courage he created the atmosphere of his clients' living dreams. Emulated, parodied, indefinable, at his best sublime, his oratory has resonated over the decades and whether rationalised as skilful psychology or romanticised as some sort of mystical empathy with his juries, it amounted to a kind of genius.

When I started at the Bar I was told about the concept of total advocacy. You began to win your case as you drove into the court car park, I was told. It was all about the way you treated the security men and the court ushers, the canteen lady and the clerks. You had to behave as though you were the winner before you got anywhere near the actual trial; every member of the public who saw you might be on the jury, or their friend might be, or their mother. Utter confidence is catching; you should never betray indecision or tiredness or self-doubt except in those rare circumstances when vulnerability will make you more attractive. You should behave as though the result for which you strive is a foregone conclusion. In writing this book I began to realise that Marshall was the ultimate exponent of total advocacy; he lived his entire life as though the world was one huge courtroom and its inhabitants a universal jury to beguile. He cared little or nothing for the restraints of his profession, or for the discipline of the law; but he introduced the concept of compassion into a legal system in which it was lacking, was universally adored and trusted by those whom that system is meant to serve, made speeches of such extraordinary power that they have lived on for more than a century and, most important of all, saved many lives. No other lawyer could claim that.

Although in 1934 Elna refused to co-operate in a film about her father's life, saying, in the richest of ironies, that she feared that it would be 'sensationalised', his legend has gone on and on. After the most famous legal biography ever written came dozens of reminiscences in newspapers and magazines, and eventually in 1947 a Hitchcock film in which the hero was inspired by him.[24] There followed radio and television series, a novel and whole books on each of his famous trials. In 2015 he was someone's *Mastermind* subject. A bus in Brighton has been named after him. He would have loved all that.

Appendix

The correspondence reproduced here is a selection from some of the letters generated in the aftermaths of many of Marshall's great trials; short extracts can be found elsewhere in the book but they are all worth including in detail, since they encapsulate more than any narrative the world Marshall inhabited. Stress and joy, rank ingratitude and extreme adulation, passionate beliefs, and struggles with objectivity, self-reproach, grief and loss and triumph all mingled in trials more intense than can be imagined nowadays. The letters show how Marshall both thrived on, and suffered from, all these experiences and through them achieved his ambition to live a life of 'life and death, freedom and imprisonment, facts not principles'.

The Marie Hermann trial

After she was released from prison, Marie Hermann instructed solicitors to obtain precise accounts of the money provided by Madame Tussauds for her defence. This was the reply:

> Dear Sir
>
> We saved your client from the gallows.
>
> Yours sincerely, Arthur Newton.

The trial of the Yarmouth murderer Herbert Bennett

After the trial, Marshall wrote in distress to Forrest Fulton, his early mentor, who was by then Recorder of London:

> My dear Fulton
>
> I am much concerned about that man Bennett, worthless scoundrel tho' no doubt he is. The more I think of it the more convinced I am that he never murdered that woman. That he

got her down to Yarmouth, meaning to take all her goods and chattels from Bexley Heath, I have no manner of doubt, but I cannot believe he murdered her. You see it was absolutely impossible to try him fairly, as the evidence of the 'chain' unless destroyed was conclusive against him, and although the jury were satisfied the chain found in the prisoner's possession was not the same as the one photographed on the dead woman, yet both the Chief Justice and Gill were satisfied it was the same chain and, being satisfied of that, it was a physical impossibility for the Crown mind to be absolutely impartial … The identification too – when the papers publish a photograph of the accused person, in the town where identification is to take place, and print into the photograph a moustache which does not exist in the original plate. Then too the highly unsatisfactory character of the hotel evidence – where nothing was known by the waiters on enquiry by the police the morning of the murder but every detail remembered six weeks later after Bennett is arrested and the chain found in his box. My object in writing to you is to discharge what I feel is a duty I owe. Personally I cannot see any better fate for a man of that criminal nature than a painless and easy death, but that is not the question, you know very well; and I am not the sort of man to worry unnecessarily about anything, least of all a worthless life like that but honestly and solemnly I do not and cannot believe he murdered his wife. My own theory of it is that he did go to Yarmouth, that he did write the letter and he did take his wife out that night, [but on] leaving her, some prowling scoundrel saw her golden hair and golden chain and beguiling her to the beach for sexual purposes, she resisting, there was a struggle, an attempted rape and murder … As to the prisoner's conduct after the murder, it is absolutely consistent with the theory that, having wished her dead … and having been at Yarmouth, he was afraid to admit he recognised by the description in the papers that it was his wife who had been murdered … And now I will bother you no further, but I want you to see Ritchie [the Home Secretary] and tell him that tho' as an advocate I am barred from expressing an opinion in court, yet as a man, after the trial is over, I say this: that I would not personally, knowing all I do know, take the responsibility of hanging that man … The chain found was not the chain and I will prove that to anyone in five minutes with the beach photograph and a strong microscope ... I, too started with a certain conviction of his guilt, and have come now to the contrary opinion ... I know it detracts from any credit due to me for the conduct of the case, for tho' it may be a matter of great merit to make a fine defence on behalf of a guilty man it is discreditable to have been unable to convince the jury of the innocence of a man you yourself believe to be innocent.

Yours always, E. Marshall Hall.

The Hettie Chattell libel case and its aftermath

During the period when the persecution by the press was becoming intolerable, Marshall wrote to Thomas Marlowe, the Editor of the *Daily Mail*:

Dear Sir,

I have had my attention called to the report in your issue of February 3rd of [a case in which he was involved]. I notice that, for some reason known only to yourselves, my name has been altered, after the type has been set and spaced, from 'Mr Marshall Hall KC' to 'Mr M. Hall KC'. For myself it matters not whether you print my name properly or not at all but what does matter is this careful sub-editing lends colour to what I have been told is a fact, viz. that some member of your staff has a personal grievance against me. I have been loath to believe it, but I must say that a good deal of colour is leant to the statement by the way your paper has treated me during the last three years. A straw shows which way the wind blows, and that anyone on the staff should have taken the trouble to alter Marshall into M but leave the valuable spacing, shows that an amount of care and attention is lavished on my name in your reports which is far in excess of my deserts. The curious coincidence is that if by any manner of means the report of a case in which I have been engaged can be made to seem to reflect upon me in the smallest degree, the sub editing is all the other way. The value of space is nothing, the 'Marshall' is put into capitals and it is thought worthy of a full capital headline for you to print 'MR MARSHALL HALL AGAIN'.

Yours very truly E Marshall Hall.

The trial of the Seddons

After the trial, the Attorney General, his opponent, wrote to Marshall expressing his admiration:

My dear Marshall

Quite frankly and sincerely, not as A-G but an old friend, do let me say how much I admired your defence and whole conduct of the Seddons' case. Your five minutes outburst for Mrs Seddon made a most powerful impression; and in my view did much – if not the most – for her acquittal. His case was such a terribly difficult one – the chain was as complete as circumstantial evidence can make it – and you had a very hard task, when it was so plain to all that the man had a covetous nature and was such a shrewd cunning fellow. But I didn't mean to discuss the case. I wanted to say ... that it was a really magnificent forensic effort and the whole defence was conducted by you in accordance with the highest traditions of our profession. I know you won't think it impertinent for me to write this to you. It is meant, and will be understood by you, as the expression of an opponent who loves to see work well and nobly done – and of a friend who has always received such generous (over generous, I think) recognition from you.

I am so glad I went away before the verdict was given ...

Yours ever Rufus D Isaacs.

The brides in the bath trial

The Bishop of Croydon, sent to administer the Holy Sacrament to Smith in his condemned cell was unnerved to be met with Smith's request that he publish a letter in which Smith continued to express his innocence. The Home Secretary refused to allow its publication and the Bishop appealed to Marshall. This is Marshall's reply.

My Lord

Your letter re G. Smith has interested me very much. I am afraid you had not all the material upon which to base a satisfactory opinion as to his guilt or innocence. On his own admission, the man was abnormal; and the admitted and undisputed evidence against him, especially two letters in his own handwriting, only one of which has ever been made public, proved conclusively that he was a thief, a liar, and utterly devoid of any sense of decency in his treatment of women. It was because I knew of the overwhelming prejudice against him ... that I most reluctantly acceded to his request that I should defend him, and this I did at great pecuniary and personal sacrifice. But the man was so unlike any other of his type that, after thirty two years' experience I felt interested; and, up to a point I hoped to save him from the extreme penalty of the law. The moment, however, that the judge, and the Court of Criminal appeal, decided that the evidence of all three deaths was admissible against him, I knew that the case was hopeless as no jury, and very few men, will ever except a theory of triple coincidence to explain what would otherwise has a criminal aspect attaching to it. The motive in all three cases was so strong and the series of similarities in all three cases overwhelming.

Personally I have seen some extraordinary coincidences happening in every-day life – for instance, I have seen the same number come up five times consecutively on a roulette table. Some years ago at Bournemouth, P.H. Morton (an old Cambridge colleague of mine), playing golf with me on the public course holed out the first hole twice the same day in one stroke. The odds against both these events are incalculable. Only a few days ago Lord Carnarvon tells me that he and two friends were playing cards at the club and they had to cut for deal; all three cut a three. They cut again; all three cut a seven; they cut a third time; all three cut an ace. My maths are rusty; but I believe the odds ($52 \times 51 \times 50$) 3 to 1 would represent them. Therefore I have not eliminated the coincidence theory, more especially as in the Highgate case – Lofty – I am extraordinarily sceptical as to the cause of death.

But alas, allowing for all of this, I have most reluctantly come to the conclusion that Smith was responsible for the deaths of all three women, directly or indirectly. That he did not drown them in any of the ways suggested by the evidence or the ex parte suggestions of the judge, I am convinced; but I am equally convinced that it was brought about by hypnotic suggestion. I had a long interview with Smith, under very favourable circumstances, and I was convinced that he was a hypnotist. Once accept this theory and the whole thing … is satisfactorily explained and it also accounts for his very firm assertion of his innocence of murder, he having satisfied his conscience that the act was induced by his will, and became to all intents a voluntary act on the part of the woman.

Obviously it is very difficult to write fully upon this subject; but if it interests you perhaps we might meet some day and talk it over. It interests me from all points of view and I am one of those who think that no man is too bad to try to save. I wrote Smith a letter, in reply to one he sent to me protesting his innocence, and I implored him to take the chaplain or someone into his confidence before the end came. I also told him that I was convinced, as well as I could be convinced of anything, that he was responsible for the deaths of all three women, and I further told him that to my mind the means he employed was some sort of hypnotic suggestion. This letter was of course private, and marked not for publication. He did not answer it and no doubt, after hearing my four hours speech on his behalf, he felt it difficult to realise that I believed him guilty. He could not distinguish between the advocate who tries to insist that the onus of legal proof has not been discharged by the Crown and the human individual who, outside his professional duties, finds it impossible, knowing all the facts, to accept the theory of coincidence. I am indeed glad, my lord, that you saw him and did all I am sure you could do for a man in his position. The value of human life has, alas, been gravely reduced by the lamentable slaughter that is going on of our bravest and best at this moment. But it is a great tribute to our judicial system that, at a time like this, this man was tried with all the care and precision as if we had been in the midst of peace.

I judge no man: I know my own life too well to dare to judge others; but in my heart I feel that it was better for this man to die, even if he were technically innocent, though morally guilty. He apparently died bravely, though with his morbid and abnormal nervous system he must inevitably have suffered acutely, and, though you and I probably look on a future state from a different point of view, I am convinced that he has passed from one plane of existence, direct to another, where he will have the chance to prepare for that ever upward movement that our immortal beings must eventually attain to. Please forgive this long letter. Large sums of money have been offered me to write for publication practically what I am now writing you but my personal and professional environment make it impossible.

I have no copy, and I have written as I feel, but I should esteem it a great favour if, after you have read it, you would return it to me, so that I may keep it with other documents concerning this most extraordinary case. As to the letter written to you by Smith, if the authorities see no objection to its publication, I see none.

I am my lord yours very sincerely,
E Marshall Hall.

The green bicycle trial

These are the letters exchanged between Marshall and Ronald Light after the extraordinary acquittal:

Dear Sir

The very first letter I am writing since my release, is of course, to you.

I cannot find words to express how deeply grateful I am for your great and successful efforts on my behalf. It seems rather feeble to say 'Thank you' for saving my life, but I feel sure you understand what I think. Your speech to the jury was simply great and practically obliterated any previous impressions they had obtained ... I shall always remember you with the deepest gratitude.

Yours sincerely R Light.

Dear Sir

Thank you for your letter which I much appreciate. Quite apart from the matter which caused so much anxiety ... may I in all kindness and great sincerity express the hope that you will realise that life is a serious thing, and that work and self-denial are the only means to happiness. Please convey to your mother my sympathetic regards, and you will, I am sure, forgive me if I say that you can best show your gratitude to me by making her life happier in the future than I fear it has been in the past. I am indeed glad to have been of service to you, and through you, to her.

Yours very faithfully Edward Marshall Hall.

The murder at the Savoy

Madame Fahmy's letter of passionate gratitude written as soon as she arrived at her hotel on the evening of her release and Marshall's response in the French of which he was very proud. The warmth of his response is in marked contrast to his reply to Light:

Cher Mâitre

J'arrive, et dans cette ambiance de bonheur un regret m'attriste, celui de n'avoir pas vous prendre la main et de vous dire merci. Mon émotion était si grande que vous me pardonnerez d'avoir fermé les yeux et de m'être laisser emmener.

Votre profondément reconnaissante

M. Fahmy.

Chère Madame

Je vous remercie beaucoup pour votre depêche, et votre lettre si bien reconnaissante. Quant á moi, je n'ai fait rien au dessus de mon devoir, et c' était a vous et le témoignage que vous avez si bravement donnée au coeur que le resultat si heureux était en effet dû. Je regette aussi que je ne pouvais pas vous féliciter personnellement apres le 'verdict' mais j'ai bien compris que vous étiez enfin á peu près epuisée par les évenèments des six derniers jours. J'espère que l'avenir vous donnera beaucoup de moments heureux pour remplacer les misères passées. C'est encore une fois que 'la vérité c'est triumphante'. Agréez madame, mes sentiments bien empressés a vous.

Edward Marshall Hall.

[Dear Maitre

I am here, and in this atmosphere of happiness I have a regret which saddens me, that I have not been able to take your hand to thank you. My emotion was so great that you will forgive me for having closed my eyes and allowing myself to be led away.

Your profoundly grateful
M. Fahmy.

Dear Madame

I thank you very much for your haste and your grateful letter. As for me, I have done nothing beyond my duty and the happy result was due to you and the evidence that you have so bravely given from your heart. I also regret that I could not congratulate you personally after the verdict, but I have well understood that you were drained by the events of the last six days. I hope that the future will give you many happy moments to replace past miseries. Once more truth was triumphant.

I send you my best sentiments
Edward Marshall Hall.]

The Crumbles murder trial

After the trial, Marshall wrote to his opponent Charles Gill:

My dear C-

Last night at Lady Elveden's Herbert Jessel's wife came up to me and told me that Maud Baxter [a witness in the trial] had been in her employ as a kitchenmaid … and that she was obliged to discharge her summarily for lying and immorality.

Having regard to the admissions that were made this may well not be of the importance that it otherwise would have, but personally I never believed her story that she met the two men [Field and Gray] … on the day of the murder … I expect that illogical recommendation was due to the summing up. What a pity he can't sum a case up instead of making a speech for the prosecution.

I am glad it is over my friend, it worried me that it took so much out of you. It really isn't worth it, but it was pleasant to go back to old times again and though as you said, there are some things that you and I both did over which we might wish to cast the veil of oblivion yet give me the time over again and I believe we should do much the same as we did before.

How little the outside public understand these cases. They talk about Greenwood and the Green Bicycle, those cases were child's play compared to this and it is only the expert like yourself who can realise the real difficulty in a case like the Crumbles murder is to put any sort of defence that does not turn round and hit you in the face.

Never have I been at such a loss for something to say and never was I more pleased to come to the end of a case.

God bless you-take care of yourself and don't do any more murder cases …

Yours ever Marshall
I hope I didn't bother you too much at Lewes.

Acknowledgements

My grateful thanks:

To Jilly Austwick, whose family inherited Marshall Hall's papers, for all her unfailing help and kindness in allowing me free access to the papers that remained, for sending me further items over the years as she stumbled on them and for giving me endless support and encouragement.

To the late Miranda, Countess of Iveagh and Andrew and Jamie Smiley, her brothers, who embraced my project with enthusiasm and allowed me access to their fascinating family papers. Miranda was very ill when I first contacted her; despite that, I experienced the charm that I later understood to be legendary. I am very sad she did not live to see the book finished.

Without the kindness of these two families, the book would never have been written.

To Margaret Clay, the Inner Temple librarian, and all the Inner Temple Library staff, and to Celia Pilkington and Lesley Whitelaw, the archivists at Inner Temple and Middle Temple respectively, whose knowledge, unremitting cheerfulness and energy made the whole project take flight. The staff in the library have uncomplainingly lugged books of press cuttings up and down stairs and advised me on topics relating to the project however obscure.

To the archivists at Christie's auctioneers; the Savoy Hotel; Eton College; the Rothschild Archive; the Garrick Club; the Beefsteak Club; the Swiss Church in London; Hertfordshire Archives and Local Studies; the BBC Written Archives Centre; the National Archives at Kew; the National Archives of Australia; St John's College, Cambridge archives; Cambridge University Archives; Churchill College, Cambridge archives; the Parliamentary Archives; East Sussex Archives; Chardstock Historical Record Group and Peter Wood, who has researched St Andrew's College, Chardstock; Queen's College, Harley Street; and the National Records of Scotland. To the librarians at the British Library; the National Library of Australia; the Harry Ransom Center, University of Texas at Austin; Cambridge University Library; Eastbourne Library; and the London Library; and to Muriel McCarthy of Marsh's Library in Dublin for her hospitality in the library whilst I was researching papers stored in Dublin. All these people responded with great kindness to my (in some cases) many requests.

To Matthew Williams and Rusty Maclean at Rugby School for all their help and permission to use quotes from the house book of Philpott's House (now Cotton House) and to use the photograph of the house cricket team.

To Dr Anthony Morton, curator of the Sandhurst Collection, and for permission to quote material from the Sandhurst Gentlemen Cadet Register.

To David Rymill, archivist to the Highclere estate, for all his help and to Lord and Lady Carnarvon for allowing me to spend a day at Highclere Castle researching their visitors' books.

To Burt Brill and Cardens Solicitors, who now occupy Marshall Hall's childhood home at 30 Old Steine, Brighton and who allowed me to visit. To Kat Kimber at the Marlborough Pub and Theatre, Brighton, who showed me the scene of the Lucy Packham killing. To St John's College, Cambridge for allowing me to see Marshall Hall's old rooms. Also to Lewes Crown Court for allowing me to see papers displayed in the robing room.

To Vernon Marshall, Keith Lesley, Shirley Leslie and David Cressy Hall, all of whom did their utmost to assist in my researches into the possibility of Marshall having fathered an illegitimate son and agreed to DNA tests with great good humour. My thanks also to Dr Turi King, lecturer in genetics at Leicester University, who advised in relation to those tests. The fact that they were negative in no way detracts from the help the two families gave me.

To Bevis Hillier for his kind permission to use material quoted in his book *The Virgin's Baby: The Battle of the Ampthill Succession* published by Hopcyn Press in 2013.

To Sheila Wood, who entertained me in her home and shared some of her family history with me.

To John Labouchere, who has helped me in relation to Marshall's sister Ada's family.

To John Bowker, who shared with me recollections of his father, Edgar Bowker, who was Marshall Hall's faithful clerk and friend, and to Robin Soule, who helped with the history of all Marshall's clerks.

To Matthew, my own faithful clerk and friend, and to his team of clerks who rallied round with their usual good humour when I made wide-ranging pleas for help.

To all those members of my chambers, 1 Crown Office Row, who have helped and encouraged me on what must have seemed to them an unending project.

To Peter Howe, Timothy Duke, Rupert Prior, Laurence Davies, Lachlan Munro, Richard Parsons, the late Sir David Penry Davey, Malcolm Spence QC, Francois Velde and Patrick Carnegy, fifteenth Earl of Northesk, all of whom answered queries on widely varying subjects as I pursued alleys blind and otherwise.

To Nicky Matthews for all her help and kindness with the word processing.

To my old friend Michael Howard QC, who introduced me to Marshall Hall in the first place and who read the completed book and commented on it with his usual (constructive) acerbity.

To another old friend, Gregory Chambers, for accompanying me on a research trip to Jersey and to David Gainsborough Roberts, whose extraordinary collection of Edward Marshall Hall memorabilia we went to see. My thanks also to David for allowing me to reproduce Robert Wood's portrait of Marshall Hall.

To Andrew Riddoch, my publisher at Wildy, Simmonds & Hill. This is my first book. Andrew guided me throughout with kindness, enthusiasm and humour and the required degree of firmness. I can never be sufficiently grateful.

To my family: my sister Pip for all her generous help, not least thinking of the title, and Max Cutting, my nephew, a professional film maker and photographer, who helped me with the photographs.

Lastly to my dear Roger, who drove me about, stood around in wet graveyards, helped me when technology threatened to defeat me, read the book and made many helpful suggestions, and put up with interminable agonisings during the creative process. I am very lucky to have him.

This book has been some years in the writing and I have had so many acts of kindness along the way; I can only hope none have slipped my memory or my notes. I deeply appreciate all the help I have been given. Equally, I have endeavoured to obtain all relevant permissions; if any have been overlooked, I offer my apologies and an assurance that any omissions will be rectified in subsequent editions of this book.

Select Bibliography

Legal background

Richard L Abel, *The Legal Profession in England and Wales* (Basil Blackwell, 1998).

Archbold's Criminal Pleading Evidence and Practice, 20th–30th editions (1888–1938).

D J Bentley, *English Criminal Justice in the Nineteenth Century* (Hambledon Press, 1998).

Sir Patrick Devlin, *Trial by Jury* (Stevens & Sons, 1956).

John C Goodwin, *Insanity and the Criminal* (Hutchinson, 1923).

J R Lewis, *The Victorian Bar* (Robert Hale, 1982).

Harry Potter, *Hanging in Judgment: Religion and the Death Penalty in England* (Continuum, 1993).

Robert Stevens, *The English Judges: Their Role in the Changing Constitution* (Hart, 2002).

William A White, *Insanity and the Criminal Law* (Macmillan, 1923).

Legal reminiscence and biography

Edward Abinger, *Forty Years at the Bar: Being the Memoirs of Edward Abinger, Barrister of the Inner Temple* (Hutchinson, 1930).

Gilchrist Alexander, *The Temple of the Nineties* (William Hodge, 1938).

F W Ashley, *My Sixty Years in the Law* (Bodley Head, 1936).

George Pleydell Bancroft, *Stage and Bar: Recollections of George Pleydell Bancroft* (Faber & Faber, 1939).

Dudley Barker, *Lord Darling's Famous Cases* (Hutchinson, 1936).

Earl of Birkenhead, *Law, Life and Letters* (2 vols, Hodder & Stoughton, 1927).

Lord Birkett, *Six Great Advocates* (Penguin, 1961).

Augustine Birrell, *Sir Frank Lockwood: A Biographical Sketch* (Smith, Elder, 1898).

Ernest Bowen-Rowlands, *Seventy Two Years at the Bar: A Memoir* (Macmillan, 1924).

A E Bowker, *Behind the Bar* (Staples Press, 1947).

A E Bowker, *A Lifetime with the Law* (W H Allen, 1961).

Henry Hawkins Brampton, *The Reminiscences of Sir Henry Hawkins, Baron Brampton* (Thomas Nelson, 1904).

Lewis Broad, *Advocates of the Golden Age: Their Lives and Cases* (John Long, 1958).

Sir Edward Clarke, *The Story of my Life* (John Murray, 1918).

Hon. Stephen Coleridge, *Quiet Hours in the Temple* (Mills & Boon, 1924).

John Ellis, *Diary of a Hangman* (True Crime Library, 1996).

Lord Hailsham, *A Sparrow's Flight* (Collins, 1990).

Sir Patrick Hastings, *The Autobiography of Sir Patrick Hastings* (Heinemann, 1948).

Nina Warner Hooke and Gill Thomas, *Marshall Hall: A Biography* (Arthur Barker, 1966).

Travers Humphreys, *Criminal Days: Recollections and Reflections of Travers Humphreys* (Hodder & Stoughton, 1946).

H Montgomery Hyde, *Lord Reading: The Life of Rufus Isaacs, First Marquess of Reading* (Heinemann, 1967).

H Montgomery Hyde, *Norman Birkett: The Life of Lord Birkett of Ulverston* (Hamish Hamilton, 1964).

Stanley Jackson, *The Life and Cases of Mr Justice Humphreys* (Odhams Press, 1952).

David Lewer, *A Spiritual Song: The Story of the Temple Choir and a History of Divine Service in the Temple Church, London* (Templars' Union, 1961).

Geoffrey Lewis, *Lord Hailsham: A Life* (Jonathan Cape, 1997).

Robert Low, *The Lawyers* (Garrick Club, 2011).

Edgar Lustgarten, *Defender's Triumph* (Allen Wingate, 1951).

Edward Marjoribanks, *The Life of Sir Edward Marshall Hall* (Victor Gollancz, 1929).

Malcolm Spence, *The Chambers of Marshall Hall: 125 Years* (Aeneas Press, 2005).

Derek Walker-Smith and Edward Clarke, *The Life of Sir Edward Clarke* (Thornton Butterworth, 1939).

Roland Wild and Derek Curtis-Bennett, *'Curtis': The Life of Sir Henry Curtis-Bennett KC* (Cassell, 1937).

Sir Ellis Hume Williams, *The World, the House, and the Bar* (John Murray, 1930).

The trials

Notable British Trials series (William Hodge).

Winifred Duke (ed), *Trial of Field and Gray* (1939).

Winifred Duke (ed), *Trial of Harold Greenwood* (1930).

Basil Hogarth (ed), *Trial of Robert Wood: The Camden Town Case* (1936).

Eric R Watson (ed), *Trial of George Joseph Smith* (1922).

Filson Young (ed), *Trial of the Seddons* (1914).

Famous Trials series (Geoffrey Bles):

The Trial of Herbert John Bennett (the Yarmouth Beach Murder) (1929).

John Benson, *The Wolverhampton Tragedy: Death of the 'Respectable' Mr Lawrence* (Carnegie, 2009).

C Wendy East, *The Green Bicycle Murder* (Alan Sutton, 1993).

Bevis Hillier, *The Virgin's Baby: The Battle of the Ampthill Succession* (Hopcyn Press, 2013).

Roy Jenkins, *Sir Charles Dilke: A Victorian Tragedy* (Collins, 1958).

Frederick J Lyons, *George Joseph Smith: The Brides-in-the-Bath Murders* (Duckworth, 1935).

Sir David Napley, *The Camden Town Murder* (Weidenfeld & Nicolson, 1987).

Jane Robins, *The Magnificent Spilsbury and the Case of the Brides in the Bath* (John Murray, 2010).

Andrew Rose, *The Prince, the Princess and the Perfect Murder* (Coronet, 2013).

Andrew Rose, *Scandal at the Savoy: The Infamous 1920s Murder Case* (Bloomsbury, 1991).

H R Wakefield, *The Green Bicycle Case* (Philip Allen, 1930).

General

Countess of Carnarvon, *Lady Almina and the Real Downton Abbey: The Lost Legacy of Highclere Castle* (Hodder & Stoughton, 2012).

Earl of Carnarvon, *No Regrets* (Weidenfeld & Nicolson, 1976).

Richard Davenport-Hines, *Ettie: The Intimate Life and Dauntless Spirit of Lady Desborough* (Weidenfeld & Nicolson, 2008).

Harry Furniss, *The Two Pins Club* (John Murray, 1925).

Anita Leslie, *Edwardians in Love* (Hutchinson, 1972).

Angus McLaren, *A Prescription for Murder: The Victorian Serial Killings of Dr Thomas Neill Cream* (University of Chicago Press, 1993).

Robert Sackville-West, *The Disinherited: A Story of Family, Love and Betrayal* (Bloomsbury, 2014).

J B Hope Simpson, *Rugby since Arnold: A History of Rugby School from 1842* (Macmillan, 1967).

Jane W Stedman, *W S Gilbert: A Classic Victorian and His Theatre* (Oxford University Press, 1996).

Stephen Wade, *Conan Doyle and the Crimes Club: The Creator of Sherlock Holmes and His Criminological Friends* (Fonthill, 2013).

Geoffrey Wansell, *The Garrick Club: A History* (Garrick Club, 2004).

Sources and Notes

Many of Marshall Hall's large collection of papers were destroyed after Edward Marjoribanks' 1929 biography had been written, or have been dispersed since. The residue is now in my possession. Marjoribanks quoted many of Marshall Hall's documents verbatim. I have checked the accuracy where possible. The references given are either to the page of Marjoribanks' book on which the document is reproduced or to Author's Collection. Many of his letters are undated though the chronology can usually be inferred from their contents.

Marshall Hall's thirty-eight volumes of press cuttings are now in the possession of Inner Temple Library. I have drawn heavily on them. Where possible I have given the name and date of the newspaper; where, as is often the case, these details are not apparent from the cutting, I have referred to the number of the press cuttings volume.

Other sources are widely distributed in archives and private collections and the details are provided in the relevant endnote.

There have been two previous biographies of Marshall Hall: the 1929 Marjoribanks biography and *Marshall Hall: A Biography* by Nina Warner Hooke and Gill Thomas, published by Arthur Baker in 1966. Where I have relied on material from them I have checked the accuracy where possible. The 1966 book was written in consultation with Marshall Hall's daughter Elna. Where it gives details of Marshall Hall's family life which are unverifiable, I have assumed them to be accurate whilst remembering that a daughter's perspective of her parents and their marriage is a very particular one.

Abbreviations for sources most frequently referred to are:

M'banks	Edward Marjoribanks, *The Life of Sir Edward Marshall Hall* (Victor Gollancz, 1929), fourth impression
ITPC	Inner Temple Press Cuttings, collection of Sir Edward Marshall Hall KC, Inner Temple Library
NA	National Archives
PA	Parliamentary Archives

Chapter 1: 'The last moment'

1. *Daily Telegraph*, 19 December 1907.
2. Frederick Edwin Smith, 1st Earl of Birkenhead, *Law, Life and Letters* (2 vols, Hodder & Stoughton, 1927), vol 1. Smith was Lord Chancellor 1919–22.
3. £1,000, roughly the equivalent of £108,000 today.
4. EMH's complaints about the Inland Revenue were frequent, eg in letters to Charles Gill (Charles Gill private collection) and to Ralph Blumenfeld, PA BLU/1/10/HA1-6.
5. Now Sussex Gardens.
6. Forerunner to the present Palace Pier, situated a little further to the west.
7. A 'saloon pistol', a small rifle chiefly used in shooting galleries.
8. *White's Directory of Derbyshire 1857.*
9. In the 1861 census, of the fifty-three private houses fifteen were occupied by members of the medical profession, most of them with large families, amongst the clergymen, army officers and gentlemen of independent means. Next door to the Halls at number 31 lived Philip Rowell, a watchmaker. In later life EMH spoke often of the watchmaker and jeweller who had sparked his lifetime's interest without naming him. It seems unlikely to be a coincidence.
10. The contemporary equivalent of today's magistrates' court.
11. In slightly different versions they were recounted many times; see Edward Marshall Hall, 'In the Days of My Youth', *MAP Journal*, 2 March 1901.

Chapter 2: 'Splendid types of English public school life'

1. Arthur was brother to the far more famous Henry Labouchere, who after a romping youth at Eton (where he developed a passion for gambling) and Cambridge (where he was accused of cheating) via an interlude in Mexico with a lady circus performer settled down to a celebrated life as a wit, publisher, theatre owner and Liberal MP. Arthur seems to have had the same eccentricity without his brother's looks and talent. Horse mad, he regularly travelled to Biarritz taking his pack of hounds with him. When Ada died, Arthur, then sixty-two, married a nineteen-year-old, Dorothy Timson, by whom he had a daughter.
2. Latterly heated with 800 radiators, it was restored by the film star Oliver Reed and is now flats.

3. Author interview with John Labouchere.

4. Letter quoted in M'banks, p 28.

5. Edward Marshall Hall, 'In the Days of My Youth', *MAP Journal*, 2 March 1901.

6. P J Wood and Chardstock Historical Record Group, *A History of Education in Chardstock and All Saints 1712–2009* (Chardstock Historical Record Group, 2009).

7. Ibid.

8. Ibid.

9. Ibid.

10. In adult life EMH deeply regretted this; see for example correspondence with John Lane, John Lane Company Records, box 30, folder 6 (1906–1922), Harry Ransom Center, University of Texas at Austin.

11. Now Cotton House.

12. Cotton House Archive, Rugby School.

13. He was still fulminating aged forty-two; see 'In the Days of My Youth'.

14. EMH, correspondence to St John's College, Biographical Records, St John's College, Cambridge.

15. Ibid.

16. Room K5, South Court; see G C Moore Smith, 'List of Past Occupants of Rooms in St John's College', *The Eagle*, vol. XVI (1895).

17. Marshall Hall, 'In the Days of My Youth'.

18. Article in *Le Figaro* in 1863; 'Le peintre de la vie moderne'.

19. *The Standard*, 28 June 1879.

20. *Aberdeen Weekly Journal Shipping Intelligence*, 4 August 1879.

21. Of Edward's journal only the brief extracts quoted in M'banks now remain, but other journals written on similar voyages on the *Hydaspes* still exist, enabling a picture to be built up.

22. A bread pudding containing fruit and cheese.

23. Mr Purves (ed), *The Hydaspes Gazette: a weekly newspaper published on board the Hydaspes, commander, E S Babot, on her voyage from Sydney to London* (Dunn, Collin, 1875).

24. Ibid.

25. Ibid.

26. On 17 July 1880 she went down off Dungeness in dense fog.

27. *Bendigo Advertiser*, 21 October 1879.

28. Shipping Intelligence, ibid.

29. W Russell Grimwade, *The Bohemians Melbourne: A Chronicle of the Bohemians in Five Periods from 1875–1931* (Specialty Press, 1931).

30. Shipping Intelligence, *Melbourne Argos*, 6 March 1880.

31. Marshall Hall, 'In the Days of My Youth'.

32. No photograph that can be reliably identified exists.

33. *The Times*, 20 June 1882.

34. *The Times*, 10 June 1882.

Chapter 3: 'Words can never tell my grief'

1. All quotations from EMH's diaries are as quoted in M'banks, pp 74–6. EMH never intended them to be seen and directed their destruction in his will. In what seems a betrayal of trust by the executors access was granted to Marjoribanks prior to the direction being carried out. Marjoribanks quotes selectively, constrained by the reticence of the time. That selection and some pretty broad hints by him as to the reasons for the problems are the only record we have of the honeymoon.

2. Ethel's fear of pregnancy is well documented, as is her insistence that her doctor had warned her about an anatomical deformity and its consequences. However, it is clear from evidence given at the trial of her killer that her doctor had merely told her she would require special attention when pregnant.

3. Edward Clarke, *The Story of my Life* (John Murray, 1918).

4. The other two, Gray's Inn and Lincoln's Inn, are situated on the other side of Fleet Street.

5. See *The Times*, 23 December 1881 and 1 November 1882.

6. Edward Marshall Hall, 'The Bar as a Career: Advice to Aspirants', *The Visitor*, 8 April 1905.

7. Gilchrist Alexander, *The Temple of the Nineties* (William Hodge, 1938).

8. No relation, but a colleague and, at the end of his life, patient of Edward's father.

9. Serjeants were an ancient order of senior barristers that dwindled from the 1850s onwards, ultimately entirely superseded by that of Queen's (or King's) Counsel.

10. He was Baron of the Exchequer of Pleas; the ancient post was later abolished and the Court of Exchequer absorbed into the High Court of Justice.

11. Demolition was recommended as early as 1878. Work began in 1902 when Newgate was pulled down. The present building opened in 1907.

12. Up to the late nineteenth century, public admission to watch the major trials was primarily by ticket or by invitation.

13. *Evening Standard*, 26 July 1920.

14. Travers Humphreys, *Criminal Days: Recollections and Reflections of Travers Humphreys* (Hodder & Stoughton, 1946).

15. Edward Marshall Hall, 'How I Became a Barrister', *The Tatler*, 6 April 1904.

16. Quoted in M'banks, p 472.

17. Sir Patrick Devlin, *Trial by Jury* (Stevens & Sons, 1956).

18. R Thurston Hopkins, *Life and Death at the Old Bailey* (Herbert Jenkins, 1935).

Chapter 4: 'Violent passionate extraordinary advocacy'

1. There have been many Beefsteak Clubs. This one was the successor to the earlier club presided over by Sir Henry Irving which met at the Lyceum Theatre. It moved from the Folly to Mayfair and ultimately in 1896 to Irving Street, near Leicester Square, where it remains to this day in a wonderful room hidden away up an anonymous staircase.

2. W S Gilbert, letter, 6 June 1876, Gilbert papers, British Library, WSG/BL Add MS 49304.

3. Henry Irving, Squire Bancroft, Charles Wyndham, George Alexander, Allan Aynesworth, Seymour Hicks, Herbert Beerbohm Tree, Henry Labouchere (the last was related to EMH, his sister having married Henry's brother Arthur), W S Gilbert and Arthur Sullivan.

4. Arthur Pinero, Wilkie Collins, George and Weedon Grossmith, F C Burnand and Frank Yardley (also a famous cricketer).

5. Harry Furniss and Edward Linley Sambourne.

6. J R Lewis, *The Victorian Bar* (Robert Hale, 1982), p 120.

7. *The Times*, 17 May 1882.

8. It is interesting that during Marshall's defence speech in the case in which he made his name (see chapter 6) he referred to the style of his opponent's advocacy as 'laboured and theatrical'; his opponent in that

case was Sir Charles 'Willie' Matthews, eight years Marshall's senior and a renowned advocate of the histrionic type.

9. Remark by Charles Gill, quoted in M'banks, p 53.

10. 'Temple Life', *Temple Bar*, vol 35 (1872).

11. Evidence by EMH in the Laermanns trial; see chapter 5.

12. Ironically given his fame as a criminal defender on capital charges, on EMH's death *The Times* refers to the Dilke trial as 'perhaps the most important case in which he was concerned'. It was typical of the intellectually superior attitude to criminal law in some quarters.

13. The private appointment of Attorney General or legal adviser within the royal household is not the same as the political appointment of Attorney General as a law officer of the Crown.

14. M'banks, p 52.

15. 'Famous QC defends small boys', *Manchester Evening News*, 2 March 1926.

16. *Pall Mall Gazette*, 11 July 1887.

17. See D J Bentley, *English Criminal Justice in the Nineteenth Century* (Hambledon Press, 1998), p 124.

18. Letter from EMH to Gill, Charles Gill private collection.

19. M'banks, p 52.

20. Evidence in Laermanns trial; see notes on chapter 5.

21. It is a measure of his devotion to his parents that EMH directed in his will that his ashes should be buried in their grave.

22. Exhibited in Laermanns trial; see notes on chapter 5.

23. Ibid.

Chapter 5: 'Mysterious death of a barrister's wife'

1. All details in this chapter not otherwise referenced derive from the NA file relating to the prosecution of de Ponthieu and Laermanns, CRIM 1/33/5.

2. Gentlemen Cadet Register, Sandhurst Collection.

3. Ibid.

4. The romantic story that he was summoned to her deathbed, arriving an hour too late, as recounted by Marjoribanks is incorrect according to EMH's own evidence to the coroner.

5. *The Times*, 16 June 1890.

6. Now ivy-clad ruins.

7. The family name, changed by his parents, was Abrahams. Newspaper reports use the names interchangeably.

8. He wrote a (very long) book called *Forty Years at the Bar* (Hutchinson, 1930), an awful lot of which is given over to explaining why he had not made mistakes in particular cases despite what others said.

9. Now the crown court.

10. In the catalogue it is entitled 'Laermaus'.

11. Until its rebuilding in 1907.

Chapter 6: 'God never gave her a chance'

1. His lucky number was eleven. When his lucky tie pin with eleven jewels was stolen he petulantly changed the number to another which he refused to divulge.

2. M'banks, p 80.

3. The client was Lord Arthur Somerset, one of many of the upper classes suspected of being clients of a male brothel in Cleveland Street, off Tottenham Court Road.

4. The trial of Frederick Seddon, in which EMH defended Seddon (see chapter 11).

5. The trial of Adelaide Bartlett.

6. The court was inaugurated in 1907 and first sat in May 1908. Prior to this, the Court for Crown Cases Reserved heard only appeals on questions of law reserved for their consideration by the trial judge. There was no right of appeal and it heard a tiny number of cases each year.

7. ITPC, vol 2.

8. *The Art of Acting: A Discussion by Constant Coquelin, Henry Irving and Dion Boucicault* (Columbia University, 1926).

9. 'Chamber of Horrors: the actual trunk and all the relics now on view, admission one shilling', *The Times*, 4 July 1894; 'Surpassed all previous August crowds', *The Standard*, 7 August 1894.

10. Respectively Sir Richard Webster KC, later 1st Viscount Alverstone; Sir Robert Reid, later 1st Earl Loreburn, Lord Chancellor under Campbell-Bannerman; Sir Charles 'Willie' Matthews; and Sir Horace Avory.

11. ITPC, vol 1.

12. Ibid.

13. Giving a theatrical performance on the radio as Serjeant Buzz-Fuzz in the trial scene in Dickens's *Pickwick Papers* with his friend Henry Dickens KC, son of the author, performing with him. See also chapter 18.

14. ITPC, vol 1.

15. Alfred Hall died less than two years later in 1897. Marshall spoke ever after of his gratitude for his father's support.

Chapter 7: 'Vote for my daddy, Marshall Hall'

1. EMH gives the Savoy as his place of residence in the certificate for his marriage to Hetty Kroeger in 1896.

2. Now part of the Savoy Grill.

3. There are no guest records for this early period though we know that Claude Monet had an arrangement as to a cheaper room such as this in 1899, 1900 and 1901; Savoy Archives.

4. Marshall and Hetty's daughter Elna, born in 1897, was unaware of it until her teens when she stumbled on the information in *Who's Who*.

5. Now Sussex Gardens.

6. The house is described in *World* magazine, 12 June 1901.

7. Quoted in M'banks, pp 174–5.

8. Ibid.

9. Ibid.

10. Ibid.

11. Letter to Elna, author's collection.

12. Ibid. The reference is to Rufus Isaacs KC, later 1st Marquess of Reading and Viceroy of India, a close friend of Marshall's.

13. Queen's (or King's) Counsel are the most eminent members of the Bar, appointed by letters patent granted by the monarch. The exchange of gowns on appointment gives us the term 'taking silk' for becoming a QC, who may also be referred to as a silk. All barristers who have not taken silk are called juniors whatever their seniority. The first KC was appointed in 1603 and the practice continues to this day, although now encompassing eminent solicitors as well as barristers.

14. Letter to the junior of the Sussex sessions, 12 November 1898, now in Lewes Crown Court Robing Room.

15. The last execution of a mother for the killing of her new-born child had been in 1849.

16. Hansard, HC Deb, 7 March 1904, vol 131, cols 278–9.

17. The 1922 Infanticide Act did not define the term 'new-born'; later the statutory definition was under one year.

18. See chapter 9.

19. The play was titled *Murder at the Marlborough*, written by John Montgomery.

20. In an early speech to the Southport electorate Curzon informed them that he 'preferred Brighton', a sentiment EMH probably shared, though he had the charm and tact not to articulate it.

Chapter 8: 'Outrageous gutter rags'

1. The equivalent of the tabloids. Broadsheets such as *The Times* cost one penny.

2. All details relating to the Bennett trial not otherwise referenced derive from *The Trial of Herbert John Bennett (the Yarmouth Beach Murder)*, Famous Trials (Geoffrey Bles, 1929) or the NA file relating to the prosecution, CRIM 1/65/2.

3. EMH's privately held view was that Bennett had been a Boer spy, a view which holds some force given the mysterious and short visit to a war zone and Bennett's subsequent free spending.

4. *Australian Sunday Times*, 7 April 1907.

5. Strictly speaking, of course, on Queen Victoria's death QCs became KCs; in fact the new King decreed that all those already in office should for the time being retain their original appointments. The metamorphosis to KC seems to have occurred gradually as new appointments were made by the King, KCs from the outset.

6. In those days the defence did not have to give advance notice of an alibi as they do now.

7. The honesty of the witness was never doubted and after the trial in an unusual move Alverstone wrote to the witness to tell him that the consensus was that he had honestly mistaken the date.

8. *The Times*, 4 March 1901.

9. Hansard, HC Deb, 14 March 1901, vol 90, cols 1561–2.

10. Quoted in M'banks, p 164.

11. *Daily Express*, 7 March 1901.

12. *Daily Express*, 23 March 1901.

13. *The Visitor*, 19 March 1901.

14. M'banks, p 171.

15. They were far ruder about Winston Churchill, making his debut at around the same time: 'His tone was lacking, he had a detracting lisp and anything in the way of inspiring eloquence was not yet apparent' (*Manchester Guardian*, 27 May 1901).

16. On one occasion, after a much publicised accident in a hansom cab, he campaigned for the glass windows to be replaced by celluloid. An objection was raised that celluloid was too inflammable. Marshall attempted to set fire to a piece in the House of Commons lobby in an attempt to prove that the objection was ill founded.

17. *Evening News*, 18 March 1901.

18. *Candid Friend*, 28 June 1902.

Chapter 9: 'Disgraceful conduct'

1. See for example *Vanity Fair*, 24 September 1903: 'The British jury believes in him and the British public admires him but Lord Justice Mathew is supposed not to love him.'

2. Marshall always attributed the animosity to be in part due to this but it was not a generally held view and Mathew's close friendship with Edward Carson, the most ardent of anti-home rulers, belies it.

3. Who, as F E Smith, had had his own reputation for fearless wit at the expense of the judges in front of whom he appeared.

4. Earl of Birkenhead, *Law, Life and Letters* (Hodder & Stoughton, 1927), vol 1.

5. *Daily Mail*, 15 June 1903.

6. Quoted in Derek Walker-Smith and Edward Clarke, *The Life of Sir Edward Clarke* (Thornton Butterworth, 1939).

7. *Taylor v Taylor*.

8. ITPC, vol 5.

9. *Daily Mail*, 9 June 1904.

10. Letter quoted in M'banks, p 184.

11. Letter from EMH to Charles Gill, Charles Gill private collection.

12. Letter from EMH to Charles Gill, Charles Gill private collection.

13. Ever since his 1896 illness he succumbed frequently to colds and chills and it had been the beginning of phlebitis, which caused increasing pain for the rest of his life.

14. *Southport Guardian*, ITPC, vol 3.

15. EMH sold the Vulcan to a younger member of the Bar, Henry Curtis Bennett, for two hundred pounds and went on to newer and ever flashier models. Curtis Bennett's clerk was horrified. It might be all right for Marshall Hall, he said, but he could not claim decent fees if a young member of the Bar turned up at the police court chauffeur driven (Roland Wild and Derek Curtis-Bennett, *'Curtis': The Life of Sir Henry Curtis-Bennett KC* (Cassell, 1937)).

16. Collin Brooks, *More Tavern Talk* (James Barrie, 1952).

17. He named his infant son, born in 1905, after him: Anthony Alfred Harmsworth Marlowe.

Chapter 10: 'A simple matter of a moment'

1. All details relating to the Wood murder trial not otherwise referenced derive from the transcript of the trial in Basil Hogarth (ed), *Trial of Robert Wood: The Camden Town Case*, Notable British Trials (William Hodge, 1936).

2. Now Agar Grove.

3. Only one, Mary Kelly, was murdered in her room. The sadistic evisceration and mutilation were hallmarks of a very different kind of murder.

4. Most famously by Patricia Cornwell in *Portrait of a Killer: Jack the Ripper – Case Closed* (Little, Brown, 2002).

5. For example John Van Druten's play *Somebody Knows* (Victor Gollancz, 1932); Patrick Hamilton's novel *Twenty Thousand Streets under the Sky* (Constable, 1935), in which a character, significantly called Jenny, is modelled on Emily Dimmock; and a novel by Ernest Raymond, *For Them that Trespass* (Cassell, 1944).

6. This book is not the place for a detailed analysis of the law on this fascinating subject. Those interested should turn to D J Bentley, *English Criminal Justice in the Nineteenth Century* (Hambledon Press, 1998).

7. Henry Shee QC, a distinguished advocate, was briefed for the prosecution in a murder trial shortly after the introduction of the 1898

Act. The accused chose to give evidence. Shee cross-examined for a few minutes and then said to the judge: 'My Lord, I am not accustomed to this class of work' and sat down. The trial continued and the accused was convicted and sentenced to hang.

8.   Nowadays he would be lucky to get one.

9.   See chapter 3.

10. A description of the court at the outset of the trial from the *Pall Mall Gazette*, 12 December 1907.

11. Untitled newspaper cutting, 20 December 1907, ITPC, vol 8.

12. Many of these, now long forgotten, were at the time of such great fame that they attracted almost as much press attention as did the opening of the trial. Amongst the famous names were glamorous actresses (Lily Elsie, Gertie Millar, Mrs Beerbohm Tree), actors (Sir George Alexander, Oliver Asche, H B Irving) and writers (Hall Caine, George Sims, Sir Arnold Wing Pinero).

13. The Old Bailey then sat six days a week.

14. The jury were at this time kept in isolation throughout the trial from oath to discharge with no newspapers or contact with the outside world permitted. The description of their activities derives from an untitled newspaper cutting, 16 December 1907, ITPC, vol 8.

15. The consensus at the time was that this was when the verdict was won, though, in a curious volte-face from his conduct during the trial, the judge at the eleventh hour indicated to the jury that the evidence was in his view not strong enough for a conviction. Marshall's petulantly expressed theory that the judge was trying to steal his thunder was, given the inconsistency of the judge's attitude, probably correct.

16. ITPC, vol 8.

Chapter 11: 'The scales of justice'

1.   Letter from EMH to Charles Gill, Charles Gill private collection.

2.   Description of EMH's room taken from 'KCs and Their Chambers', *Strand Magazine* (1903), vol 25, no 146.

3.   Portrait of EMH by Robert Wood reproduced in plate section.

4.   So called because of its size and difficult handling.

5.   Historically the Bar of England and Wales has been divided into circuits or regions for ease of administration. Barristers elected to join the

circuit on which they intended principally to practise, in EMH's case the South Eastern.

6. There is no transcript of the Lawrence trial. All details not otherwise referenced derive from newspaper cuttings in ITPC, vol 9.

7. Human and animal blood could not be definitely differentiated until 1901.

8. The first conviction on fingerprint evidence in a British court was in 1902.

9. *Archbold's Criminal Pleading Evidence and Practice* (Sweet, 1886).

10. He continued to do so throughout his life, never admitting the pragmatic reality that he failed to secure the brief owing to a fall out over fees. Marshall's clerk Edgar Bowker eventually gave the true account in his book *Behind the Bar* (Staples Press, 1947).

11. Newton's career of sailing close to the wind ultimately led to a three-year prison sentence in 1913 for his part in a fraudulent investment scheme.

12. All details relating to the Seddon trial not otherwise referenced derive from Filson Young (ed), *Trial of the Seddons*, Notable British Trials (William Hodge, 1914).

13. It features as one of the classic murders in George Orwell's essay 'Decline of the English Murder', the type of murder that makes ideal reading after Sunday lunch, pipe in hand, cup of tea at elbow. By now Edward VII had died and George V was on the throne, but I use the term 'Edwardian' here as it is frequently used to cover the period up to the outbreak of the First World War.

14. At the end of the trial after Seddon had given evidence and prior to speeches Willcox was recalled by the prosecution and attempted to explain away the evidence relating to the hair. He said it had been contaminated by blood-stained fluid seeping from Miss Barrow's body post mortem. Whether correct or not Seddon had by then sealed his own fate.

15. Bowker, *Behind the Bar*. It was a rape case at Leicester.

Chapter 12: 'I have shot him – he dared me to do it'

1. Correspondence in NA, TS 18/247. For an account of this, see Robert Sackville-West, *The Disinherited: A Story of Family, Love and Betrayal* (Bloomsbury, 2014), p 135.

2. The Countess of Carnarvon, *Lady Almina and the Real Downton Abbey: The Lost Legacy of Highclere Castle* (Hodder & Stoughton, 2012), p 214.

3. The Earl of Carnarvon, *No Regrets* (Weidenfeld & Nicolson, 1976), p 93.

4. And of the Houses of Parliament.

5. In fact he resigned in 1916, causing a by-election; he gave Hetty's ill health and the demands of work at the Bar as his reasons.

6. Horace Avory, Montague Lush, Eldon Bankes, Thomas Horridge, Thomas Scrutton, John Simon and Rufus Isaacs, all great names in their day.

7. In one trial a witness referred to a man as NBG. What did it mean? the judge asked. Prosecuting counsel said he had been informed it referred to naval officers and stood for 'Navy Blue and Gold'. An incredulous Marshall got to his feet. It stood for 'No Bloody Good', he said to the delight of the public gallery. The use of such language by the professional classes in a formal environment was unheard of.

8. There is ample, albeit anecdotal, evidence for this. The biography approved by Elna refers to his infidelities; see Nina Warner Hooke and Gill Thomas, *Marshall Hall: A Biography* (Arthur Barker, 1966), p 180. When researching this book I was contacted by a lady whose great-aunt was reputed to have had an affair with him, though I could not substantiate it. In his own chambers the stories were legion. On one occasion it is said a girl was concealed on an outside balcony when Hetty called unexpectedly.

9. Evidence of Jean-Louis's brother Amédée Miéville to the House of Lords, House of Lords Sessions papers 1842, vols 16–25.

10. Charitably attributed by Hetty to his increasingly painful phlebitis.

11. Author's collection.

12. All details relating to Jeannie Baxter's trial not otherwise referenced derive from ITPC, vol 11.

13. Account in M'banks, p 320.

14. *Daily News*, 13 January 1922.

15. Jane Robins, *The Magnificent Spilsbury and the Case of the Brides in the Bath* (John Murray, 2010), p 102.

16. Law Report, Court of Criminal Appeal, *The Times*, 24 June 1913.

Chapter 13: 'Nearer, my God, to Thee'

1. At the Yarmouth Patriots' Demonstration, 19 September 1914.

2. At the Mile End Recruiting Rally in May 1915.

3. East Toxteth meeting, reported in *Liverpool Courier*, January 1910.

4. All details relating to Smith and the Brides in the Bath trial not otherwise referenced derive from Eric R Watson (ed), *Trial of George Joseph Smith*, Notable British Trials (William Hodge, 1922) or the NA files CRIM 1/55 and MEPO 3/225B.

5. F D Mackinnon, 'Scrutton, Sir Thomas Edward (1856–1934)', rev Hugh Mooney, *Oxford Dictionary of National Biography* (Oxford University Press, 2004).

6. *Daily Dispatch*, 4 July 1915.

7. Havelock Ellis, quoted in Watson, *Trial of George Joseph Smith*.

8. John Ellis, *Diary of a Hangman* (True Crime Library, 1996), p 125.

9. Letter from EMH to Lord Edmund Talbot, quoted in M'banks, p 185.

10. Quoted in Robert Stevens, *The English Judges: Their Role in the Changing Constitution* (Hart, 2002).

11. He had been educated at Wimborne Grammar School and King's College London.

12. Letter from Lord Edmund Talbot to Andrew Bonar Law, PA, BL/82/4/11.

13. Letter from EMH to Lord Edmund Talbot, quoted in M'banks, p 377.

14. Son of Charles Dickens.

15. EMH in a letter to Sir Charles Gill told him that it was Hetty's wishes that she should be Lady Marshall Hall; Charles Gill private collection.

Chapter 14: 'It's a shame!'

1. A E Bowker, *Behind the Bar* (Staples Press, 1947), p 234.

2. At this time there was no statutory definition of provocation and it was permitted as a defence reducing murder to manslaughter only in defined and extreme cases.

3. A Berserker was an ancient Norseman famous for fighting with uncontrolled ferocity.

4. All details relating to Holt's trial not otherwise referenced derive from newspaper cuttings in ITPC, vols 14 and 15.

5. Or, as his counsel Henry Curtis Bennett put it to the jury: 'A member of a class whose type of life brought them many men friends.'

6. Blackwell had also been a member of the Atkin committee.

7. Correspondence with regard to Edward Flavell's sentence, NA, HO 144/22088 and HO 144/220.

8. Ibid.

Chapter 15: 'A strange magnetic quality'

1. All details relating to the Green Bicycle murder not otherwise referenced derive from the (edited) transcript of the trial in H R Wakefield, *The Green Bicycle Case* (Philip Allen, 1930) or from the NA file DPP 1/61.

2. Wakefield, *The Green Bicycle Case.*

3. C Wendy East, *The Green Bicycle Murder* (Alan Sutton, 1993).

4. The prosecution brief in the NA presents a more dubious picture of Light's character. Much of it was rumour and conjecture but it recorded that Light was court-martialled for forgery and sentenced to twelve months' military detention prior to discharge. More significant perhaps was the indecent photograph and ladies' underwear found in his room. None of this was referred to at his trial nor could it have been.

5. George Pleydell Bancroft, *Stage and Bar: Recollections of George Pleydell Bancroft* (Faber & Faber, 1939).

6. Later a distinguished judge in the Court of Appeal and one of the British judges at the Nuremberg trials.

7. Lord Birkett, *Six Great Advocates* (Penguin, 1961). The admiration was not originally shared by EMH. A few years previously he had appeared against Birkett in a small case in Birmingham which Birkett had won, to EMH's fury. 'A most offensive young man,' he said afterwards. But he nonetheless recognised his promise. Shortly after the Green Bicycle case he offered Birkett a place at 3 Temple Gardens. Birkett moved to London and a glittering career.

8. Letter from EMH to Charles Gill, Charles Gill private collection.

9. *Illustrated London News,* 29 October 1921.

10. All details relating to the trial of Harold Greenwood not specifically referenced derive from the transcript of the trial in Winifred Duke (ed), *Trial of Harold Greenwood,* Notable British Trials (William Hodge, 1930) or the NA files DPP 1/57, ASSI 72/46/7, HO 144/11780 and MEPO 326/B.

11. Provided by Instone Airlines, a firm started in Cardiff in 1919 and subsequently well known for its pioneering flights which included the first ever transport by air of a racehorse in 1921.

12. *The Nation*, 13 November 1920.

13. Commentary in Duke, *Trial of Harold Greenwood*.

14. This included the obligatory £100 the client had to add to the brief fee if he wanted to be defended by a barrister who did not practise on the circuit in which the case was to be heard. The barrister in question then paid this to the circuit administrator.

15. A slight misquote from *Othello*.

16. The prosecution had the last word according to the rule that a defendant who called witnesses relinquished his right to the last word before the summing up. Nowadays the defendant always has the right to the final speech.

Chapter 16: 'Unsuitable for the eyes and ears of pure women'

1. Bodkin's concerns and the belief of the police are set out in correspondence between Bodkin and Charles Gill; Charles Gill private collection.

2. Police report in NA, MEPO 3/275.

3. Letter from Bodkin to Charles Gill, Charles Gill private collection.

4. Charles Gill private collection. Rupert Gwynne had been a barrister in Marshall's chambers at 3 Temple Gardens.

5. All details relating to the Crumbles murder not otherwise referenced derive from Winifred Duke (ed), *Trial of Field and Gray*, Notable British Trials (William Hodge, 1939) or the NA files DPP 1/56, MEPO 3/272–81 and T/161.

6. My own theory, unsupported by clear evidence and arising from a flavour in the newspaper reports and trial transcripts, is that Irene, who was sexually experienced and reasonably sophisticated, may have alluded to the closeness of the friendship between the two men and touched a very raw nerve.

7. Letter from EMH to Charles Gill, Charles Gill private collection.

8. The picture, by Douglas Granville Chandor, was in the 1919 Royal Academy Exhibition. It was the artist's first major commission and led to one to paint the Prince of Wales and to the establishment of his name.

9. All details relating to EMH's executorship for Sir Alfred Rothschild derive from the Rothschild Archive, London, 000/154 and 000/174.

10. See Dennistoun v Dennistoun divorce, discussed later in the chapter.

11. PA, BLU/1/10/hai-6.

12. The Sex Disqualification (Removal) Act 1919. The Act was initially interpreted to mean that the jury must be composed of equal numbers of men and women. The Court of Appeal ruled that this was wrong; the jurors were to be drawn randomly from the same box. The consequence was that the overwhelming majority were still men.

13. Letters, *Daily Mail*, 31 January 1921.

14. The Matrimonial Causes Act 1857.

15. A proposed clause that a wife's grounds should include adultery committed by the husband in the conjugal residence was firmly rejected.

16. All details of the Russell divorce not specifically referenced derive from ITPC.

17. These passages, not published in the press, are part of the original trial transcript and are quoted in Bevis Hillier, *The Virgin's Baby: The Battle of the Ampthill Succession* (Hopcyn Press, 2013).

18. Now the Supreme Court.

19. Quoted in the report of the Royal Commission on Divorce 1912.

20. All details of the Dennistoun divorce not specifically referenced derive from ITPC.

21. In his autobiography, *The World, the House, and the Bar* (John Murray, 1930), p 157.

22. Quoted in Hillier, *The Virgin's Baby*.

Chapter 17: 'God's great Western sun'

1. Letter from EMH to Charles Gill, Charles Gill private collection.

2. The outer chamber had been discovered in 1922 but the sealed inner chamber with all its treasures was not opened until February 1923.

3. All details relating to the Madame Fahmy trial not otherwise referenced are derived from ITPC and the NA files CRIM 1/244 and DPP 1/74.

4. This theory is the subject of a fascinating recent book, Andrew Rose, *The Prince, the Princess and the Perfect Murder* (Coronet, 2013).

5. *Reynolds's Weekly Newspaper*, 16 September 1923.

6. An allusion to Rudyard Kipling, 'Oh, East is East, and West is West, and never the twain shall meet' ('The Ballad of East and West').

7. Correspondence between the Batonnier, the Attorney General and EMH quoted in M'banks, pp 449–50.

8. *St James Gazette*, 31 August 1892.

9. Quoted in M'banks, p 461.

10. This story is recounted by EMH in a contributory essay in *The Survival of Man: A Study in Unrecognised Human Faculty* (Methuen, 1909). Co-contributors included Sir Arthur Conan Doyle and Sir Oliver Lodge. The latter was a distinguished physicist as well as Boyd Carpenter's indirect predecessor as president of the Society for Psychical Research.

11. Catherine Wingfield, *Guidance from Beyond* (Philip Allan, 1923).

12. Sir Arthur Conan Doyle, 'Three Notable Recruits'.

13. EMH made these remarks at a meeting of the National Laboratory for Psychical Research on 28 September 1926. Interestingly, there were two other KCs in the audience.

Chapter 18: 'You damned swine, you have seduced my wife'

1. See Heather Shore, 'Criminality and Englishness in the Aftermath: The Racecourse Wars of 1920s', *Twentieth Century British History*, vol 22, no 4 (2011), pp 474–97.

2. Letter from Hetty to Elna, author's collection.

3. Innocent had retired. This one went by the more pedestrian name of Bucket.

4. The studio ultimately became the more famous Walton Studios. The film is included in the British Film Institute's '75 Most Wanted' list of lost films.

5. No recording exists. The broadcast was on 5 November 1925 on all stations in the evening.

6. Hugely popular and now forgotten, he was a prolific novelist.

7. Charles Dickens, *The Pickwick Papers* (1837).

8. Sir Ellis Hume Williams, *The World, the House, and the Bar* (John Murray, 1930).

9. The case was that of Jean-Pierre Vacquier, a French national convicted in Britain of murdering his mistress's husband with strychnine. EMH's highly unusual role as a prosecutor came about because the case was to be held in Guildford. As EMH was Recorder (part-time judge) of Guildford, the DPP probably instructed him as a matter of courtesy.

10. Letter from EMH to John Lane, 2 December 1920, John Lane Company Records, box 30, folder 6 (1906–1922), Harry Ransom Center, University of Texas at Austin.

11. Letter from EMH to Ralph Blumenfeld, PA, BLU/1/10HA1-6.

12. Now in Pakistan.

13. See Angma Dey Jhala, *Courtly Indian Women in Late Imperial India* (Pickering & Chatto, 2008).

14. All details relating to the Stella Maris trial derived from ITPC.

15. Avory was famous for what was regarded as the encapsulation of the philosophy of capital punishment: sentencing a murderer to death, he said: 'You too shall die.'

16. It continued to be so until 1961.

17. M'banks, p 476, misquotes this, changing 'peculiar' to 'great' and omitting the last reference to the public, which Avory probably intended as a gentle dig; he despised Marshall's populism and thought the acquittals he gained were usually undeserved by the accused.

Chapter 19: 'Some great statue of mourning'

1. *Daily Sketch*, 28 April 1927.

2. My own guess, for what it is worth, is that it contained letters. Valuables seem unlikely given Louisa's own financial circumstances.

3. The Sir Edward Marshall Hall Trust for Needy Members of the Inner Temple exists to this day.

4. Christie's Archives.

5. Sir Frank Lockwood, a fellow barrister and politician (see chapter 7), was also a skilled cartoonist who contributed drawings to *Punch*. He amused himself during trials by producing sketches of his opponents and the judge which were much sought after by their subjects; many barristers had Lockwood cartoons on their wall commemorating trials in which they had appeared with him.

6. The terms of the will were: 'I direct my trustees to destroy all my letters and private papers other than those my trustees think I should wish delivered to any person or persons affected thereby.' This plainly envisaged the return of a personal document; it was not a carte blanche to hand papers over to a biographer nor could it have been interpreted as such.

7. 'Pop' is the exclusive and long-established Eton society; membership (which is by election and is much sought after) carries with it special privileges.

8. The classics degree at Oxford.

9. See M'banks, p 432.

10. It is fair to say that his family would not share my view; his stepfather was devoted to him, as was his stepbrother Quintin (see note 17 below), eight years younger than Edward. He writes movingly of Edward's charm in his autobiography *A Sparrow's Flight* (Collins, 1990); though I note that even his family made jokes about his social aspirations.

11. All these characteristics are painfully apparent in his letters to his friend and confidante Lady Desborough; Hertford Archives, DERV C1774.

12. Ibid.

13. Ibid.

14. Churchill College Cambridge Archives, Hailsham papers, GBR/0014/ HAIL HAIL 4/3/1.

15. Ibid.

16. Letter from Edward Marjoribanks to Hetty, author's collection.

17. Quintin Hogg, later second Viscount Hailsham and, like his father Douglas, Lord Chancellor.

18. See Cyril Connolly, *Enemies of Promise* (Penguin, 1938), p 198. Connolly had been at the receiving end of some of the beatings.

19. 'Westminster Morning to MLD': 'Is it nine years or just a little while | since on that flaming summers day | for the last time he turned to me that smile so gay …'

20. Letter from Edward Marjoribanks to Lady Desborough, Hertford Archives, DERV C1774.

21. Curiously they all died in the spring, a season in which one would have expected a certain optimism; Llewelyn Davies and Buxton in May 1921 and Marjoribanks a decade later in April 1932. Perhaps it was the optimism that they found hard to cope with.

22. The seventh Earl Beauchamp's homosexuality was revealed by his brother in law, the Duke of Westminster. Beauchamp fled, intending to commit suicide on the continent, but had a change of heart and remained in exile.

23. His observation that Ethel was the kind of woman 'who should only be married to a man who could dominate her' is an example.

24. *The Paradine Case* (1947); the young Gregory Peck plays a startlingly handsome barrister who collects jewellery.

Index

References are to page numbers. EMH refers to Edward Marshall Hall.